Acclaim for *Creating Restora*

Beginning with her courageous assertion, "There simply is no place for punishment in schools," Martha Brown provides a map for replacing punishment with restorative processes that are healing, produce lasting results, and are cost effective. She recognizes that RJ is not an easy fix, but she makes a compelling case for teaching our youth the values used in circle processes to resolve conflicts, because they strengthen the school community and will also serve them throughout life. This important contribution to Restorative Justice literature takes a conclusive stand for leaving zero tolerance in the dust bin of educational theory and, instead, investing our time, energy, and tax dollars in school-wide restorative practices.

— Sylvia Clute, President, Alliance for Unitive Justice

Deep relational ecologies are the heart of RJE. Within this deeply reflective ecology, Martha Brown maps out how we are all practitioners, researchers, trainers and theorists. To engage in this transformational journey at the core of educational praxis, we must learn and grow together. RJE is a journey, not a destination. Martha has gathered the wisdom of our times through engaging the voice of students, teachers, administrators, academics and practitioners. With this visionary map in hand, we are ready to take the next steps.

— Brenda Morrison, Author and Director of the Centre for Restorative Justice and Assistant Professor in the School of Criminology, Simon Fraser University

I have very much enjoyed reading Martha's book. It has re-invigorated my passion for the work I do in and with schools. It has also reassured me that the challenges I see schools facing in the UK are very similar to those in the US. Bringing about culture change along relational and restorative lines is not easy, and Martha has painstakingly showed why this is. However, even piecemeal implementation can make a huge difference to school culture and relationships. Martha has shown this to be the case, whilst never relinquishing her belief in the potential of a systemically implemented relational and restorative approach across a whole school community.

— Belinda Hopkins, Author and Director, Transforming Conflict, National Centre for Restorative Approaches in Youth Settings, Berkshire, UK

At the end of the reading the book, I can only breathe a sigh of gratefulness for such a comprehensive, careful, caring, daring, bold, and compassionate description of the reality of implementing and sustaining RJE. I think you have caught the ethos in the words and descriptions. You have been very respectful, caring, and accepting of what it is to be human.

— Dorothy Vaandering, Author and Professor of Education
Memorial University of Newfoundland, NL, Canada

This book is perhaps one of the best books on restorative justice in schools written. It's a "must read" for anyone interested in a truly honest and practical approach to becoming a fully restorative school.

— Randy Compton, President, Co-Founder Restorative Solutions, Inc.,
Boulder, CO

In *Creating Restorative Schools*, Martha Brown describes directly the challenges and benefits of moving the entire school staff towards a restorative culture. The process is not a straight line, and the side roads are many. The story of the two schools' paths provides directions and cautions, essential insight for any educator working to implement Restorative Justice in Education principles and practices in their school.

— Nancy Riestenberg, Restorative Practices Specialist,
Minnesota Department of Education

Creating Restorative Schools

The HOPE talking piece on the cover photo belongs to school board member Nina Senn, of the Oakland Unified School District in Oakland, California, USA. In the spring of 2015, it was passed between the superintendent, school board members, and each attendee during a school board meeting. It then traveled and was used in restorative Circles at five different schools with youth and adults, including Libby Schaaf, Oakland's mayor, and then came back for a student-led Circle with the school board. Circle participants spoke of their hope for themselves, their community, and their city.

Photo credit: Josh Egel for Oakland Unified School District, Restorative Justice. Reprinted with permission from David Yusem, OUSD's Restorative Justice program facilitator.

CREATING RESTORATIVE SCHOOLS

Setting Schools Up to Succeed

MARTHA A. BROWN, PhD

FOREWORD BY KATHERINE EVANS, PhD

Living Justice Press
St. Paul, Minnesota

Living Justice Press
St. Paul, Minnesota 55105

*For information about permission to reproduce selections from this book,
please contact:*
Permissions, Living Justice Press, 2093 Juliet Avenue, St. Paul, MN 55105
Tel. (651) 695-1008 or contact permissions through our website:
www.livingjusticepress.org.

Library of Congress Cataloging-in-Publication Data
Names: Brown, Martha A., 1966– author.
Title: Creating restorative schools : Setting schools up to succeed /
Martha A. Brown, Ph.D. Description: St. Paul, Minn. : Living Justice Press,
2017. | Includes bibliographical references and index. | Description based
on print version record and CIP data provided by publisher; resource
not viewed. Identifiers: LCCN 2016058414 (print) | LCCN 2017022178
(ebook) | ISBN 9781937141226 (ebook) | ISBN 9781937141219 (trade pbk.) |
ISBN 9781937141226 (eBook)
Subjects: LCSH: School environment—United States. | School improvement
  programs—United States. | Community and school—United States. |
  Restorative justice. | School environment—California—Oakland. |
  Educational change—California—Oakland. | Community and
  school—California—Oakland.
Classification: LCC LC210.5 (ebook) | LCC LC210.5 .B76 2017 (print) |
  DDC 371.2/070979466--dc23 LC record available at
  https://lccn.loc.gov/2016058414

ISBN-13: 978-1-937141-21-9
eBook ISBN: 978-1-937141-22-6

22 21 20 19 18   5 4 3 2 1

Copyediting by Cathy Broberg
Cover design by David Spohn
Interior design and typesetting by Wendy Holdman
Diagram and chart production by Martha Brown, Loretta Draths, and
  Wendy Holdman
Printed by Sheridan Books, Ann Arbor, Michigan on Nature's Book
  recycled paper

Unless otherwise indicated, photos and images courtesy of the author.
Names of both individuals and schools have been changed to protect
identities.

To Kathy

My partner, friend, sometimes editor/proofreader, and eternal optimist. I am forever grateful to you. You always believed that someday I would write a book. Here it is.

To Shirley Brown

Although you are not with me on this physical plane anymore, you are alive in my heart and in my music. I know you are proud of your baby.

Contents

List of Abbreviations and Terms

BART	Bay Area Rapid Transit
CASEL	The Collaborative for Academic, Social, and Emotional Learning
CRT	Critical race theory
DHP	District hearing process
EMU	Eastern Mennonite University
GFSA	The Gun-Free Schools Act
LGBTQIA+	Lesbian, gay, bisexual, trans, queer/questioning, intersex, asexual, and all other sexualities, sexes, and genders not included in these few letters
NCLB	The No Child Left Behind Act
OCR	On Campus Reflection room at Davis Middle School
OUSD	Oakland Unified School District
PACT	Panthers, Academic achievement, Community building, and Total health: an advisory class at Davis Middle School
PBIS	Positive behavioral interventions and supports
PD	Professional development
PLCs	Professional learning communities

P.R.I.D.E.	Davis Middle School's values: Positivity, Respect, Independence, Determination, and Empathy
PTSA	Parent Teacher Student Association
RFP	Request for proposals
RJ	Restorative justice
RJ facilitator	The term used by OUSD for on-site RJ coordinators
RJE	Restorative justice in education
RJOY	Restorative Justice for Oakland Youth
RPs	Restorative practices
RTI	Response to intervention
SEL	Social and emotional learning
SRO	School resource officer (also called school police or school security officer [SSO])
SSO	School security officer (the term used by Oakland schools for SRO)
SWRPs	School-wide restorative practices
UK	United Kingdom
USDOE	United States Department of Education
USDOE OCR	United States Department of Education Office for Civil Rights
USDOJ	United States Department of Justice

List of Pseudonyms

Davis	**Davis Middle School**, a school with resources, a student waiting list, and three years' experience in creating a restorative school
Stan Paulson	Principal, a White man
Riordan	Assistant principal, a White man
Cameron	RJ facilitator, an African American man
Acke	RJ facilitator, an African American man
Eric	School security officer, an African American man
Sandra	School security officer, an African American woman
Miss Jenner	Sixth-grade teacher at Davis, a White woman
Grant	**Grant Middle School**, an underfunded, "take all" school, recently traumatized by six months of a punitive interim principal
Elena Baez	Principal, a Latinx woman
Antonio	RJ facilitator, a Latinx man
Patrisse	School security officer, an African American woman
Carson	School security officer at the adjacent school, an African American man
Caridad	Family engagement coordinator (a grant-funded position), a Latinx woman

Miss Zang   Sixth-grade teacher at Grant, a Chinese-
             American woman

Note: It was not part of my study to ask people how they self-identify regarding race and ethnicity. The identifications named here reflect their phenotype, which also indicates how students would most likely perceive these educators: "Does this adult look like me, and might he or she have had experiences because of race and culture similar to what I am having in school, family, community, and society?" I include these identifications because of the impact that race and ethnicity have on schools, youth, and the RJE work as well as to show these schools' commitment to hiring a diverse staff that reflects a diverse study body.

Lists of Figures and Charts

List of Figures

List of Charts

Acknowledgments

I have had the honor and privilege of being on this journey with hundreds of people who taught me, coached me, encouraged me, put up with me, and supported me through six years of graduate school and ultimately the writing of this book. Here, I name but a few, while holding the rest in deep gratitude.

This book would not exist without the brilliance, patience, and wisdom of Denise Breton, my editor, and Kay Pranis, senior editor. Their voices ring loud and clear throughout this manuscript, as they filled in my gaps and made it a complete, genuine representation of what RJE is and can be. You made me better—you made the book better—you make the world better. Thank you.

A heartfelt thanks to Kathy Evans for being excited enough about this book to write the foreword—on top of everything else that you do to move RJE forward in teacher education and in the world. Your support is priceless to me, as are your own contributions to the new field of RJE! Thank you for your guidance and friendship over the years. And thank you and Dorothy Vaandering both for the wonderful gift of the *Little Book of Restorative Justice in Education*.

Those of you who have taken the time to read this book and engage its ideas with your comments and reviews have made a huge contribution toward validating this work. In particular, Dorothy Vaandering, Sylvia Clute, Brenda Morrison, Belinda Hopkins, and Nancy Riestenberg took the time to make suggestions that vastly improved the book. I appreciate you so much!

Kathy Wickwire, my partner, has sacrificed much to give me the time and space to write both my dissertation and now this book. She has been my greatest friend, cheerleader, and support. Thank you.

Thanks to all of the wonderful, amazing, and incredible administrators, teachers, principals, RJ facilitators, students, school resource officers, and support staff in the OUSD who volunteered to participate in my study and who are the heart and soul of this book. David Yusem opened the door to me and the rest was magic. I hope your words and actions that inspired me so much can now inspire millions.

I am grateful for my students at Florida Atlantic University and Simon Fraser University who allow me to bring Circles into our virtual and digital classrooms. You are my greatest teachers.

Finally, I thank you, my readers, for wanting to learn more about RJE and for being willing to do the often hard but also often inspiring and joyful work of paradigm shifting and creating restorative schools. I wrote this for you.

With utmost gratitude,
Martha A. Brown
2 February 2017

Foreword

One of the great joys of my work as an education professor at Eastern Mennonite University (EMU) is collaborating with teachers and school administrators, counselors, students, and other school staff about restorative justice in education (RJE). In addition to sharing some of my knowledge about RJE, I have learned so much from the amazing educators and students I have been able to interact with. Much of that collaboration has been with local school districts in the Shenandoah Valley, including the Harrisonburg City Public Schools here in Harrisonburg, Virginia, where EMU is located. In addition to the current cohorts of educators who are enrolled in the graduate program in RJE at EMU, there are many other educators and community members working together to facilitate more restorative justice school practices in the area. It's exciting to see the momentum growing and the commitment, not simply to implementing a program, but to building a culture. It is this type of culture shift that we are advocating for in Harrisonburg and it is the type of culture shift that Martha promotes in this book.

When Dorothy Vaandering and I wrote *The Little Book of Restorative Justice in Education*, we intended it as a framework, a compass pointing toward the principles, values, and foundations of RJE. At the end of the book, we called for restorative justice practitioners to work together to share ideas about what works and what doesn't work in their schools and communities and for educational researchers to provide more data that supports and informs the applications of RJE. Educators in Harrisonburg, Minneapolis, Houston, Denver—and count-less other places—are enacting these restorative principles in creative and powerful ways. Martha's book adds to the grow-ing body of research by documenting the applications of RJE in two middle schools in Oakland, California.

In her first chapter, Martha defines RJE as a "whole-school approach that prioritizes relationships, builds community, cre-ates just and equitable learning environments. . . . [R]estorative schools support struggling students, teach peaceful conflict resolution, and repair relationships after a harm has occurred."

In *The Little Book of Restorative Justice in Education*, Doro-thy and I define RJE as "facilitating learning communities that nurture the capacity of people to engage with one another and their environment in a manner that supports and respects the inherent dignity and worth of all" (p. 8). According to both of these definitions, RJE is a holistic and comprehensive approach, impacting the way we interact at the individual, organizational, and community levels. It must impact more than simply the way we do school discipline; it has to impact the way we do school, including how we speak to students in the hallways, the way we engage with parents and care-givers, and the way we design our curriculum and our ped-agogy. When RJE is implemented solely as a way to address students' "misbehavior," we miss opportunities to address the underlying causes of those behaviors; often those causes are rooted in relational issues, such as disengagement, mistrust, cultural barriers, implicit biases, microaggressions, lack of safety, and a host of other issues that impede effective learn-ing. A holistic approach to RJE, as Martha describes in this book, seeks to address those underlying causes.

When RJE is put forth as an alternative to discipline, schools might actually experience a reduction in suspensions and expulsions. Without the cultural shift, however, we might simply be masking underlying issues that may still result in disproportional rates of discipline, increased frustration on the part of faculty who feel like nothing is being done to address misbehavior, continued lack of achievement, and a general lack of safety for everyone. Unfortunately, we have seen this too often in schools that received grant funding to implement a program while failing to do the hard work of creating a more restorative environment.

Conversely, when RJE is introduced as a shift in culture, we address the underlying issues that hinder learning; we focus on meeting students' emotional and social needs, not simply their academic needs—realizing that they are all intertwined; and we challenge injustice and inequities that often are causing toxic and unproductive learning environments. This shift not only addresses discipline challenges, but also promotes effective learning opportunities for all students. Consistent with this holistic approach, Martha's research identified four related themes: trust, having a voice, relational culture, and a commitment to social justice.

At its core, RJE is about relationships that are characterized by respect, dignity, and mutual concern. There's an acknowledgment that we are all interconnected and that what happens to each of us impacts all of us. Driven by values, RJE is an ethos, not simply a set of practices or processes, but rather a way of being that guides those practices and processes. Effective educators know this; when relationships in the classroom and school are healthy, learning is facilitated. For example, attachment theory has stressed the importance of children and youth having significant adults in their lives; RJE practices build in opportunities to foster those types of healthy attachments by working *with* students to resolve challenging behaviors rather than relying on punitive measures that ultimately interfere with healthy relationships.

Working *with* students, rather than doing things *to* them or *for* them, promotes social engagement rather than social control. This ethos doesn't just show up when we are addressing student behavior, but can impact our pedagogy as well. For example, Erich Sneller is a chemistry teacher at Harrisonburg High School and a participant in the RJE graduate certificate program at EMU. As we were discussing the impact of social engagement and social control, Erich talked about how in his chemistry labs, having students simply follow a set of instructions for completing the lab can easily become social control, but involving them as part of the problem-solving process related to the lab promotes social engagement. Students aren't simply passive recipients but are actively engaged as chemists; this not only promotes their learning, but also builds positive interactions with Erich around chemistry.

One of the greatest contributions of Martha's book, in my opinion, is in the way she establishes a more direct connection between the principles and practices of RJE and the important research on social and emotional learning (SEL). For those in the RJE community, Circle processes have consistently demonstrated the potential for assisting students and educators in developing social and emotional competencies such as self-awareness, social awareness, self-regulation, empathy, decision making, and problem solving. Many schools are already committed to promoting social and emotional competencies, so the links between RJE and SEL are important places for building on what is already happening. For example, Christy Norment is a school counselor at Harrisonburg High School and a participant in the EMU RJE graduate program. She facilitates Circle processes as a way of collectively solving classroom challenges. When teachers and students come together, with the help of a well-equipped facilitator, to resolve issues in the classroom, not only are they building a shared responsibility for the learning environment, but they are also creating spaces where students learn important problem-solving skills.

Relational ecologies are a primary aspect of RJE, but simply being relational is insufficient without concurrently committing to address injustice and inequity. Restorative justice must be about justice—and no less so in educational contexts. We can no longer talk about achievement gaps without acknowledging, along with Gloria Ladson Billings and many other critical educators, that there are instead opportunity gaps. As we pursue restorative justice in education, we have to talk about educational justice. This means responding to historical harms that have primarily impacted people of color, those with severe financial inequities, members of the LGBTQIA+ community, students with disabilities, and other marginalized youth. RJE that is holistic beckons us to ongoing professional development in antiracist pedagogy, culturally relevant teaching, and inclusive education. It calls us to examine issues of power and privilege, implicit bias, and microaggressions that create unsafe educational spaces for both students and teachers. Holistic RJE requires that silenced perspectives are lifted up and that students and teachers are invited into decisions about school policy and practice. Martha's research reminds us that a commitment to social justice must be part of the work of RJE.

Finally, Martha's work in this book reminds us that implementing RJE practices requires more than a few add-ons; the work of building more restorative school cultures requires a paradigm shift—and those don't happen overnight. RJE is not a quick fix. It is about changing school culture or, as we say in *The Little Book,* changing the way we do things around here. Change is messy, nonlinear, and unpredictable. There are things we can do to facilitate it, but with all our best intentions, sometimes it shows up or doesn't in the most random of ways.

Based on her research, Martha offers some suggestions for how we might facilitate this type of cultural shift. Martha and the educators she worked with in Oakland understand the current context of public schooling and the challenges that schools face; yes, there are barriers, but in the face of these barriers, schools are continuing to move toward more restorative educational cultures.

Martha emphasizes that having support from district administration is crucial; however, initiatives cannot be mandated from above. Without sufficient buy-in from members of the learning community, mandated initiatives not only violate the principles of RJE—setting it up for ultimate failure—but can also violate trust and exacerbate ineffective relationships in a building.

For example, Harrisonburg City School District has over fifty different languages represented and is home to students from more than forty different countries. Many students each year are newcomers and many have arrived as refugees. Dr. Scott Kizner, superintendent, and April Howard, director of Student Services, are committed to improving the learning environments for this diverse mix of students in the district and realize that in order to build a restorative school culture for all of those students, there needs to be a variety of supports. Dual language programs have been designed, after-school programs are in place, and the district is committed to building more trauma-informed education. District administrators are supportive of RJE and work with other staff and building administrators to find innovative ways to build a more restorative culture without mandating more programming for those educators who haven't yet been convinced of the efficacy of RJE. The result is perhaps a slower cultural shift, but one that has stronger foundations and greater buy-in.

We need more institutional support for RJE; yes, funding is tight for educational institutions, but as Martha notes, we have a choice about how we will invest the monies we do have. Investing monies in capacity building creates a more sustainable shift in RJE; providing ongoing professional development for educators within the building, rather than bringing in experts from outside, is not only economically prudent but also ensures that the RJE efforts are led by those who understand the context in which those efforts are being made. What works in one space may not work in another and what might be essential in one school might matter less in another.

One of the ways we are doing that in Harrisonburg is by preparing educators to be RJE leaders in their buildings through a partnership between Harrisonburg City Schools and EMU. EMU offers a graduate certificate in RJE that ensures a depth of knowledge in both theory and practice. Educators, including teachers, administrators, school counselors, family-school liaisons, and behavior specialists, take classes together that are designed to facilitate their ability to lead the efforts to build more restorative school cultures. At Harrisonburg High School, a critical mass of educators has completed the certificate program and they are now doing their own professional development within their school. We believe this to be a more sustainable model for implementing RJE than models where outsiders are coming in and doing trainings for a day, without attending to the unique needs of the school and without attending to the depth of knowledge needed to implement RJE with fidelity to the values and principles of RJE. It also honors the existing expertise of those educators, building on what they know and bring to the learning experience.

In conclusion, decades of zero tolerance policies have proven ineffective at addressing the learning needs of students and creating safe and effective learning communities. Refusing to see that the cost of educating our young people is less than the cost of incarcerating them, we have often persisted on resorting to the same old punitive measures that have accomplished nothing and, in many cases, have exacerbated school failure. We must repeal these policies and replace them with policies that have been proven to actually work to make schools safer. Martha's research supports the effectiveness of RJE and its potential to do that. She reminds us that we all pay for the costs of zero tolerance policies and their impact on our youth and children. Money spent on expensive policing could be more wisely spent meeting the needs of our youth and children, equipping them with the social and emotional skills, as well as academic proficiencies, needed to succeed and contribute to our world.

Henry Giroux, in his critique of zero tolerance policies, argues that "rather than attempting to work with youth and make an investment in their psychological, economic, and social well-being," these laws and policies are "designed not only to keep youth off the streets, but to make it easier to criminalize their behavior."[1] Restorative justice in education actually reverses that trend and seeks to make an investment in the well-being of not only our students, but all those involved in our educational systems. As Martha points out, while zero tolerance policies offer a quick response with no sustainable solutions to the underlying problems, RJE asks us to invest now in our youth with a promise of relational dividends later.

We still need more research on the efficacy of RJE in various contexts, but Martha's book offers great insight into the work happening in two Oakland schools. Consistent with other research, the centrality of relationships and the emphasis on social justice ring strong through her writing. I am grateful for this book and hope that it will provide a strong grounding for educators seeking to advocate for and implement RJE in their classrooms, schools, and districts.

Katherine Evans, Associate Professor of Education
Eastern Mennonite University
February 2017

Creating a Restorative School in Stages

> Restorative practices in schools, the workplace, and the greater community seek to effect culture change. Restorative approaches argue for an all-encompassing philosophical orientation that informs all practices, policy, and everyday interactions and learning—grounded in community, relationships, and connection. It requires conceiving of restorative justice as a worldview; its core attributes of respect, equality, empathy, forgiveness, and community are present and intentionally reinforced in every place imaginable.
>
> ■ Nailah Peters, M.Ed., RJ facilitator, Salvation Army

Have you ever wondered why all those children in Pink Floyd's hit song "Another Brick in the Wall" are screaming, "HEY! TEACHERS! LEAVE US KIDS ALONE!" Have you ever thought about what can be done to make going to school a positive experience for all students? If so, then you are in the right place. You are about to venture deeply into two middle schools that, by adopting school-wide restorative practices (SWRPs), are using a new model for doing school. This is the story of how principals, staff, and students confronted decades of racially discriminatory discipline practices and embraced a philosophy that centers on relationships with all students. It is the story of people who, despite ever-changing district, state, and federal requirements and mandates, have committed themselves to making sure that every child who goes to their schools is treated with respect, listened to, valued, and welcomed into the diverse school community. It is the story of restorative justice in education in two middle schools in the

Oakland Unified School District, located in California's East Bay Area, an urban center that the media has called one of the most diverse and dangerous cities in the United States.

As you read, I invite you to re-vision how we do schools and, perhaps even, how we do RJE. What can we learn from these two middle schools about implementing RJE so we can tap into its full power?

▨ The Story of Julio

My journey to writing this book and the work I do today began while I was teaching at a public school in Florida. I was struggling to understand why my administrators seemed to care more about high-stakes test scores than about students. Today, I know this is a systemic issue stemming from federal and state policies that tie school funding and teachers' jobs to student scores on standardized tests. Nonetheless, what I was witnessing every day eclipsed this bigger picture, as it did for the students. I was very disturbed by how my school approached teaching, learning, and student discipline, and how the school's culture was negative, oppressive, and depressing—not at all conducive to teaching and learning. One experience in particular highlighted how harmful school discipline had become, not only to the students but also to the relationships between adults and students in the school. I was a brand-new teacher in an urban high school situated in a working-class Latinx neighborhood, and this is the story of Julio.

Someone had been pulling the fire alarm all week, and our classes were interrupted at least once a day for three or four days. It was an annoyance for sure. With every alarm, we had to evacuate the buildings until the fire department gave us the all clear. To find the person pulling the alarms, school police put a salve on the alarms that was visible only under a black light. One day during my class, the alarm sounded. While we were evacuating, the boy who pulled the alarm high-fived one of my students, whom I will call Julio, leaving some residue on his hand. Half an hour later when we were back in the classroom, the armed school police officer entered my room and set up the black light in my closet. He called my students, one by one, into the closet and placed their hands under the black light. Julio's hand lit up under the light. In response, the officer handcuffed Julio and led him out of my class, while my other students and I watched in shock and horror. I followed them into the hall and told the officer that Julio had never left my sight and was in my classroom when the alarm went off. I made it clear that there was no way Julio could have pulled the alarm. But my proclamation of Julio's innocence fell on deaf ears. Julio was escorted to the office for what I assume was some sort of interrogation that lasted until Julio's mother came in and encouraged him to name his friend.

This situation could have been an opportunity for a student to bond with an adult in the school who trusted him and stood up for him. Instead it became a chance for the police officer to break any existing bonds of trust and socialize Julio for the prison culture. To this day, I wonder how this experience affected Julio, who was a good kid and one of my best students. I know the effect it had on me—it made me an advocate for restorative justice.

Learning from Two Middle Schools in Oakland

To better understand what is happening in schools, I chose to pursue a doctorate in Curriculum and Instruction. My area of specialization was restorative justice. And to learn more about restorative justice in education, I partnered with the Oakland Unified School District (OUSD) to conduct a study of two of their middle schools that had been using school-wide restorative practices (SWRPs) for about three years before I arrived.

My study represents a snapshot in time through the voices of administrators, staff, and students, all of whom were dedicated to improving their schools. Their challenge was to help each other shift from a punitive, zero tolerance discipline mind-set that regularly excluded students to embracing inclusive restorative approaches that keep students a part of the school community. This is no small task, and their journey continues.

Through their perceptions, I learned many important lessons about the struggle to implement SWRPs with fidelity and the positive outcomes that can occur, even when implementation has its ups and downs and may be incomplete. What I present here are not conclusive findings but thoughtful reflections based on observations and dialogue with those closest to the work.

One finding, however, is conclusive for me: I support RJE as a whole-school reform; I do not promote using restorative practices solely to create a kinder, gentler way of excluding and punishing students. Research has repeatedly shown that this approach is not effective, nor does it create the long-term personal and systemic changes that our schools need. Each time a school district "throws RJ" at the problem of discipline and expects a quick fix without providing adequate training, personnel, funding, support, and *time,* it provides more ammunition for staunch zero tolerance advocates who want to prove that RJE "does not work." My hope is that the policy makers and district administrators who read this book learn more about what RJE is, how it is implemented, and its potential for creating safe schools and positive learning environments.

Implementation Science: Four Stages of Implementing School-Wide Change

How do schools bring about change? The most successful change efforts occur when teachers, leaders, staff, students, and community members come together to create a shared vision and then decide how they want to bring that vision to life. Rarely do top-down initiatives work or last.

Developing a shared vision is the first step of implementing restorative practices. Fidelity of implementation is key for creating restorative schools, as these two middle schools experienced, and implementation science has much to tell us about the process.[1] One the greatest challenges of implementation is that it does not happen all at once, like flipping a switch. Rather, implementation is a process, and like most processes, it has stages—with challenges distinct to each stage.

Nancy Riestenberg, Restorative Practices Specialist at the Minnesota Department of Education, explores the stages of implementing school-wide restorative practices in her article "The Restorative Implementation: Paradigms and Practices." She describes the four stages—exploration, installation, initial implementation, and full implementation—and what they look like in schools:

> The question at hand for schools looking to implement Restorative Measures is how to start? The basic answer is to look to implementation science, and follow the interconnected stages of exploration, installation, initial implementation and full implementation. Build a diverse team that has authority. Get buy-in from the faculty and staff, the family members and the students. Collect data and analyze it. Make sure the leadership in the school supports the approach. Have meetings, train people. Coach. Train again. Re-allocate resources, adjust policy. Review data, disaggregate data, make decisions based on data. Report to the community and the school board. Engage in a continuous cycle of improvement. You know, run a school.[2]

To understand what the two middle schools I studied were experiencing, it's critical to recognize the four stages. Neither school was at the fourth stage. Full implementation takes more than three years to reach, and one school had a major setback during the process. In the early stages, schools have a foot in both punitive and restorative approaches. The adults are still learning *how* to practice restorative approaches and *why* this is important to do school-wide. The students are wondering if they can trust the adults to use the restorative approach consistently. Gaining confidence in restorative practices takes time and experience. And yes, both students and staff will occasionally revert to familiar responses. But mixing in punitive approaches reduces the impact that restorative practices have on school culture.

Indeed, lack of fidelity to RJE can give rise to serious, even dangerous, confusions: "Does RJ 'work' for everyone?" "Maybe RJE is not effective with this or that group." "Maybe we should not even try using restorative practices with a marginalized group if we have decided RPs do not bring positive change for them." I want to make my position clear up front: *RJE works for everyone.* Every RJ/RP practitioner I know affirms this view. When issues of effectiveness arise, the group that needs to consider changing is not the students but the adults. As the adults practice RJE, the students respond. A school cannot achieve overnight the consistency, continuity, and fidelity that RJE requires to "work." We have to start somewhere, though, which is where the four stages of whole-school implementation come in.

Restorative practices are so different, if not totally foreign, from how most educators think about schools and school discipline that they need ample time to process how distinct a restorative school really is. Fully adopting SWRPs involves shifting how people think about relationships, schooling, discipline, teaching, learning, and even how to *be.* Having worked in restorative practices for roughly two decades, Nancy Riestenberg emphasizes that fidelity to RJE takes practice:

Implementation science developed in part to help ensure that a practice would be done to fidelity, and that students benefit from the practice. There is no short cut to Carnegie Hall: one has to practice, practice, practice. . . . The restorative philosophy is a paradigm shift in the way adults and students work together. Implementation is a process, not an event. We do things best that we have learned deeply.[3]

Chart I.1 (page 8) outlines the four stages of implementing school-wide restorative practices.

Creating Restorative Schools: Setting Schools Up to Succeed

Creating Restorative Schools explores the journey of two schools to eliminate zero tolerance discipline policies and create a healthy atmosphere that supports positive development, teaching, and learning. The idea is to set schools up to succeed by making them places where students, teachers, and staff want to be; where they feel safe, trusted, and accepted; and where they experience care and belonging. This book offers on-the-ground information about RJE values and processes that districts, schools, and communities can use to develop their own restorative initiatives that are successful and sustainable.

Sometimes, though, in the rush to *do something* about suspension rates and disproportionate disciplining, districts set themselves—and RJE—up to fail. Let me give you an example. In early 2016, a large, diverse, urban school district in Florida issued a fifty-five-page request for proposals (RFP) for implementing RJE in two middle schools as a *pilot program*. The first thirty-five pages were filled will legal jargon that only lawyers could understand. The rest outlined the expectations of the awarded provider: they were to plan the initiative, train staff, implement the program, and evaluate RJE in the schools, *all*

Chart I.1. Four stages of implementing school-wide restorative practices	
STAGE	DESCRIPTION
Exploration *"Should we do it?"*	Decision of making a commitment to adopt and enact the processes and procedures to support implementation of SWRPs with fidelity. Creating a shared vision that embraces diverse perspectives and allows for the nuances of school culture and context. Developing an RJ community.
Installation *"Let's get ready to do it!"*	Training staff and setting up infrastructure required to successfully implement SWRPs. Involvement of students, staff, families, and community members. Creation of a core team to plan, hold the vision, implement and collect data.
Initial Implementation *"Let's do it!"*	Adoption of SWRPs into all systems within the school. Staff members are actively engaged in the practices. Students and families are knowledgeable about practices and active participants. Clear evidence of restorative practices is visible. Data collection is ongoing.
Full Implementation *"Let's make it better!"*	Data has been collected and reviewed with all stakeholders. Ongoing professional development for all staff. Benefits are present, celebrated, and made known. Reflection happens and adjustments are made as needed.

Source: Adapted from the Minnesota Department of Educations' *Trainer's Guide for Working with Schools to Implement Restorative Practices* by Kara Beckman and Nancy Riestenberg. They adapted this chart from the Los Angeles County Office of Education.

in just one year! As much as I want to work with school districts wishing to shift from punitive to restorative, I tossed that RFP into the recycling bin. The school district's RFP for a one-year pilot program told me this: (1) the school district really did not understand what RJE was about; (2) they were looking for a quick fix to discipline problems; (3) they did not understand that any successful whole-school reform initiative takes four to five years; and (4) they were not willing to commit to funding RJE for more than one year. This district was setting itself and RJ practitioners/trainers up to fail by expecting too much in a short period of time without making a long-term commitment to resources and training.

Studies and evaluations about RJE agree: RJE, *when implemented with fidelity*, has the power to make schools safer, increase student achievement, improve school climates, empower students to solve problems nonviolently, and change lives. Achieving all this takes *time*.

Creating Restorative Schools aims to support schools and communities in moving toward restorative practices in three ways. First, it articulates a framework for thinking about restorative practices by considering a school's "relational ecology"—how people in schools relate to each other on a daily basis. This includes how people talk with each other, how the staff, principal, and faculty relate with students and each other, and the quality of interactions throughout the school setting. These issues help uncover a school's relational ecology (see figure 1).

Why do we need yet another term for something so basic? *Relational ecology* focuses on relationships, which is the absolute foundation of restorative practices. And it says the relationships in a school form a living system, like an ecology in nature. When we nurture our relationships in a school, we are feeding and nurturing the school's ecology, which, as in nature, values and sustains every person and relationship within it.

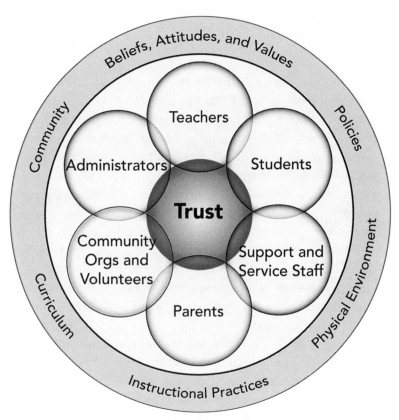

Figure 1. Factors influencing a school's relational ecology

Second, *Creating Restorative Schools* is about change and how to foster it: it's about the kinds of relational ecologies that support school-wide change. The book also explores how school-wide restorative practices change the ecologies—the quality of relationships—within a school. *Creating Restorative Schools* argues that we cannot separate a school's relational ecology from its capacity to change. The two are intimately related. Positive relational ecologies enable people throughout the school community to embrace change: to reflect, make adjustments, persevere, support each other, and succeed in transforming their school cultures. In turn, school-wide restorative changes improve a school's relational ecologies.

In the two schools I studied, this cycle continued even when school personnel changed and new students entered the school community. As time went by, staff and students alike became more familiar and comfortable with restorative practices. While many studies focus strictly on quantitatively measurable outcomes, such as reduced suspensions and expulsions, my study examined what actually occurred in schools daily to prevent or decrease conflict, violence, and other behaviors that traditionally result in student suspensions or expulsions.

Third, *Creating Restorative Schools* considers the change process on three levels: organizational, individual, and instructional or pedagogical. Because schools are incredibly dynamic environments, we cannot expect to implement RJE school-wide in a nice, clean, linear fashion. Change is messy, setbacks occur, and old habits return. The need to re-evaluate and refocus efforts is not a sign of programmatic failure. In fact, this very process creates a spiral of energy that propels people forward and renews their dedication. This is a message that policy makers and administrators desperately need to hear.

What do we really need to talk about for schools to be successful in shifting to RJE? Of course, measuring how suspensions or disproportionate disciplining go down and how students' test scores go up as schools become safer and more caring places are important; these markers confirm that RJE is good for schools. But *Creating Restorative Schools* invites a deeper conversation. Its aim is to delve into what generates these positive outcomes. For this, we need to discuss how to cultivate trusting, caring relationships in schools, how essential these relationships are to our nation's young people, and how to sustain a school's positive relational ecology over time and through the inevitable comings and goings of both staff and students. Many youth are hurting and carrying trauma. Many of the adults in schools are struggling as well. Developing trusting, caring relationships in schools through RJE can heal, empower, and generate enormous changes in how we do school.

◾ The Book's Organization

The book is divided into four sections. Section 1 sets the stage for this study. Chapter 1 lays out the challenge. The current model of education is failing us; schools are in crisis. In contrast, RJE offers schools an opportunity to become positive learning communities by building relationships and teaching lifelong skills for resolving differences and repairing harms.

Chapter 2 begins with where many schools are now: coping with the harmful effects of zero tolerance discipline policies. This chapter summarizes research findings on the impacts of zero tolerance: it has been a disaster.

Chapter 3 introduces RJE in detail and describes other initiatives that work well with RJE, including social and emotional learning (SEL) and Positive Behavioral Interventions and Supports (PBIS). The chapter also introduces the three-tiered pyramid of RJE practice—a framework for implementing RJE in schools.

Section 2 describes the context—the physical, human, and institutional landscape—in which this study took place. Chapters 4 and 5 describe each of the two middle schools.

Section 3 presents the study's findings. Chapter 6 addresses the question, "What do the relational ecologies of schools practicing school-wide restorative practices (SWRPs) look like?" Four themes emerged: trust; being heard; a student-centered, relational-based culture; and a commitment to social justice.

Chapter 7 considers a further question, "What changes occurred at the organizational, individual, and pedagogical levels in schools that adopted SWRPs?" This chapter identifies organizational changes that took place across the entire school. It also discusses what impeded change and threatened program fidelity.

Chapter 8 examines how the people—the principals, teachers, and students—were able or unable to incorporate restorative and relational practices into school life, especially into daily classroom teaching.

Chapter 9 investigates the larger issue of how relational ecology affects change and vice versa. The chapter also identifies why students and teachers may perceive restorative approaches as "not working for all students."

Section 4 offers insights gained from the study. Implementing RJE involves change. How do schools find the strength to face this change? And how can we use what we have learned to set schools up to succeed?

Chapter 10 explores how relational ecology and change interact: a school's relational ecology influences its capacity to change, and change affects the school's relational ecology.

Chapter 11 maps out and offers recommendations on shifting to a restorative school and implementing RJE. The hope is that the practice of RJE can become more widespread, supported, and utilized.

As you read this book, you will undoubtedly bring your own experiences, beliefs, and practices into the stories. You may find themes, situations, people, or occurrences that are familiar, or you might gain new insights. I hope for a little of both. I believe there is much to be learned from the people in these two schools and from my own experiences as an RJE researcher.* These voices can, I hope, ripple out into communities across the country to inspire change and re-create our nation's schools.

---

* The author's original dissertation included more than 2,000 in-text citations that referred to hundreds of authors whose ideas are represented in this book. The author agreed, for purposes of readability, to eliminate these in-text citations, which are fully available in her dissertation "Talking in Circles: A Mixed Methods Study of School-Wide Restorative Practices in Two Urban Middle Schools" (see the bibliography).

Making the Shift from Punitive to Restorative Schools

CHAPTER 1

From Zero Tolerance to Restorative Schools

Schools in Crisis and Change

US schools are both engulfed in crises and engaged in change. Some schools feel like prisons and treat students like prisoners; others hold spaces for learning that inspire and energize students and teachers alike. Schools in change prove that schools in crisis need not remain there.

First the crises. In far too many schools, neither students nor teachers feel safe. Teaching to the test has replaced meaningful teaching and learning. Teachers fear for their jobs if their students perform poorly on national tests. Yet despite this pressure, the United States lags behind many other countries in academic achievement. Racial disparities are raging. More than sixty years after the Supreme Court ruled segregated schools unconstitutional in *Brown v Board of Education,* an enormous achievement gap remains between White students and students of color. High suspension and low graduation rates among students of color suggest that schools are not only failing to educate these students but also targeting them for exclusion to raise test scores, which determine a school's funding. More middle-class White parents are pulling their children out of public schools, opting for homeschooling or private schools. Public schools with limited resources and even less political support struggle to find the best ways to educate students living in poverty, immigrant children, students with special needs, and students who require high levels of emotional support. On top of these crises, the traditional education model—involving competition and coercion, rules and punishment, fear of failing, learning by rote—does not equip students for today's fast-changing world. Nor does it help new generations develop the social and emotional and cooperative skills that many jobs require and that bring out our best as human beings. Most of all, far too many schools are not happy places. Though our brains are wired to take joy in learning, attending these schools feels more like doing time.

■ Restorative Justice in Education: A Paradigm Shift

Rather than continuing down this road of school failure, growing numbers of schools are forging a new path. Restorative justice in education (RJE) is blazing this trail, presenting a new paradigm for how we do school. RJE is a whole-school approach that prioritizes relationships, builds community, and creates just and equitable learning environments. RJE draws all members of the school community together to create learning environments where everyone is safe, respected, valued, and honored. A values-based philosophy grounds restorative practices (RPs), which foster social and emotional learning, community, trust, equity, and student engagement. From these foundations, restorative schools support struggling students, teach peaceful conflict resolution, and repair relationships after a harm has occurred. RJE is not new or untested. Many schools in Australia, the United Kingdom, Canada, and the United States have been practicing RJE for more than thirty years. We know it "works"—for everyone.

Not that implementing RJE is without challenges. The greatest challenge facing large-scale implementation of school-wide restorative practices (SWRPs) is that RJE requires an enormous paradigm shift—a fundamental change in attitudes, beliefs, behaviors, and assumptions. This is hard to do, as most of us have been schooled in the old model; its thought patterns are ingrained and reinforced by society. Even though we strive to shift, old habits sneak in to frame our thinking—we may not realize how much. These habits are why, after thirty years, the vast majority of schools in the United States continue to punish and exclude students for adolescent behaviors—each time increasing the risk that the student will drop out and end up in the criminal justice system.

Along with the paradigm shift that's required by individuals, the next major challenge is institutional change. This means changing not only the ways that individual schools operate, but also the way that the larger educational system functions. Administrators, school board members, state and federal education departments, state legislators and Congress, as well as the public: all these players affect the institutional setup for schools. Implementing RJE involves all of us. The good news is that this shift is already under way, both here and around the world.

Given these challenges, the RJE paradigm shift requires support. Obviously, we need policy makers on board, since federal and state funding policies, laws, and mandates hold the current model in place. Decision makers need to entertain ways of doing school beyond the traditional model. They definitely need to let go of the zero tolerance paradigm and repeal all policies that support it.

Who provides the momentum for changing laws and policies? We do. While a 8 January 2014 "Dear Colleague" letter from the US Department of Education (DOE) and US Department of Justice (DOJ), Civil Rights Division, recommended that schools replace suspensions and expulsions with restorative justice, this idea did not start at the top. The federal government was responding to a grassroots movement of parents and community members fed up with how schools have been excluding youth—disproportionately youth of color—and putting them on the road to prison. Advocates of restorative justice energize this movement by educating both the public and policy makers about RJE and why it deserves our support.

Since decision makers—whether within a school, on a school board, in a legislature, or within a family or community— weigh costs and benefits to choose their course, let's look at how we might assess the costs and benefits of both the current zero tolerance model and the restorative model.

Zero Tolerance Paradigm: On-the-Spot Benefit; Costs Forever After

"Benefit": On the spot and done with. Zero tolerance discipline policies set a uniform range of punishments for breaking rules. School administrators and teachers work from a discipline matrix that restricts their decision-making ability, much like mandatory sentencing laws restrict judges. The matrix is set. It provides little to no flexibility and certainly does not allow educators to consider circumstances that drive behaviors. The benefit is that the matrix makes life simple for school administrators and teachers. In the matrix, every undesirable behavior or broken rule has a punishment assigned to it, allowing for quick and efficient responses to undesirable behavior.

Costs to society, justice, and democratic values. But zero tolerance discipline policies come at a great cost to individuals, families, and communities. When we are talking about children, there is no "done with." School efficiency turns out to be school failure. The costs to society for zero tolerance policies, which feed the school-to-prison pipeline, have been enormous. What often starts as a broken rule in a school ends up ruining a young person's life. Locked in a facility, youth cannot contribute to their family or community, their critical years for learning and forming character are stolen from them, and they often end up with a criminal record that follows them through life.

In the name of discipline, millions of students—primarily Black and brown males—are pushed out of schools and onto the streets. There, without guidance and supervision from caring adults, they follow street rules. Law enforcement policies, such as "Stop and frisk" that target young men of color, have allowed police to sweep massive numbers of young people into juvenile detention facilities. Many of these facilities are owned and operated by private corrections companies that, to be profitable, require large numbers of incarcerated people. In this case, "profitable" means charging taxpayers. Yet, as taxpayers, we would do better to send young people to college, since a year at college costs less than a year in prison. With college, society could reap the benefits of knowledge and creativity as the young people enter the workforce. As it is, released from prison, adults, now no longer youth, face an uphill struggle to contribute to society.

We all pay for the mass injustice of the zero tolerance system. Our society pays a devastating price in moral integrity when we operate in a way so contrary to our democratic and humanitarian values.

Costs to schools. Youth, their families, and society are not the only ones to pay the price. Schools pay, too, in both money and time. Zero tolerance policies have cost school districts millions of dollars to implement. They have been led to a police-state mind-set, investing in metal detectors, armed school police (called "school resource officers" [SROs] or "school security officers" [SSOs]), surveillance cameras, drug-sniffing dogs, computerized visitor sign-in systems, and locked doors and gates. In his book *Governing Through Crime*, criminologist and sociologist Jonathan Simon refers to these as "fortress tactics."

Yet zero tolerance policies do not get to the root of why

students act as they do, nor do they build good relations. So, after the punishment is meted out, the cycle continues. Punishment and exclusion produce anger and shame, and students often express these emotions in ways that disrupt the learning environment or that lead to conflict and violence. Students who are temporarily removed from classrooms are sent back into them without any reintroduction or reintegration process. The repeated removal and return of students disrupts the learning environment; tension between teachers and students mounts; and ongoing and unresolved conflicts—among students or between students and teachers—intensify. The school environment created by zero tolerance policies takes an emotional toll on everyone.

Costs to learning. Nor are zero tolerance policies conducive to learning. Students who attend schools equipped with human control technologies and armed police officers experience tremendous stress from being treated like "criminals." With cameras and police everywhere, students feel and react to the constant threat of punishment for even minor rule infractions. Seeing School Resource Officers (SROs) rush in, overpower, and handcuff a student traumatizes the class. Schools need to be places where students want to be and where they feel safe: they should never, under any circumstance, feel like prisons. Yet this is where zero tolerance policies have pushed schools: controlling students outweighs teaching them.

Costs to social and emotional health and development. Since 1998, the new field of positive psychology—which explores what makes for a satisfying life—has greatly influenced how we think about relationships, learning, and discipline. Interdisciplinary research in early childhood education, educational psychology, and child/youth/human development consistently finds that when students have trusting relationships with adults, they bond to their schools better. When students form these attachments, they are much less likely to exhibit problematic behavior and are more likely to behave in ways that foster healthy relationships. Not only is this bonding critical for human development, but research shows that, when students feel connected to their schools, they become better students and take their education more seriously.[1]

By contrast, authoritarianism in the classroom or school does not foster attachment, connection, or relationships but serve only to force compliance. In US schools, that means compliance with historically White, middle-class rules, procedures, and expectations.

The urge to force compliance is one of the old paradigm habits we have to watch. It is appropriate if the building is on fire. Otherwise, it is far better to teach and model how to develop positive, mutually respectful relationships by resolving problems in good ways.

Evidence baseless. While the next chapter gives an overview of the research on zero tolerance policies, to my knowledge, not a single study shows that zero tolerance produces desired behaviors or higher student achievement. Not one shred of evidence. Rather, researchers and practitioners in criminal justice, education, psychology, sociology, and mental health counseling have documented the negative impacts of zero tolerance policies, fueling the movement to call for their repeal.[2] Simply put, zero tolerance is *not* an evidence-based approach for making schools safer or for helping students succeed in school.

The policies persist, however, for several reasons. First, like popping a pill, these responses are quick and simple. Second, policy makers have for decades lacked the political will to revoke zero tolerance policies, despite evidence of their harms. Perhaps most of all, zero tolerance policies continue because our culture is vested in force-and-punishment thinking. Punishing is an emotional response. Carried into schools, zero tolerance is an emotional response to student behaviors deemed undesirable, no matter how miniscule. It is time for today's policy and decision makers to reject zero tolerance policies and instead support RJE, an approach to schooling and positive discipline that has decades of research, evidence, and experience behind it.[3] Yes, making the shift involves up-front costs, but the short- and long-term benefits more than justify the expense.

RJE Paradigm: Up-Front Costs, Benefits Forever After

RJE builds a school community. First the benefits. The main purpose, and one of the great benefits, of RJE is its ability to build community among students and teachers. Community develops when restorative processes are used across all school environments, particularly in the classroom. When individuals feel a sense of belonging and acceptance, they are far less likely to do anything to harm one another. Typically, students who bully, commit acts of violence, or disengage from learning are those who do not "fit in," who feel alienated or isolated, and who lack a meaningful connection to the people around them. RJE is about acceptance, inclusion, and community.

The restorative process uses conflicts and harms to build relationships. Community is, of course, most tested when a person acts in a way that disrupts community or causes harm. Restorative principles map a response that repairs broken relationships, builds them where they did not exist before, and strengthens relationships all around. How? The first step is to find out what happened and what lies behind the behavior. An RJE response brings community members together to listen, hear the stories of all those involved, address needs, and engage in problem solving. The idea is to use the experience for social and emotional growth and transformation. Once a clearer picture of what happened emerges, the group turns to repairing harm as a means to establish good relations. When a person in a community commits a harm, he or she then has an obligation to repair the harm. Other community members deserve and expect that. Yet they also share a responsibility for harms that happen in their midst and for finding ways to put things right.

A positive social and emotional learning process. The time that this process takes, often in Circles, is not time away from learning. It is time well spent in a different kind of learning—a collaborative development of social and emotional skills essential to becoming a healthy, responsible, balanced adult and good citizen. Moreover, each time a class or group works through issues, those issues are less likely to resurface. Social and emotional skills do not develop overnight; neither can they bloom in social isolation. RJE is the work we do together to expand students' social and emotional capacities for learning in community, so that when students turn to their coursework, they learn far more readily.

Fosters collaborative skills. Indeed, collaborative learning strategies are widely promoted as an effective way to engage students and to have them take responsibility for their own learning. In schools where students constantly bicker and fight with each other, teachers are less apt to use collaborative learning in their classrooms, because the students lack the social and emotional skills needed to work as a team. Yet these are the very skills that today's employers seek. In schools that practice RJE, teachers use learning activities that allow students to work cooperatively on projects, so they develop social and emotional skills while mastering the curriculum at the same time.

Good for learning. The biggest benefit from RJE is that schools become positive places of learning. Restorative processes make it clear that every single person in the class is valued, respected, honored, deserving of an education, and a vital member of the classroom and school community. Through trust-building and conflict-resolution processes, students learn how to interact with others in positive ways. Students feel safe, heard, and trusted, which allows them to focus on their schoolwork.

In restorative schools, the learning environment is effective and efficient. Students spend time engaging with each other and the lessons; teachers focus on those who need help; and discipline problems do not hold center stage. When conflict occurs during cooperative learning activities, students are equipped to resolve conflicts peacefully, often without needing adults to step in.

Peacemaking as a way of life. Once a school makes the shift to RJE across all school environments, less time and fewer resources are needed for discipline problems, simply because fewer problems arise. Research and evaluations of RJE here and abroad show that behavioral problems decrease when problems are handled restoratively.[4] When a harm does occur, restorative processes teach conflict resolution as a way of life, a way of being together. John Paul Lederach, who studies conflict transformation internationally, describes conflict as a natural and healthy part of human relationships. How we handle conflict reflects our social and emotional health. When students learn through restorative practices, like Circles, how to productively and respectfully handle conflicts, they are learning vital life skills and nonviolent ways to resolve conflict. By helping to build generations of peacemakers, RJE can have a profoundly positive impact on our collective future.

And now the costs: savings in time and money. Creating a restorative school requires a commitment of time and money—no question. Personnel: restorative schools hire RJ facilitators, also called RJ coordinators, preferably more than one. RJE consultants and coaches support the school through the transition and continue to provide RJE knowledge and experience. Trainers and trainings are essential, both initially and regularly. Some schools integrate training as a year-round program. Resources—such as books, manuals, visuals, and materials for Circles—provide critical support. And time: restorative schools create time for restorative practices, which are all about building relationships—the lifeblood of a restorative school community. As we all experience in life, building relationships takes time.

While we should certainly acknowledge these expenses, also consider what a school saves in both money and time. A school does not have to hire SROs. Expensive policing and fortress tactics are unnecessary as well. As school-generated trauma goes down, students are happier, which means the school needs fewer crisis management personnel. Less time is spent on discipline issues, which means administrators and teachers become more effective, and students learn more. Up and running, a restorative school saves time and money and aligns schools with their overall goal: not to discipline or control but to educate.

These savings to schools say nothing of the savings to society. We taxpayers do not have to fund as many juvenile detention facilities and prisons, neither do we have to create social nets for people whose lives have been ripped apart by early incarceration. We do not lose the knowledge and creativity of all those whose education was cut off. Instead, we reap the benefit of millions of productive citizens who are healthy and happy and who create healthy and happy families and communities. As in school, so in life: healthy and happy people can use their minds and energies far more effectively in addressing the issues our world faces.

■ What Does the Shift Entail?

Investing in students. Faced with a decision, we all weigh costs and benefits. However, the cost-benefit model comes from business, and I do not advocate approaching schools as if they were businesses. Educating new generations is our responsibility as humans, not an opportunity for marketplace profits. If the business model is instructive at all, then it teaches us that successful businesses invest in their people. As a nation, we need to invest in our people, and our people are our students.

Rethinking why we educate youth. In the big picture, why do we have schools? Today, people generally agree that we create schools because free, democratic societies need a well-educated citizenry capable of making decisions and solving complex problems. Peter Senge and Justin Reich, professors at the MIT Sloan School of Management, believe that schools need to help students prepare to do the work that computers cannot do well, which include communicating to a diverse audience and solving problems when the resources needed to solve the problem are not clear, nor is the solution. The "pay-off" for quality public schools is a strong, vibrant democracy and students who are equipped for today's workplaces, which are diverse and changing.

Indeed, schools need to help young people develop into creative, competent, healthy adults. While graduating students certainly need a knowledge base, technical skills, and workplace literacy, they also need much more:

- They need to think critically.
- They need to possess emotional literacy and social and emotional skills.
- They need to have empathy, which is our species' protective mechanism against harming others.

- They need conflict-resolution skills and the ability to listen to, appreciate, and work well with people who are different from them.

The skills that restorative schools build are essential for success in a globalized economy where a person's team member may be halfway around the world. They are the same skills that contribute to a person's sense of well-being. Meaning matters, and schools succeed when they help students learn how to connect with meaning in their lives. By nurturing meaningful relationships, the whole person, and the school community, restorative schools not only resolve the behavioral problems in schools but also hold the promise of bettering society and humanity.

Rethinking punishment and accountability. Despite its widespread use, punishment fails to produce the desired results. Rather, it produces stigmatizing shame, which leads a person to withdraw, act violently against others, self-harm, or develop other unhealthy behaviors, including addictions. There simply is no place for punishment in schools. There is a place, however, for students to learn how to hold each other accountable for their actions in a restorative way.

Relationships in a community interweave individual and collective accountability. The individual does not bear the entire weight of a harm or its repair. Bystanders and supporters have a role and a responsibility as well. Classmates, for example, play a part in either egging on or deescalating conflicts, fights, or bullying. They decide whether to reach out in friendship or to exclude. Many choices by many people contribute to an event. Restorative practices use events as opportunities to cultivate, among other things, civic responsibility—a sense of sharing responsibility for the integrity and well-being of a community.

Committing to whole-school restorative practices. In recent years, some schools and school districts have attempted to adopt restorative practices, but they have used them only as an alternative to suspension or as a kinder, gentler way to punish students. Research on RJE shows this does not produce systemic change. RJE needs to be implemented throughout the entire school community for it to improve the school climate, promote social and emotional competency, reduce suspensions, and increase student achievement.

So far, we have examined the costs of zero tolerance and RJE and have begun to explore what is involved with shifting from punitive to restorative practices. Now, we will take an in-depth look at how zero tolerance discipline policies have turned schools into hostile environments, particularly for students of color. These policies, combined with other factors, formed a perfect storm that has ravaged the landscape of education.

CHAPTER 2

Zero Tolerance: A Disastrous Policy

Understanding What We Want to Change

Restorative justice is a philosophy, a set of values, and a radically transformational way of being in the world. It includes processes for healing, reparation, and restoration. Most of all for education, restorative justice is a way to transform schools into communities where individuals experience joy in learning together.

That said, why might a book on restorative justice in education (RJE) include a chapter on zero tolerance discipline? Because I believe we need to understand the policy and political climate we seek to change. To tell that story, I present the history, use, and results of zero tolerance discipline policies in schools. Schools adopting school-wide restorative practices (SWRPs) are "in recovery" from decades of failed zero tolerance policies and practices. From a harsh, punitive atmosphere, RJE transforms schools into caring, collaborative learning communities where people are not just "tolerated" but welcomed.

To appreciate this sea change in school climate, we begin with where many schools are now: coping with the harmful effects of zero tolerance. For the past twenty-five years, fear of violence, the dehumanization of students, and the demonization of teachers have led to policies and practices in US schools that have caused much hurt and harm, and in some instances, trauma. How did we go down this road?

◼ The Origin of Zero Tolerance: A Response to Gun Violence

Since the turn of the twentieth century, schools have been considered the most important gateway to citizenship. As a society, we ask our public schools to help us produce free and responsible, capable adults. However, since the 1980s, sociopolitical conservatism and a "tough on crime" criminal justice philosophy have led to the widespread use of punitive disciplinary policies, commonly referred to as "zero tolerance." These punitive policies have excluded millions of students, many of whom have ended up in the juvenile or criminal justice systems. This outcome, commonly called the "school-to-prison pipeline," has been criticized as discriminatory, unjust, and undemocratic.

During the 1980s and 1990s, Washington's political leaders and policy makers spouted a narrative coded with fear, with race-based fears playing a big role. The narrative was that juvenile crime rates were on the rise, youth gangs were becoming more deadly, and urban adolescent males—code for non-White, especially Black youth—were becoming remorseless, psychopathic "super-predators" capable of committing heinous crimes. This narrative was not the reality; it did not reflect the facts. Nonetheless, Congress passed the Gun-Free Schools Act in 1994 (GFSA). This act prohibited guns within 100 feet of schools with the intent of transforming schools into safe havens free from gun violence.

Yet, the GFSA did not reduce violence in schools. Instead, on its heels came unprecedented school violence: in the 1996–97 school year, 10 percent of schools reported at least one violent crime. The 1998 shooting in Jonesboro, Arkansas, and the 1999 massacre at Columbine High School in Littleton, Colorado—both involving White male youth shooters—escalated the public's fear that schools were no longer safe places for their children. Policy makers at the federal and state levels, acting against the wishes of many Columbine parents, reacted viscerally to the school shootings by passing laws that changed school buildings, school cultures, and even the way teachers taught lessons and managed behavior in their classrooms.

The same year that the Gun-Free Schools Act passed, Congress also passed the Safe and Drug-Free Schools and Communities Act (Safe Schools Act) of 1994. Prior to this law, President George H. W. Bush convened a national conference of governors to frame a national education agenda and to set goals to achieve by the year 2000. Goal six referred specifically to school discipline, stating that "every school in America will be free of drugs and violence and will offer a disciplined environment conducive to learning."[1] By linking drugs to violence and a lack of discipline to crime, goal six essentially transformed schools into an arm of the criminal justice system.

The passage of these two laws—the Gun-Free Schools Act and the Safe Schools Act—led more than 90 percent of US schools to implement zero tolerance policies for weapons possession. More than 80 percent of schools revised their disciplinary codes to make them more restrictive and punitive.[2] Police, juvenile justice agencies, and schools cemented close relationships with each other during this time, as certain criminal justice theories and practices took hold in the US public and hence in public schools. For example, theories of deterrence and rational choice claim that criminals or rule breakers will stop their wrongdoings if they are sufficiently afraid of punishment or imprisonment. These theories became common underpinnings in school discipline policies and practices. Essentially, from this point forward, the US Department of Education governed teaching and learning in schools, while the US Department of Justice managed school culture and discipline.

From Criminalizing Youth Behavior to Creating Prison-Like Schools

The focus on punitive measures in the public and political arenas took its toll: student behavior became increasingly criminalized and schools operated more like prisons. Zero tolerance policies shifted responsibility from the adults in the schools and the school as a whole to the individual students. Schools focused on student "failure" and responding to it with punishment by exclusion. Yet the public discourse did not raise some important questions: Are schools failing our children, children of color in particular? Is school failure the real issue, not because school staff are bad people but because the punitive system sets schools up to fail in educating their students?

Instead of addressing this larger systemic issue, the policies wrote off—sacrificed—individual students and sent an intimidating message to groups.[3] Just as mandatory sentencing laws reduced judges' ability to use their own discretion, school discipline codes limited teachers' responses to students' behavior. The mantra became "If you do that, then this will happen to you—no questions asked."

A distinctive change in attitudes and beliefs about adolescent behavior followed. Behavior that would have been considered normal acts of mischief or rebelliousness in the 1970s—things that most of us did, were encouraged to do by our peers, and were often, in fact, developmentally appropriate—were treated as criminal acts in the 1990s. We refer to this change as the criminalization of behavior. Policy makers and school leaders continually expanded their lists of "offenses"— including nonviolent behaviors—that they would no longer tolerate.

The tools of the criminal justice system became dominant technologies in schools, and some educators began to reframe students as a population of potential victims and perpetrators.

Figure 2. High school built like a prison, complete with tower

Since the passage of the Gun-Free Schools and Safe Schools Acts in 1994, both prisons and schools have been increasingly restricted from doing more than sorting and warehousing people. Within a very short period of time, school policies made it acceptable and sometimes mandatory to punish children by depriving them of an education.

No Child Left Behind and Push Out

The No Child Left Behind (NCLB) Act of 2001 included many provisions relating to student behavior and required schools "to provide civic education materials and services to address specific problems such as the prevention of school violence and the abuse of drugs and alcohol."[4] Like the 1994 Safe Schools Act, NCLB required states to track and report the number of violent incidents in schools. By linking student achievement to school funding, the NCLB created a great incentive for schools to push out low-performing students. Zero tolerance policies and their wide net of criminalized behaviors provided the legal means to do just that. The result was a "perfect storm" (see figure 3) comprised of federal and state policies, public opinion, and educator attitudes that converged directly upon students and left in its aftermath increased suspensions and expulsions, high minority dropout rates, and vast numbers of youth referred to the juvenile justice system.

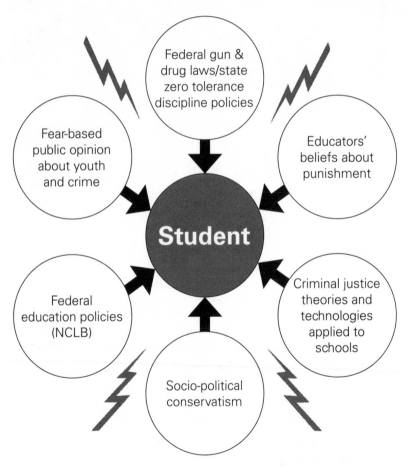

Figure 3. The "perfect storm" of policies, beliefs, and discourse

▨ School-Community Bonds Broken

Zero tolerance policies, as well as other elements of the perfect storm, failed to recognize that the strength of students' relationship with their school, particularly their bonds with the adults in their school, can predict their behavior. Exclusionary policies, such as zero tolerance, break the bonds among students and their schools and invite hurtful, and sometimes violent, behaviors. If students do not care about the people around them or, worse yet, feel that the people in schools do not care about them, then they feel no obligation to follow school "rules" and norms.[5]

Relationships in schools took a hit when School Resource Officers (SROs) became commonplace. At this point, teachers, counselors, and other school personnel were pushed out of their roles to teach and model prosocial behavior. SROs took over and essentially conditioned students for a life behind bars. Indeed, the very presence of SROs in the schools eroded the relationship between teachers and students. The adults began to subconsciously see students—particularly students of color—as future prisoners in need of exclusion or coercive control, and this created a self-fulfilling prophecy: many students who were suspended one or more times soon found themselves in the hands of the juvenile or criminal justice systems. On top of it all, racial stereotypes have long portrayed Black males as unsalvageable, making their future role as prisoners rather than neighbors, scholars, professionals, and leaders seem inevitable.

Although parents and policy makers believed that schools would become safer with fortress tactics and zero tolerance policies, quite the opposite occurred. The physical security procedures created an emotional backlash in students: disorder increased in the schools. Just as in Julio's case, which I described in the introduction, students reported feeling mistrusted or even provoked by SROs. They recognized that their schools looked and felt like prisons and that they were viewed as delinquents instead of as students. Zero tolerance became the problem, not the solution.

Zero Tolerance Fails to Serve the Purpose of Education

The American Psychological Association's 2008 Zero Tolerance Task Force concluded that zero tolerance policies not only fail to achieve the goals of an effective system of school discipline but also run counter to healthy child and adolescent development. Because zero tolerance does not promote or teach desirable behaviors, school psychologist Dr. David Hulac and his colleagues found that fortress tactics and punishments may actually encourage more aggressive behavior.[6] The tactics cease to be punishing and, instead, reward students who do not want to be in school anyway. If a disciplinary system's effectiveness is measured by how well it teaches students to peacefully solve problems and conflicts, then zero tolerance policies have been worse than a failure: they have been a disaster. Belinda Hopkins, the director of Transforming Conflict in the United Kingdom, states:

> The system of rewards and sanctions often implemented by schools to ensure compliance of the school rules suggests a lack of understanding by the staff themselves of the purpose of rules. If compliance is the sole intention, and failure to comply the only interpretation given to unacceptable behavior, then a vital and important lesson in developing intrinsic pro-social motivation and an inner autonomous moral compass is being lost.[7]

▣ Racial Bias in Teacher Attitudes and Racialized Discipline Policies

The teacher, in most cases, is the catalyst in the disciplinary process. Therefore, teacher attitudes need examining as well. Do some teachers prefer zero tolerance discipline policies, for example, because these policies make someone else responsible for dealing with challenging student behavior? Moreover, the ways that teacher attitudes affect discipline raise questions of social and racial justice: How much do teachers' racial and cultural biases affect how they interact with students of a different race or culture? And how much do racial and cultural biases influence how teachers and administrators perceive student behaviors: which behaviors do our schools' policies let pass and which do they label as "criminal"?

I enter into this section on teacher bias fully aware that not all teachers support zero tolerance policies. Plus, some teachers may not be aware of the biases they subconsciously harbor. I would argue that the majority of White middle-class teachers—and I am White middle class—have not examined their White racial identity and have little to no understanding of how White privilege affects our approach to teaching students of color.[8] As multicultural educator Gary Howard says, "An unexamined life on the part of a White teacher is a danger to every student."[9] Whether biases are hidden or out in the open, implicit or explicit, they often persist, and our collective history of racial biases affects what happens in the classroom. Think about it: who could perform to their potential in a racially unsupportive or even hostile social and emotional climate?

Extensive research supports this assertion. Given the disproportionate numbers of Black and other minority students being suspended and expelled under zero tolerance policies, researchers have studied the role that teacher attitudes and behaviors play in disciplining students of diverse races.[10] White middle-class teachers, who account for more than 80 percent of the teaching workforce in US schools, are often unfamiliar and uncomfortable with the more active style of communication among many African American adolescents, for example. We "may interpret the impassioned and emotive manner popular among young African Americans as combative or argumentative."[11] Several studies on school discipline found that the most frequent reason for referring students to the office were insubordination and defiance.[12] Additionally, most discipline problems were considered norm-violating, not maladaptive (behaviors meant to reduce anxiety but having dysfunctional or non-productive results).

Other studies have revealed unrecognized teacher biases that led them to commit microaggressions against minority students. These are everyday expressions that denigrate, though usually without an intent to harm. They occur because of ignorance—both a lack of experience with people of a different background and a lack of critical awareness on issues of White privilege, race, and culture. Microaggressions, according to psychologist Derald Wing Sue, include statements that repeat or affirm stereotypes about the minority group or subtly demean it, that seek to deny the perpetrator's own bias, or that minimize real conflicts between the minority group and White society.[13] Examples of microaggressions include asking questions like, "What are you?" denying the possibility of having any bias at all, assuming Asian or Latinx students were not born in the United States, or making comments to Black students about being intelligent, pretty, or articulate, as if these qualities are unexpected. However unintentional, White teachers' microaggressions negatively affect minority students' behavior and academic performance.

Racial and cultural biases may be one reason behind teachers' disproportionately referring African American and other students of color to the office for discipline. School psychology professor Russell Skiba asked African American students what was not working for them in school. They reported that conflict in the classroom arose primarily due to a lack of respect from the teachers, differences in communication styles, disinterest on the part of teachers, and teachers pushing them "to the edge."[14] Indeed, a number of researchers have attributed the perceived misbehavior of African American students and the resulting differential treatment and disciplinary actions they received to cultural differences, systemic racism, teacher biases, misunderstandings, and fear.[15] To say the least, zero tolerance discipline policies, the criminalizing of misbehavior, and racial biases have created unwelcoming learning environments and unhealthy relational ecologies in schools, particularly for students of color.

The outcome—now multigenerational—has been disastrous for students, families, and communities of color. African American males have been harmed by zero tolerance policies more than any other group, resulting in the well-documented phenomenon known as "disproportionate disciplining." African American students account for only 15 percent of all K12 students in the United States, yet they make up 35 percent of all students suspended once, 44 percent of students suspended more than once, and 36 percent of students expelled. African American and Latinx students comprise 50 percent of all students involved with arrests or referred to law enforcement.[16] Research has shown that students who are suspended even once are more likely to drop out of school, so disproportionate disciplining contributes to already low graduation rates for African Americans and disproportionately high arrest and incarceration rates. The school-to-prison pipeline is filled with Black and brown young men.

School Push-Out: A Civil Rights Issue for Our Time

Despite continued support among certain populations and policy makers, zero tolerance discipline policies are now recognized as being blatantly discriminatory to students of color, particularly African American, Latinx, and Indigenous males. The Dignity in Schools Campaign, the US Department of Education Office for Civil Rights (USDOE OCR), and the US Department of Justice (USDOJ) state outright that punishing and pushing out students of color has created a crisis in the American education system. After President Obama's administration introduced the Supportive School Discipline Initiative in Summer 2011, the federal government acknowledged that zero tolerance policies have caused disproportionate disciplining of primarily African American males and that this outcome has become one of the most pressing civil rights issues of our time.

On 8 January 2014, the Obama administration took action: the USDOE and the USDOJ joined forces to issue federal guidelines for school leaders wishing to draft and implement new discipline policies that do not discriminate against racial or ethnic groups. The guidelines made it clear that policies that unfairly target or affect certain groups in word or application would be considered discriminatory. Two of the most important components of the new guidelines are that schools return the power to solve behavior problems to teachers, counselors, and administrators and that SROs and other law enforcement officials are involved only as the last resort. The clear aim is to encourage school districts to create positive environments and to prevent behavioral incidents by revising their disciplinary policies. The guidelines named restorative justice as an important approach that schools can and should use. Today, many school districts are exploring how to implement RJE across schools and districts because of the federal government's endorsement of RJ as a viable alternative to zero tolerance.

A Paradigm Change Under Way

Adopting more effective discipline policies means changing school culture. Schools need to function as communities, and that means building trusting relationships. Such deep change—rethinking habits ingrained by several decades of zero tolerance—calls for a shift in funding, thinking, and organizational behavior.

When relationships among students, teachers, and administrators are strained by the constant threat of punishment and by a school culture of authoritarianism, control, domination, and outright harm to students, it is difficult to enact meaningful change. Is it impossible to achieve deep change in our schools? Certainly not, but it will take significant effort and a public education campaign. A sea change in how we educate youth will require policy reform on federal, state, and local levels. It will require changing how we educate administrators and teachers to handle student misbehavior. It will also require changing how the school community's adults—parents, school board members, and community members—engage each other.

These changes are already happening. Schools nationwide are replacing zero tolerance with restorative approaches. Indeed, one by one, schools and districts across the country are adopting values and practices that teach students prosocial behavior. When this happens, positive and safe school environments follow. Restorative justice in education is changing how people in schools think and relate to each other. It is even changing the curriculum and how it is taught.

The rest of this book is dedicated to explaining how RJE, when implemented as a school-wide reform, creates schools where teachers want to work, where students are excited to learn, and where relationships are the highest priority. The next chapter explores what restorative justice means in schools, especially when it is used with other initiatives that promote prosocial behavior.

CHAPTER 3

Understanding Restorative Justice in Education (RJE)

▪ What Is Restorative Justice?

Howard Zehr, a leader in restorative justice (RJ), defines restorative justice as "a process to involve, to the extent possible, those who have a stake in a specific offense, and to collectively identify and address harms, needs, and obligations, in order to heal and put things as right as possible."[1] Brenda Morrison, director of the Centre for Restorative Justice and criminology professor at Simon Fraser University, expands that definition. For her, RJ is "both a process and a set of values" that focus on "addressing basic social and emotional needs of individuals and communities, particularly in the context of responding to harmful behavior to oneself and others."[2] Whereas traditional criminal justice removes the victim from the process, defines crime as an offense against the state, and frequently seeks punishment over reparation, RJ offers a humanizing and humane response to harms.

▪ Restorative Values

Values drive restorative justice processes. RJ values include being inclusive, building relationships and communities, minimizing stigmatizing shame, and reintegrating those who have caused harm. Contemporary restorative justice looks to the time-tested values of Indigenous peoples for its philosophical foundation, because these values have sustained relationships and communities over millennia. For this reason, RJ values have been linked to the philosophies and practices of Indigenous peoples worldwide, including, for example, Navajo peacemaking; *Ubuntu** philosophy in Africa, spiritual beliefs shared by many religions; Asian conflict resolution; and Maori ways of living in community.[3] Brenda Morrison writes that restorative values are "about healing rather than hurting, moral learning, community participation and community caring, respectful dialogue, forgiveness, responsibility, apology, and making amends."[4] Howard Zehr believes that our interconnectedness underlies the values of restorative justice: "We are all connected to each other and to the larger world through a web of relationships. When the web is disrupted, we are all affected."[5]

People engaged in RJ describe restorative values in different ways. Morrison, for example, lists overarching values of RJ, while Kay Pranis, international trainer and author in the field of peacemaking Circles and restorative justice, differentiates between process values and individual values: process values nurture relationships in groups, and they also connect individuals with the values of their best selves. Chart 3.1 illustrates this range of values.

Restorative justice operates from a value-based philosophy that, as Morrison says, ultimately "grounds and enhances our notions of freedom, democracy, and community—it is the heart of responsible citizenship."[6]

The Indigenous values and practices that RJ draws on can help restore humans to our natural ways of being. These practices can be used across cultures and ethnicities; they carry as much power in today's high-tech world as they did millennia

---

* *Ubuntu*, a Nguni Bantu term translated as "humanness," conveys an attitude of "humanity toward others." Philosophically, it affirms a universal bond that connects all humanity.

Chart 3.1. Overarching, individual, and process restorative values		
OVERARCHING VALUES	INDIVIDUAL VALUES	PROCESS VALUES
Empowerment	Respect	Respect
Honesty	Honesty	Individual dignity
Respect	Compassion	Inclusion
Engagement	Open-mindedness	Responsibility
Voluntarism	Patience	Humility
Healing		Mutual care
Restoration		Reparation
Personal Accountability		Non-domination
Inclusiveness		
Collaboration		
Problem solving		

Adapted from Morrison, *Restoring Safe School Communities*, p. 167; Pranis, "Restorative Values," p. 72.

ago around a campfire. Since the contemporary RJ movement began in the 1970s, more societies, regions, and countries have adopted restorative practices into their criminal justice, juvenile justice, and educational systems. RJ's focus on values makes the process both highly contextual and adaptable. Although RJ is not a panacea, many of us believe it is a more just, equitable, fair, and humane way of being.

How Is Restorative Justice in Education Different?

RJ has been migrating from juvenile justice settings into schools for several decades now to keep youth in schools and to prevent early incarceration. In the process, practitioners have been adapting RJ to school uses. In *The Little Book of Restorative Justice in Education*, Katherine Evans, education professor at Eastern Mennonite University in Virginia, and Dorothy Vaandering, education professor at Memorial University of

Newfoundland in New Labrador, define restorative justice in education (RJE) in this way:

> [T]he term *restorative justice in education* can be defined as facilitating learning communities that nurture the capacity of people to engage with one another and their environment in a manner that supports and respects the inherent dignity and worth of all.[7]

Their definition embeds learning in communities that operate on relationship-oriented values—values that good relationships require: respect, mutual appreciation, and trust that learners will be valued and treated well and with dignity.

The new language of RJE reflects how restorative justice values, philosophy, theory, and practices (RJ) are being

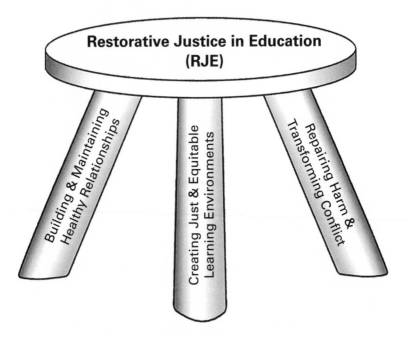

Figure 4. Foundational concepts of RJE

applied and modified for the school environment (E). Restorative justice in education means creating a restorative justice environment—using restorative practices to create a truly just and equitable environment for learning. Figure 4 illustrates the foundational concepts of RJE. "School-wide restorative practices" (SWRPs) is another key term emerging from the RJE movement in schools, and it comes up a lot in this book. It refers to the practice of using restorative values and processes in all school environments, a practice that incorporates both the preventative and responsive aspects of restorative justice. Researchers and practitioners in different parts of the world use terms like restorative approaches or restorative measures; in this book, we will use SWRPs and RPs.

Restorative Processes in Schools

Historically, the three restorative processes most often used in schools are Circles, conferences, and mediation. Each approach embodies the values of restorative discipline and asks the following questions:

1. Who has been hurt? *or* Who has been affected and how?
2. What are their needs?
3. Whose obligations are they? *or* How can we put right the harm?
4. What are the causes?
5. Who has a "stake" in this?
6. What have we all learned that will help us make different choices next time?
7. What is the appropriate way to involve stakeholders in an effort to put things right?[8]

Each approach serves distinct purposes and is useful in different situations. Circles have become the most common restorative approach used in schools for at least two reasons. One is their versatility. The other is that no other RJ process builds relationships and community as effectively across school environments as Circles do. Building community is central for RJE, and Circles provide the process to do it.

Chart 3.2 describes and summarizes how these three restorative processes are being used in schools.[9] Those trained in restorative practices—teachers, administrators, counselors, RJ coordinators and facilitators, and community members— try to match the restorative process to the intensity of the harm. As chart 3.2 indicates, conferences and mediation are more disciplinary in nature and are suited for intensive or targeted interventions. That said, mediation is being critically examined, and some practitioners find it to be a blunt instrument that is not always aligned with restorative values due to potential power imbalances. Others would not use conferences for bullying due to the potential for further abuses of power and victimization. The Circle, on the other hand, is considered a universal "intervention" that is both preventative and reparative; it can be used for everyday relationship building as well as for intense, severe harms, including bullying.

That said, all truly restorative practices share certain principles. They

(a) focus on relationships first and rules second
(b) give voice to the person harmed
(c) give voice to the person who caused the harm
(d) engage in collaborative problem solving
(e) enhance responsibility
(f) empower change and growth
(g) include plans for restoration/reparation

Chart 3.2. Restorative processes and their applications in schools

RESTORATIVE PROCESS	DESCRIPTION	STAKEHOLDERS (VARY BY SITUATION)	INTERVENTION LEVEL AND USES
Circles	Chairs are placed in a physical circle. Circle keepers pass a talking piece that permits only the holder to speak; the piece is passed clockwise so that all have an opportunity to speak and listen. Circles involve a number of rounds in an orderly and reflective process that reinforces the values of RJ. Any stakeholder can act as the Circle keeper.	Students Teachers RJ facilitators/ coordinators Community members Person(s) harmed Person(s) who committed harm Parents Supporters	**Universal, targeted, and intensive interventions: preventative (relationship building) and reparative** Community building Check in/out Problem solving Repairing harm Teaching and learning
Mediation includes peer mediation	A structured method in which trained mediators help people in dispute by listening to their concerns and helping them negotiate a solution.	Trained mediator RJ facilitator or counselor Person(s) who committed harm Person(s) who was harmed Parents	**Targeted and intensive interventions: reparative** Dispute resolution
Conferences	A structured meeting that includes the person(s) who did the harm, the person(s) harmed, and both parties' family and friends. The purpose is to hold the harmdoer accountable and reach consensus as to how to repair the harm. This can be done in Circle or not. The process usually results in an agreement that outlines the responsibilities of each party.	Trained facilitator RJ facilitator or counselor Person(s) who was harmed Person(s) who committed harm Parents Supporters Other stakeholders	**Targeted and intensive interventions: reparative** Simple and serious harms

Restorative processes can look different from school to school, region to region, country to country because restorative values require us to respect, honor, and incorporate the cultural values of all participants. This is important to recognize, as it prevents practitioners from automatically defaulting to Western values that may not be shared by everyone in a school. Even within a school or district, though, restorative practices are likely to evolve to reflect community norms and are influenced by various trainers. But even though restorative initiatives in schools vary greatly, as soon as practitioners stray away from core restorative values and fail to honor these restorative principles, they risk creating processes that are no longer restorative in nature and may, in fact, cause even more harm. For this reason, Restorative Justice Colorado developed a standard of practice to support best practices in the field.[10]

"Sharp End" versus School-Wide Restorative Practices

Schools use restorative practices to create positive and caring school cultures as well as to respond to harms. Belinda Hopkins refers to the latter use as RJE's "sharp end" response to specific behaviors.[11] In the early years of RJE, and still in many schools today, restorative practices were used only after a harm has been committed or in response to some offense, event, or rule violation. In these uses, RJE processes redefine accountability. They hold the person who committed the harm directly accountable, not by imposing a punishment but by working with the person to repair the harm as much as possible and to restore broken relationships. This allows those affected to heal and move forward. The RJE approach then reintegrates the person who did the harm back into the school or classroom community, a move that may happen either while the person is working toward meeting, or after the person has met, the agreed-upon obligations to put things right.

Another feature of RJE's sharp-end response is that the restorative processes reject the behavior while offering support and respect to the person. No one is a bad person for having made a bad decision or misstep. Whereas exclusionary discipline policies inflict stigmatizing shame that often leads to more isolation, alienation, and unwanted behavior, restorative practices help the person who committed the harm to learn resiliency and to become a responsible and contributing member of the school community. By creating spaces where students learn how to repair broken relationships, schools model for students healthy and productive processes for solving problems and working through conflicts.

As effective as restorative processes are for dealing with conflicts and harms, though, researchers and practitioners have found that restorative practices can be even more effective when they are adopted school-wide. With this use, the entire school community focuses on building relationships; people use restorative language throughout the school campus; teachers use restorative and relational pedagogies, such as Circles, in classrooms to build community and deliver content; and the school pulls together to emphasize positive youth development. Using restorative language means asking restorative questions when something has happened as well as when people just want to be kind, respectful, positive, and affirming in how they speak to each other.

The three-tiered pyramid model of restorative practices (see figure 5), originally developed for the mental health field, shows how universal, targeted, and intensive practices—sometimes called interventions—work together in a school. The pyramid depicts how various restorative practices are implemented along a continuum of support that ranges from universal to intensive.

As the pyramid shows, schools use Circles on all three tiers, both when problems arise and for everyday teaching and learning, problem solving, and community building.

The bottom and largest tier, tier 1, of the pyramid represents practices that occur in all school environments. Restorative schools integrate RJE practices with daily school life. These everyday practices, from speaking in restorative and affirmative ways to using Circles in the classroom, support all students and typically include practices that are both proactive and preventative in nature. A wide range of daily or regular Circles trains students in how to be together in respectful, positive, and restorative ways. These are effective tier 1 practices, as are aspects of social and emotional learning (SEL) and Positive Behavioral Interventions and Support (PBIS). The pyramid conveys the message that all students need and can benefit from tier 1 school-wide practices. It also communicates a systemic message: the school as a whole needs tier 1 practices to build the positive relationships and sense of community that tiers 2 and 3 stand on and from which they draw their strength and effectiveness. This is why tier 1 practices need to be implemented with fidelity across all school environments—most importantly in the classrooms.

The middle tier, tier 2, represents group practices for students who are considered at risk or who need support to resolve a short-term problem. These practices, more focused and reparative in nature, are of moderate intensity. The top tier, tier 3, represents practices of high intensity; they are designed to address students who appear to be having severe problems. School-wide restorative practices offer a flexible, adaptable continuum of informal and formal strategies for developing relationships, establishing trust, building community, and, when needed, responding to conflicts, struggles, and harm.

Circles can be used in all tiers. In one of her trainings,

Nancy Riestenberg described the foundational role of Circles in restorative schools:

> The Circle process is the basis for a restorative school. Understanding and experiencing the process and its applications provide the core for social and emotional learning, learning and practicing empathy, teaching, building relationships between students and students and students and teachers, and building community. Circles are the building

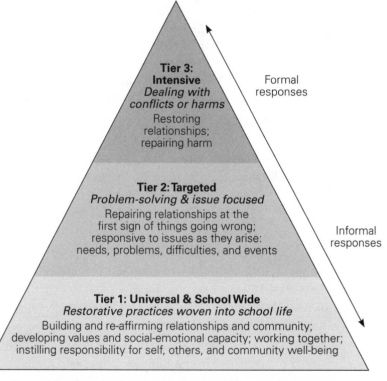

Figure 5. Three-tiered model for restorative practices. Originating in the mental health field, this three-tiered RJE pyramid concept builds on the work of Brenda Morrison and Peta Blood, both of whom adapted the pyramid model to show how restorative practices can be most effectively used in schools.

blocks for all interventions, short or long, as the process establishes the language of the restorative school. Understanding the entire process allows teachers to adapt both the principles and the practices as the situation needs.[12]

At tier 1, all staff have been trained to use restorative and affirmative language, to make relationships with students and with each other a priority, and to work together to create an environment of trust and community. School-wide restorative practices implemented at tier 1 encourage respectful listening, understanding, and appreciation, which have the effect of discouraging challenging behavior. Teachers understand that greeting students at the door with a smile and kind words of interest or welcome have immediate effects on how they feel in the classroom. Teachers then continue modeling restorative values through a variety of relational pedagogies in the classroom, such as cooperative learning activities and Circles. Across the entire school environment, tier 1 restorative practices link restorative ways of thinking and acting to developing students' capacities: they learn self-awareness, how to have healthy relationships, and how to believe in their own abilities to accomplish their goals—what Albert Bandura termed "self-efficacy."

Because zero tolerance discipline has created toxic learning environments and unhealthy relational ecologies, the question becomes, How can we reclaim our schools as places of mutual care, belonging, and community, all of which support learning? The sharp-end application of restorative processes simply will not bring about the changes we need. Therefore, along with many others in the RJE discipline, I do not advocate that schools use RJE to replace punitive disciplinary practices without also implementing community building and other universal, tier 1 preventative practices across all school environments, starting in the classroom. Only by implementing tier 1 restorative practices can schools actively prevent violence, conflict, and other problem behavior. Only by using tier 1 practices consistently can schools create a values-based community that promotes learning and reduces the need for tier 3 interventions.

Positive Behavioral Interventions and Supports

With a better understanding of how SWRPs (that is, tier 1 practices) work and why schools need them, we can examine some other school-wide approaches to discipline and behavior. One approach, which is also based on the three-tiered pyramid concept, is Positive Behavioral Interventions and Supports (PBIS). This model of skillfully reinforcing positive behaviors is already widely accepted as an evidenced-based program and is being used in more than 14,000 schools across the country. Many schools that have adopted RJE use restorative practices alongside PBIS. In fact, in some areas of the country, professional development for teachers and school leaders incorporates both approaches so that teachers learn how to respond positively to a wide range of student behaviors. Standard PBIS classroom rules, such as "be kind, be safe, be responsible," are aligned with school-wide expectations and are also congruent with restorative values. Praising and rewarding students for prosocial and expected behaviors reinforces those behaviors, increases student achievement, and decreases unwanted behaviors.

Social and Emotional Learning

Another approach to education that is proving vital for today's schools is social and emotional learning (SEL). Students today face unprecedented insecurities and fears due to increased poverty, structural and institutional racism, globalization, social media exposure, and unstable families and communities. Now more than ever, we need effective teaching methods that help students develop empathy, resilience, self-awareness, and other social and emotional skills that help them succeed, both academically and in life. Critical theorists, multicultural educators, restorative justice practitioners, and researchers also link empathy, compassion, and tolerance to creating more just schools and societies.[13]

Like RJE and PBIS, SEL builds on school-wide prevention practices. The Collaborative for Academic, Social, and Emotional Learning (CASEL) has developed five interrelated sets of cognitive, affective, and behavioral competencies that form the basis of SEL. These are best taught and modeled across tier 1. They are

1. *self-awareness:* the ability to accurately recognize our emotions and thoughts and their influence on our behavior
2. *self-management:* the ability to regulate our emotions, thoughts, and behaviors effectively in different situations
3. *social awareness:* the ability to take the perspective of others and empathize with those from diverse backgrounds and cultures
4. *relationship skills:* the ability to establish and maintain healthy and rewarding relationships with diverse individuals and groups
5. *responsible decision making:* the ability to make constructive and respectful choices about our personal behavior and social interactions

By participating in Circles on a regular basis, for example, students naturally cultivate each of these SEL competencies. Educators who practice and model the SEL competencies through restorative practices create schools and classrooms that are safe places for students to learn, grow, and form attachments to their teachers, administrators, and peers.

Connections between SEL, PBIS, and RJE

Teaching children to feel empathy toward others through both SEL and RJE helps to build healthy, safe, and positive school climates. Restorative processes create safe spaces for those on both sides of harms to talk about their experiences and share their feelings. This develops empathy on both sides. Those harmed relate what they feel and have experienced, as well as what they need for things to be right again. Those who have caused harm have a chance to see, hear, and even feel how their actions have hurt others; their own sharing helps the people who have been harmed understand what was going on in their minds when they acted as they did. These are empathy-producing moments, and they are often transformational all around, helping to counter the narcissistic tendencies that can prevent people from considering how their actions affect others.

SEL, PBIS, and RJE advocates and practitioners agree: students need their schools to provide safe environments where the adults care about all students holistically. While PBIS relies largely on extrinsic motivation to produce desired behaviors, restorative practices tap into students' intrinsic motivations: to belong to a group, to feel good about themselves and each other, and to operate from deeper levels of mutual understanding and compassion. Combining approaches that balance extrinsic and intrinsic motivations can create healthy and positive classrooms and school cultures, which in turn increase students' engagement and academic performance.

The goal to raise student academic achievement need not interfere with teachers' efforts to meet the social and emotional needs of their students. In fact, students are less likely to improve academically when their social and emotional needs go unmet. As ample cases prove, RJE, PBIS, and SEL can and do work side by side within a three-tiered framework, especially at tier 1, to create healthy relational ecologies. The practices build students' attachment and connection to each other and adults. They model ways of being that include being responsible for other members of their school community and accountable to them. Through the process, these practices often prevent challenging behaviors. When incidents do arise, schools learn how to respond to them in ways that restore and build relationships rather than exclude youth.

Brenda Morrison reminds us that

> [the] broad aim [of restorative practices] is to build the social and emotional intelligence and skills within the school community such that a normative capacity for safe and just schools can be realized. It is in the latter capacity that the development of restorative justice in schools has augmented other movements driving school safety reforms.[14]

Restorative practices reinforce social and relational competencies. As reparation and problem solving replace punishment, individuals who hurt people get a chance to develop empathy and find healing in knowing that they have made things right to the best of their ability.

Connecting SEL to Teaching through Restorative Practices

Belinda Hopkins defines relational and restorative pedagogies as methods of teaching that develop relationships and build connections with one's self, others, and the curriculum.

Relational pedagogy involves using language that "maintains connection, respect, and mutual understanding." When disconnection occurs, "reconnection is encouraged at the earliest possible opportunity, using restorative processes."[15] In her book *The Restorative Classroom: Using Restorative Approaches to Foster Effective Learning*, Hopkins teaches educators how to speak restoratively as well as how to conduct a wide variety of activities that build a restorative classroom.

Relational pedagogies, such as those described in Hopkins's book and in Carolyn Boyes-Watson and Kay Pranis's books *Circle Forward* and *Heart of Hope*, teach and model positive ways

Chart 3.3. Outcomes of restorative practices: SEL competencies	
RESTORATIVE PRACTICES USED	SEL COMPETENCIES DEVELOPED
Encourage dialogue among all those involved or affected by a situation, incident, or event	Relationship skills Self-management
Appreciate and acknowledge the differing views and perspectives that dialogue encourages	Social awareness Self-awareness
Recognize that what people do and say is influenced by their thoughts, beliefs, feelings, and unmet needs	Self-awareness
Take these thoughts, beliefs, feelings, and unmet needs into consideration in finding ways forward when planning, problem solving, or resolving conflicts	Self-management Social awareness Relationship skills
Believe that the people who have the problem are the ones best suited to find their own answers and solutions	Responsible decision making
Trust in the capacity of people to know how to find their own ways forward and the importance of letting them do this	Self-management Responsible decision making Social awareness

Adapted from Hopkins, *Just Schools*, p. 180 and CASEL, *Success in Schools*.

of relating to self and others by fostering emotional intelligence. In chart 3.3, I matched Hopkins's outcomes of restorative practices used in the classroom to SEL competencies in order to illustrate the strong connection between them.

Along with these SEL competencies, restorative practices expand students' capacities for respect and empathy—essential for good relationships and all SEL competencies.

■ RJE and Sharing Power

Restorative and relational pedagogies radically change how teachers convey authority in the classroom. This is one of the biggest challenges for teachers working in schools that adopt RJE. Hopkins addresses this struggle, which goes to the core of understanding and practicing RJE's paradigm shift. She encourages teachers to let go of traditional notions of authority and instead create classrooms where students are empowered and invited into the decision-making process. This does not mean that students no longer respect the role of the teacher, nor does it mean that teachers do not make decisions in the best interest of their students. Rather, sharing power is about bringing a deeper and more authentic respect into the teacher-student dynamic: teachers can change how they assess, evaluate, and teach students without losing their authority as teachers.

Sharing power in schools is an intentional, natural outcome of RJE. People change naturally when they engage others in relationships, and relationships are the foundation of restorative justice. In schools practicing RJE, students become more empowered because they have constant opportunities to speak and be heard. As a result, they often want to take part in creating change in their schools. While most school-reform efforts overlook the important role of students as change agents, restorative schools discover that students are absolutely essential to bringing about transformation. Many students I have spoken with love and embrace RJE, and they are eager to take part in it in their current and future schools.

The concept of power sharing seems threatening at first to many teachers and administrators. Given the habits that zero tolerance policies have created, this is understandable. Realizing the harms that can come with repressive and authoritarian methods, however, teachers in restorative schools change the ways they think, act, and relate with students. They work on changing their habits and mind-sets. This is not as simple as it sounds, even when teachers and administrators initially embrace restorative values and processes. Over time, institutional structures tend to co-opt RJ principles and instead reinforce a rule-based culture. Because falling back on familiar responses is so easy to do, adults in restorative schools regularly participate in Circles to support each other and ground themselves in restorative values.

◼ RJE as a Way of School Life

As CASEL's research on social and emotional learning shows, improving students' social and emotional competencies improves the school climate, student behavior, and student achievement. If we push these correlations further, we find mutually reinforcing connections between SEL and RJE. Alone, SEL lacks the processes for dealing with challenging behavior. RJE provides these. As schools step into their restorative potentials, teachers use restorative and relational pedagogies on a daily basis (tier 1): the very way they teach—teaching in Circles, in particular—instills social skills and cultivates relationships. These school-wide practices then provide the foundation for dealing with behavioral incidents in a restorative manner at the targeted (tier 2) and intensive (tier 3) levels. Brenda Morrison describes this framework as both "responsive to behavior and restorative to relationships."[16] Kathy

Evans and Dorothy Vaandering expand on this vision of what RJE can do for schools as a way of life:

> Restorative justice in education is a comprehensive and holistic approach to education. The types of change that we believe RJE can bring about are not limited to reductions in suspension rates, improved student behavior, or even improved academic achievement, although those outcomes are certainly included. What we hope for is the transformation of school cultures such that all members of the learning community—including students, teachers, staff, administrators, parents, and caregivers—feel that they belong. We long for schools where students and teachers are engaged in active and enthusiastic learning and where everyone—regardless of their race, gender, sexual orientation, ethnicity, religion, language, ability, or class—is valued and provided with what they need to grow and learn.[17]

Davis and Grant: Two Very Different Middle Schools

Setting the Stage

Restorative Justice and the Oakland Unified School District

The information offered so far provides background for understanding the study I conducted with the Oakland Unified School District (OUSD) in 2015. I invite you to read appendix 1 to learn more about the theories that informed my study and its overall design. This section of the book will tell the stories of the two middle schools, but first I want to talk about how restorative practices came to the OUSD in the first place.

The Oakland Unified School District is comprised of 123 district-run public and district-authorized charter schools that serve 49,600 students. Latinx students make up 41.3 percent of the district's student population, followed by 26.2 percent African Americans, 13.6 percent Asians, 11.1 percent White, 1.1 percent Pacific Islanders, 0.8 percent Filipinos, 0.3 percent Native Americans, and 3.9 percent multi-ethnic. Students who qualify for free/reduced price lunch make up 72.5 percent of the OUSD's students, and 30.8 percent are English language learners. In the 2014–2015 school year, the OUSD graduation rate was 64.2 percent.[1]

On December 16, 2009, the OUSD adopted a resolution to launch a three-year, district-wide restorative justice initiative. The program included professional development for administrators and school site staff; a set of redesigned district discipline policies; and structures and practices that promoted alternatives to suspension. The resolution acknowledged that the district had been disciplining African American students disproportionately and looked to restorative justice to change this practice. It also saw RJE as a way to promote teaching that incorporated social and emotional learning (SEL) and developed social skills. Rita Renjitham Alfred, cofounder of the Restorative Justice Training Institute, and Fania Davis, founder of Restorative Justice for Oakland Youth (RJOY), played integral roles during this stage.

In 2012, the US Department of Education (DOE) Office for Civil Rights (OCR) initiated a review of the district to determine whether African American students were being disciplined more frequently and harshly than White students. But before the investigation was completed—and without admitting any violation of Title VI of the Civil Rights Act of 1964—the OUSD entered into a voluntary agreement with the USDOE OCR to reduce disproportionate disciplining in the schools by and beyond the 2016–2017 school year. Middle schools and high schools in the district began implementing various programs within a Response to Intervention (RTI) framework, including RJE, PBIS, Caring School Community, and/or African American Male Achievement Manhood Development. Regardless of which program(s) schools chose to reduce disproportionate disciplining, the district was required to evaluate and report progress annually.

Each school developed a framework and schedule for reviewing discipline data and identifying areas where students and teachers needed more support. While I was conducting my study, the OUSD completed its first district-wide evaluation of RJE.[2]

The RJE initiative is one of many housed within the OUSD Behavioral Health Unit. To comply with the voluntary resolution, the district created a structure for establishing RJE that involved hiring staff and recruiting students to help implement school-wide restorative practices (SWRPs) in select schools. David Yusem, the OUSD's RJ program coordinator, oversees the entire program. He and his staff train and support restorative justice facilitators who work at school sites. Additionally, some schools have peer mediators—a select group of students who have been trained in restorative mediation. Peer mediators support the school by assisting with community building practices, teaching restorative skills to others, and responding to conflicts and harm in restorative ways. Finally, an advisory team of dedicated youth and adults supports the program and provides feedback. The OUSD has made a significant investment in money, resources, personnel, and time toward district-wide implementation of SWRPs.

The rest of this book is about the administrators, staff, and students in two middle schools that were in various stages of implementing SWRPs (remember the four stages explained in the introduction?). I will describe each school separately, then put what I learned together to answer the questions: What did the relational ecology of two middle schools look like after they had adopted school-wide restorative practices? And what changes occurred throughout the schools in the process?

While both schools had adopted SWRPs and were committed to restorative values and processes, startling disparities in how the two schools were funded and staffed created very different environments: stability in one school and near chaos in the other. This damaging inequity is important to recognize, especially as we consider restorative justice in the larger context of social justice. After all, how can schools become more just and equitable institutions through RJE when justice and equity are lacking in their funding and resources?

To protect the privacy of study participants and honor my agreement with the OUSD, I do not use real names in this book but have assigned pseudonyms (see the List of Pseudonyms on page XX). So, too, for the schools: I refer to one as Davis

Middle School in honor of Angela and Fania Davis, two African American women who have spent their lives confronting racism and oppression and working for social justice. I refer to the other as Grant Middle School in memory of Oscar Grant, an unarmed young Black man who was murdered by a Bay Area Rapid Transit (BART) police officer in an act of racist police brutality not far from the school. I also altered all photographs to remove any identifiers and to blur faces. When it comes to content, however, I used the exact words of those who spoke to me for purposes of this study and made only minor adjustments as needed for clarity.

I have also changed some job titles to reflect the culture of the OUSD. Whenever I speak of the middle schools or the OUSD structure, I will call the site-based RJ coordinators "RJ facilitators" to be consistent with their current job title. Also, the OUSD calls its SROs "school security officers (SSOs)", so I will use that title in the narrative as well. Other school districts may settle on different titles.

My research provides clear evidence that restorative justice in education offers schools the philosophy, values, and practices they need to create positive, healthy, just, and equitable learning environments. But implementing school-wide restorative practices is not without its challenges, and it requires change at every level: organizational, instructional/pedagogical, and individual. The more people in schools are willing and able to change, the greater the integrity of RJE's implementation and the more successful the change to a restorative school will be.

The Middle School Years: More Conflicts, Deeper RJE Practices

Both of the schools I studied were middle schools. Middle school is a tough time for many students, who must not only adapt to an organizational structure vastly different from what they knew in elementary school but also undergo unprecedented physical, emotional, social, and intellectual changes. Not surprisingly, then, students typically experience more conflict during these years. Regulatory structures exacerbate behavioral problems and further alienate struggling students by imposing punishment, especially suspensions, on those who have not yet mastered the ability to control their impulses.[3] Put positively, middle schoolers' own development spurs them to confront conflicts and learn how to resolve them, making RJE particularly critical for their stage of growth.

The challenges of the middle school years proved perfect for my study, because the students in the schools presented a wide range of experiences and struggles. For example, despite the many positive changes that students reported experiencing— and this was the overwhelming response I heard—teachers and students alike also called attention to students who were still struggling and who were not making positive changes as quickly. Of course, many issues go into this, including their emotional and social maturity levels, experience with academic success, and self-image. Some students may also be carrying trauma. And the larger context of historical, racial injustice and privilege as well as multigenerational economic inequity play a huge role in the lives of youth. For any number of reasons, some students may require a deeper commitment on the part of the adults to take a relational and restorative approach to problems that arise for them.

The wider spectrum of student responses to restorative practices gave me openings for going deeper into RJE. After all, other schools may have similar perceptions. As it turned out, these very perceptions proved most useful in pushing my understanding of RJE deeper, as they did for the schools and the OUSD as well.

And now for their stories.

CHAPTER 4

Davis Middle School: More Resources for RJE Make the Shift Easier

According to its website, Davis Middle School is an excellent school that serves a diverse population of more than 800 students. In fact, Davis is the top-performing middle school in the Oakland Unified School District (OUSD). Principal Stan Paulson told me that Davis has the lowest chronic absence rates, the lowest suspension rates, and the biggest wait list of all the middle schools in the district.

Davis sits atop a hill on a quiet street in a wealthy neighborhood. The school's mascot, the Panther, provides a strong sense of identity with the school and is promoted and reinforced throughout the school on bulletin boards, posters, and signage. Panther P.R.I.D.E. refers to the school's values: Positivity, Respect, Independence, Determination, and Empathy. An LED sign near the main entrance sends a constant stream of information to parents and community members. The sign provides a phone number for information on the Black Lives Matter movement, signaling that the movement is important to those at Davis.

The two-story school building itself is well maintained and adequately resourced. All students have access to Chrome-Books (notebook computers). Many of the classrooms are quite large. The hallways are decorated with student art and various posters. Color and light fill the school, creating an open, friendly, and pleasant environment.

Outside, a large courtyard provides a common space and connection point between the four buildings that make up the

Figure 6. Student-created mural of influential people

campus. Student-painted murals of influential people line the walls that surround the basketball courts in the back of the school (see figure 6). Like almost every school in the OUSD, Davis is a Title 1 school. The Elementary and Secondary Education Act (ESEA) categorizes schools with high numbers of children from low-income families as Title 1 schools. Schools with this designation are often eligible for additional federal funding to ensure that all children meet challenging state academic standards. According to the National Center for Education Statistics, in the 2014–2015 school year, 70 percent of Davis's students were eligible for reduced/free lunch; 30 percent of the students were not eligible because they were from middle-class families.

The Principal of Davis

In 2015, Stan Paulson, a vocal, passionate, energetic, fast-moving, and high-profile man, was in his sixth year as principal at Davis. He is a White male who wore the traditional clothing of a school principal: white shirts, ties, and suits. Although several faculty members told me that he was known for shooting from the hip, for better or for worse, I found him to be highly self-reflective about his values and leadership practices. Several teachers in the focus group believed that Stan is good at allocating resources and ensuring that the restorative justice initiative is adequately funded and staffed.

The Staff of Davis

As of March 2015, Davis's thirty-four academic teachers were diverse, both in terms of gender and ethnicity, although the majority were White (67 percent) and were women (64 percent). Only one teacher was an African American man. African Americans and Asians each made up 12 percent of the teachers, while 9 percent were Latinx. The teachers appeared to be young; many of the teachers I observed were in their twenties and thirties, while the oldest appeared to be in their fifties. Funds raised by the Parent Teacher Student Association (PTSA) allow Davis the luxury of two full-time music teachers. In addition, numerous behavioral interventional specialists, case managers, special education teachers, and counselors are on staff. All eight participants in the adult focus group I held at Davis said positive things about the school, and all of them said they loved teaching there.

In addition to the principal, staff, and teachers, certain staff members play key roles in implementing restorative justice in schools: RJ facilitators, who facilitate whole-school implementation of school-wide restorative practices (SWRPs), and school security officers (SSOs). In schools that adopt SWRPs, RJ facilitators, working with SSOs, respond to challenging behavior and situations whenever teachers feel they cannot or will not address the problem.

RJ Facilitators

When I was there, Davis had two full-time restorative justice facilitators, both of whom were African American men. I refer to them as Cameron and Acke. When Cameron started at Davis, he worked only three days a week; by the time I got there, he was at Davis five days a week. Cameron's responsibilities included training and overseeing peer mediators; training teachers; facilitating Circles at staff meetings; responding to requests for restorative interventions, such as mediations and Circles; coordinating and planning Circles to repair harms; and being available to students who just needed to talk. The PTSA raises funds to provide Davis with a second full-time RJ facilitator—a support few schools can afford. The role of this RJ facilitator, Acke, was quite different; he spent his entire day in the on-campus reflection (OCR) room, supervising students who had been sent out of class, deescalating conflicts, holding conferences, and helping students with their schoolwork. Both RJ facilitators provided support across the entire school community and worked as a team.

Cameron and Acke shared some personality traits that made them highly effective RJ facilitators. First, they clearly loved and cared about kids. Although they were in positions of authority, they were kind, approachable, caring men, who at the same time exuded inner strength and stability. In other words, they were solid. They spoke to students directly and firmly when needed, but also mentored and encouraged them.

School Security Officers

Two African American school security officers, one man, Eric, and one woman, Sandra, provided security at Davis. The SSOs were a constant presence in different areas of the school, both inside and outside, ready to respond to calls from teachers and administrators. Both Eric and Sandra had friendly demeanors and personal relationships with the students. I often saw students chatting with them during lunch and breaks and even hugging them at times. Both SSOs were trained in restorative practices, and neither carried weapons. When they were called, they approached the situation calmly. It was not uncommon to see them place a gentle, reassuring hand on a student's shoulder when they had to escort him or her to the OCR (described below).

The Students of Davis

The student body at Davis is not only racially and ethnically diverse, but also includes students from lower and upper-middle class families as well as special education students with various disabilities. What makes Davis so different from other Oakland middle schools is the large number of White and Asian middle-class students who attend. Parents compete in a lottery system for openings at the school. As a result, students from the upper and middle classes comprise approximately 30 percent of the student population. Principal Paulson believed that the concentration of middle-class students was much higher at Davis than at any other OUSD school.

According to the Center for Education Statistics, Davis

has a relatively even distribution of three racial groups in its student population: Black, non-Hispanic students are in the majority (30.1 percent), followed closely by Asian (29.5 percent) and Latinx ("Hispanic" in the report) (20.8 percent) students. White students account for 12 percent of the population, while Native or students of two or more races comprise the remainder. Because the majority (68 percent) of students who attend Davis are not from the immediate neighborhood, the student body reflects the diversity of the entire Oakland community.

On Fridays, one of the support staff likes to DJ and provides a freestyle rap session for the students during their lunch in the outside courtyard. During this time, I could see the entire student body and observe how they interacted with each other. I did not see students in homogenous groups but rather saw students making friends across class and ethnic/racial divides. Special education students danced and sang to the music along with everyone else, as this was one of the few times during the school day that they were integrated into the student body. I did not perceive any tension, and the staff and SSOs who provided oversight of the courtyard were diligent but relaxed.

■ RJ Peer Mediators

Davis has a team of seventh- and eighth-grade student leaders trained to conduct peer mediations. They are always on call to help other students with their problems. I observed Cameron as he conducted a training for twenty-four students learning how to mediate problems between their peers. One peer mediator told me, "When we mediate them [other students]—when they're done—they can mediate themselves later on if the problem arises again." Peer mediators in the focus group spoke of how being in that role made them more confident, better leaders, better students, more empathetic, and more hopeful. One teacher noted in a survey response that, of all the students, peer mediators seemed to be the most positively affected by SWRPs.

Parental Engagement at Davis

Parental engagement at Davis was very high. The school is open at all times to parents wishing to visit, and I frequently saw parents visiting the classrooms or stopping into the main office for various reasons.

Because of the school's reputation as the best middle school in the district, parent volunteers conduct tours for prospective parents, and the school has a waiting list of students hoping to attend. I participated in one such tour, which concluded in the library, where the principal, counselors, and students presented information about the school. Principal Paulson described the restorative philosophy and processes to parents. He noted that, other than bringing drugs or a weapon to school—both of which were instantly expellable offenses—all student behavior problems are handled restoratively. He explained that one of the reasons Davis is a very safe school is because the staff emphasizes building community and relationships instead of zero tolerance policies for bullying and other behaviors. Instead of suspending children who bully others, they "invite kids to tell us what's going on and who's doing what, and we seek to stop the bullying both by working with the bully and the kids being bullied." Stan emphasized to the parents that "kids make mistakes" and that the role of the school is to use those mistakes as learning experiences. The principal told the parents the same thing he said to me on our walk-through: "We don't try to punish the bad out of kids."

The Structure of Davis

At Davis, each grade level has its own wing or area. Certain classrooms and areas, such as orchestra and band classes, the cafeteria, and the outside courtyard, allow students from different grade levels to mix with each other. However, sixth-grade students are always segregated from the older students, even during lunch.

Sixth-grade students are organized into "families" that minimize the number of teachers they are exposed to and that allow teachers to better help them transition from elementary to middle school. Seventh- and eighth-graders also belong to school families.

The school runs on a ninety-nine-minute block schedule, so students see only half of their teachers every day. After each block class, students get a fifteen-minute break; it serves as a recess or snack time. While the building has a large cafeteria, most students eat lunch outside, using that time to socialize or play games on the athletic courts. In addition to gym class, these active middle schoolers have ample opportunities throughout the day to release their physical energy and give their minds a break. "A lot of teachers do an exercise break or a 'move your body sixty seconds' or stretch between instructional activities in the class," said Stan. I watched several teachers do this, and it certainly seemed an effective way to minimize behavior problems that may arise out of sheer restlessness.

Advisory Period

Many middle schools build an advisory period into their schedules so teachers can meet with small groups of students to help them with social and academic issues. At Davis, this one-hour advisory period occurs each Wednesday morning. It is up to the principal and staff to determine how to use this hour. At Davis, students are graded on goal setting and Circle participation in their Wednesday morning advisory class, called PACT, which stands for <u>P</u>anthers, <u>A</u>cademic achievement, <u>C</u>ommunity building, and <u>T</u>otal health.

■ PBIS and Other Initiatives

As discussed in chapter 3, RJE is frequently implemented alongside other behavior initiatives, such as Positive Behavioral Interventions and Supports (PBIS). At Davis, however, RJE is the preferred method for promoting healthy relationships and prosocial behavior. Principal Paulson explained how that occurred:

> Principal, assistant principals, and instructional coaches and we as a school agreed that we were falling victim to initiative burn. We were doing too many initiatives in not enough depth, and [so] we decided to not do PBIS, Positive Behavioral Interventions and Supports, as an official PBIS Cohort School. We already totally believe in positive reinforcement and P.R.I.D.E. tickets and consequence chains and narration of positive behavior. We are already doing a lot of PBIS strategies, but when we had the chance of someone [an RJE facilitator] who is really strong to work here, three days a week and then this year five days a week, I think that pushed me more toward, let's fully implement this school-wide.

Some teachers still used PBIS strategies, including reward tickets, in their classrooms; they frequently said PBIS reinforcement phrases such as, "I like how John is ready to begin"; and the PTSA ran the PBIS P.R.I.D.E. store where students redeemed their reward tickets for treats and school supplies.

■ The Restorative Justice Room

The restorative justice room at Davis is a large, sunny room next to the gym. Cameron spent much of his time in this room conducting mediations and Circles. This room is always set up to host a Circle whenever one is needed (figure 7). The room also houses a drum set and a PA system, as the school's rock band holds rehearsals in this space after school. Sometimes Cameron allowed a student to release aggression by playing

Figure 7. Restorative justice room at Davis

the drums for a while. This room is a safe space for students. Students stopped in frequently to talk or seek advice from Cameron. They can come by this room any time, not just when they are in trouble or have problems to solve. In the focus group, Cameron explained:

> You've got to do the community building aspect. If you don't do that, then the students will start looking at "Oh, I've got to go to Mr. Cameron because I've got a problem." It's not coming to me with your problem; it's coming to me to talk. I want you to come to me to talk about . . . not just problems, but tell me about the good things.

▨ On Campus Reflection Room (OCR)

The second RJ facilitator at Davis, Acke, supervised the on-campus reflection room, where he played the dual roles of teacher and disciplinarian. This room has a variety of functions: it is a place where students can go to instead of class if they think they might have a problem or conflict with a teacher or student in that class; it is where students go when they are sent out of class; it is where students serve lunch detention; and it is another room where students hold restorative conferences or mediations. OCR differs from typical in-school suspension rooms in non-restorative schools in that it provides a welcoming environment where students are greeted with the aroma of lavender, the sounds of new age music, and the sight of inspiring posters. It is both a calm room and a calming room. Students working with Acke in OCR received counseling, assistance with their schoolwork, and restorative solutions to their conflicts.

■ Reflections on Davis

Davis operates cohesively, with students, staff, and parents on the same page. Even though the students are going through enormous physical and emotional changes, Davis does not have that "crazy" feeling common in many middle schools. Most of the classroom teachers I observed had built strong relationships with their students and, as a result, students were highly engaged with their learning. When the students changed classes or were on break, they seemed to get along with each other and were generally happy. Staff were pleasant and friendly, and teachers liked their jobs. That the school is well funded certainly contributes to RJE's success. Davis is very fortunate to have two full-time RJ facilitators, a well-trained group of outstanding peer mediators, a dynamic principal, and a core group of teachers who truly believe in the power of RJE.

CHAPTER 5

Grant Middle School: Fewer Resources Pose Extra Challenges

Grant Middle School came into being in 2006 through a Gates Foundation grant that focused on creating small neighborhood schools. According to its website, Grant's mission is to interrupt the inequities in the community by ensuring that all students are academically and socially prepared for success in high school and beyond. Grant's mission statement clearly acknowledges social, political, and economic inequities, since the school primarily serves minority students from poor and working-class families.

The small school is located in an east Oakland neighborhood that is home to Oakland's largest Latinx population. Latinxs comprise almost 50 percent of the total population. Barred-up, graffiti-tagged houses, parked cars, and small convenience stores line the busy street in front of the school where cars and noisy buses continually speed by. As I prepared for my first day at Grant, Antonio, the school's RJ facilitator, advised me to make sure I got off the bus at the stop closest to the school and to refrain from walking up the street because it was not safe.

Grant shares its campus with one of the district's grade 6–12 schools. The dual campus creates challenges for keeping the two school populations separate, especially since they share the athletic fields, track, and cafeteria. The two schools connect physically, separated only by two metal doors at the end of the sixth-grade hallway. Outside, a large courtyard decorated by student-painted murals separates the two schools on one side (see figure 8).

Figure 8. One of many student-painted murals in Grant's courtyard

Physically, the school is clean, although much of the furniture in the main office and faculty lounge is old and in various states of disrepair. My first impression, based on its appearance, was that the school was under-resourced. Later, when I spoke to teachers and administrators, my suspicions were confirmed. However, all of the classrooms are equipped with SmartBoards and ChromeBooks for the students. The principal explained that the school had received a large school improvement grant that had allowed it to upgrade its technology.

Although the hallways of Grant are filled with student artwork, the school is a bit dark and cold. The few windows that exist do not let in enough sunlight to cut the chill of the Bay Area morning temperatures.

Grant is a Title 1 school. According to the National Center for Education Statistics' findings for 2014–2015, 417 of Grant's 436 students were eligible for free/reduced-priced lunch. These statistics demonstrate that 96 percent of Grant's students live in poverty.

The Principal of Grant

At the time of this study, Elena Baez had been the principal for six years; she had formerly been the assistant principal at Davis. She is a soft-spoken, calm, Latinx woman, diminutive in stature and much younger looking than she is.

Elena brought restorative justice to Grant in 2010 after participating in an RJ training with Rita Renjitham Alfred when the Oakland Unified School District (OUSD) launched its pilot RJ program. Teachers in the focus group expressed gratitude and admiration for this quiet principal who held the restorative vision. Elena explained that the decision to adopt SWRPs came from discussions with her staff about "students who we don't really know how to support." When she and her staff engaged in a visioning process, Elena said, "That's when we started saying, 'Well, if [suspending] isn't what we want, then we've got to do something different.'"

Before I arrived at the school, Antonio explained to me that Principal Baez had been on maternity leave for six months and was just returning to work. During her leave, the assistant principal became acting principal, and an interim assistant principal—one who embraced traditional, punitive discipline—had been appointed to fill that vacancy. Caridad, the school's family engagement coordinator, referred to this period as "suspension madness!" Elena had been back from maternity leave for only three weeks when I showed up at her school to do my study. She was facing the immediate and enormous task of rebuilding and reshaping her school's community and was attempting to stabilize the environment and return it to the more restorative state. Over and over again, staff told me that, in just six months, the punitive interim assistant principal had done significant damage to RJE at Grant.

■ The Staff of Grant

Again, as of March 2015, Grant's nineteen academic teachers were diverse in ethnicity and gender, more so than at Davis, with fewer White teachers (42 percent) and more men teachers (42 percent). Three teachers were African American men. African Americans and Latinxs each made up 21 percent of the teachers, while 11 percent were Asian (one declined to state). A few of the teachers appeared to be in their twenties, while several appeared to be in their late fifties or early sixties. As at Davis, the teachers' demographics did not reflect those of the students.

Grant had no music teacher on staff when I was there, so once a week, an English teacher taught a drumming class. Behavioral interventional specialists, case managers, special education teachers, and counselors provided emotional, behavioral, and academic support, but there were not enough of them to meet the needs of the students. As Antonio explained, a very effective clinical case manager and proponent of RJE had recently left the school, and her position had not been filled. Her leaving hurt the RJE initiative and increased the caseload of the remaining social workers and counselors.

I found the people who worked at Grant to be dedicated professionals committed to creating a safe learning environment and providing support to all students. The following quotations from three different teachers who participated in the focus groups reflected the passion and care that embodied the teaching philosophy at Grant:

> *Teacher 1:* The reality of a school that has as many needs as we do and then as few resources as we do—just as a material reality—for a teacher who's teaching here, we give 110 percent. There is no other place I would want to be.

Teacher 2: I like teaching here a lot. [I have] been given a lot of freedom to try new things with curriculum and teach things that I am passionate about teaching. I also really enjoy how it's forced me to think about how I relate to students in a different way.

Teacher 3: It's definitely a lot of heart and a lot of sweat that you put into this campus, to this site, and not just because you care about teaching; . . . it's a lot of really going beyond just teaching the curriculum [to] really getting to know the students. I cannot ask for a better job and a better place to teach, as far as the community goes.

Almost every teacher I met at Grant was involved in after-school programs and student activities, including tutoring, youth development, and soccer. They worked long hours and invested much of their personal time to strategizing how they could help their students feel safe and learn. They gave all they had to their students, knowing that their students lived in an unjust and inequitable society that was not going to do them any favors. So although they were caring, passionate, dedicated teachers and staff, they were also tired. The one person who seemed to have a never-ending supply of energy was Antonio, the RJ facilitator.

■ RJ Facilitator

At the time I conducted this study, Grant employed one full-time RJ facilitator, a Latinx male named Antonio who was an employee of the school district. Principal Baez told me that, despite experiencing extreme cuts to her budget, she had made sure funds were available to maintain his position. Antonio was responsible for training teachers in how to hold community building Circles. He did this training mainly during faculty meetings, where he demonstrated the process and explained the reasons for its components, and then he provided assistance to individual teachers as needed later on. He was constantly on his feet, quickly responding to behavioral incidents that occurred throughout the day. Antonio met with most students one-on-one, and he checked in with students constantly to see how they were doing and if they were upholding their values contracts or other agreements. He also hosted a parent Circle once a month. He told me how his role as RJ facilitator had changed drastically during the principal's maternity leave in 2014, when he was required to function more as a dean of discipline than as an RJ facilitator. He was still operating largely in that mode when I was present, as the school was mostly still functioning as it had during Elena's absence.

School Security Officer (SSO)

One African American SSO, a woman I will call Patrisse, provided security at Grant. She was present in the hallways during every class change as she worked to move students to their classes in a timely manner. She also responded to calls from teachers and administrators. Patrisse knew the students by their first names and had a firm but approachable demeanor. Although I did not ask her if she had been trained in restorative practices, she clearly placed relationships with the students at the heart of her work and was an integral part of the school community. Like the SSOs at Davis, Patrisse did not carry weapons.

A unique and informal relationship existed between the students at Grant and the adjacent school's SSO, a tall African American man named Carson. He often walked through the school to provide an additional SSO presence and to help staff needing assistance. Caridad told me that he came to Grant on his own because he knew the families of many students and felt responsible for them in addition to those in his assigned school. His demeanor was very authoritarian and strict, and to me, he seemed a little scary. As Caridad and I were walking through the school, we saw him publicly, and very loudly, reprimanding one African American girl student in the hallway, which is not at all a restorative practice. When I asked Caridad about his approach, she told me that he had a long-standing relationship with that particular girl and her family and that he was able to get through to her in ways that others could not. She described his behavior as "tough love, and it's familial, and then he will sit down with you and talk to you about your life. It's like the most stereotypical dad thing I have ever seen." I began to see how different people in the school displayed caring behaviors in different ways. Some students who might not respond to some approaches or people might respond to the caring reprimands of a father figure who clearly wanted what was best for them, even if he expressed it through yelling.

The Students of Grant

According to the findings for 2014–2015 of the National Center for Educational Statistics, of the 436 Grant students, 76 percent were Latinx [Hispanic], 14 percent were Black non-Hispanic, 8 percent were Asian, and less than 1 percent were Native, of two or more races, or White. According to the district website, 62.6 percent of the students live in the immediate neighborhood surrounding the school.

The student body includes "newcomers"—immigrant children just learning the English language and culture—and special education students, which is one reason that only 13 percent of the students read at grade level. The school also receives a number of students who, as a result of the District

Hearing Panel (DHP), have been expelled from other schools in the district. "We want to accept students, but that presents a new challenge when students are coming in the middle of the year . . . because they've been kicked out of another school. Then we have . . . more DHP . . . students than your typical middle school," said a teacher. There is little economic diversity among the student population, as most students come from poor or working-class families, and almost all students have high levels of social, emotional, financial, and educational needs.

Peer Mediators

At the time this study was conducted, Grant did not have any peer mediators.

Parental Engagement at Grant

Even though Grant had a full-time, grant-funded family engagement coordinator, Caridad, parental engagement at the school was low. Many of the parents are, as one teacher described, "more stable working-class people, day laborers, [and] a lot of domestic workers." Every Wednesday, Caridad sponsored a food and clothing bank in her room where parents could come and get free provisions. Caridad said the Parent Teacher Student Association was more of an informal group of parents who did not raise funds because most of them were immigrants or members of the working class. She described the PTSA to me as follows:

> We have always had a parent leader group that is sort
> of self-fashioned and self-made, like gathering together
> culturally. Their focus is to impact the school culture. Every
> year you gather the parents and you gather their concerns,

and out of that gathering of concerns a kind of working group emerges. It always happens the same time, in the morning on Wednesdays, you have that group. You have the ones that come once a month at night to have their conversation, and that's the RJ group. Then you have the governance committees which are really guiding the school budgeting process.

However, a bigger problem is safety in the neighborhood. This concern often prevents families from attending meetings or events at night. Caridad told me:

> At least five of the families that I have worked with this year have gotten mugged three blocks of here, even in the day-time. . . . It's just that getting around is a risk. It's a real risk.

Even so, Antonio hosted a restorative justice night for parents, where he used restorative practices to build community and facilitate open communication between parents and school staff. Figure 9 is a photograph of a Circle painting a group of parents made the night before I arrived at the school.

The Structure of Grant

Each grade level at Grant has its own area in the small school, which is comprised of just three hallways that form a U-shape. The doors at the end of the seventh- and eighth-grade hallway open into an outside courtyard that leads to the cafeteria. Four sixth-grade classrooms share one hallway with the special education classrooms. The sixth grade is divided into two school families, so each student has only two teachers instead of four. According to one of the teachers, sixth-graders know they can talk to or seek support from any of the four sixth-grade teachers, because they work closely together as a team.

Figure 9. Circle painting made by parents at Grant

Because Grant is a Title 1 school, students receive both free breakfast and lunch. Students enjoy a small break outdoors after breakfast as they walk with their teachers from the cafeteria back to class. During lunch, most students eat outside in the courtyard when the weather is nice; here they can also play soccer, walk around the track, lie in the grass, and enjoy the fresh air and sunshine.

Inside, the school's hallways display student artwork (see figure 10), and teachers' doors are often decorated with inspiring and welcoming signs.

The school day is made up of seven 50-minute periods, and students see all of their teachers every day. Because the school is so small, students have only two minutes to change classes; teachers, administrators, aides, and the SSO are present in the hallways to move students into the classrooms on time.

■ Advisory Period

Grant holds advisory class every morning during the first period, and the Wednesday advisory period is dedicated to conducting community building Circles. Unlike at Davis, this class is not graded.

Figure 10. Example of student artwork displayed in Grant's hallways

▨ PBIS and Other Initiatives

Grant has internal initiatives, like Positive Behavioral Interventions and Supports (PBIS) and restorative justice in education (RJE), as well as partnerships with various community members and organizations who provide additional support for the students. Grant is technically an official PBIS school. PBIS posters displaying expectations hang throughout the school to remind students of the school-wide PBIS behavioral guidelines: be safe, be responsible, and be respectful.

Before the loss of so many staff, Grant had a PBIS team who went to meetings and met with staff once a month about PBIS. This past year, however, Elena struggled with how to balance all of the professional development needs at faculty meetings. She explained:

> Because you are doing "here's my curriculum, here is my department time, here is my grade-level time, here is my PBIS time" but what we've been struggling [with] as a school is, how do we make people feel that it's one? Because it really is. But how do you make it so that it feels like it's the same thing?

In addition to PBIS and RJE, Grant has other mentoring programs. The SSO voluntarily held a support group for African American girls after school. Additionally, a male volunteer and local preacher held a mentoring Circle with boys every Monday morning. Several of the boys in my focus group spoke of how much that Circle helped them change their behavior and take school more seriously. While at the school, I also met Trestin George, who mentored young men one-on-one. Trestin was a former professional football player who now worked as an actor and lived in Oakland.

■ The Restorative Justice Room

The restorative justice room provides space for the RJ facilitator to meet with students and parents in Circle or to conduct individual conferences or mediations. The large, windowless room is decorated with posters that display the values and processes associated with restorative practices. There is no centerpiece, and the Circle consists only of hard folding chairs (see figure 11). Because the school is so small, several rooms perform multiple purposes, including the RJ room, which is also used for storing supplies.

Figure 11. Restorative justice room at Grant

The Main Office

At the time of this study, the main office was where students who had been sent out of class went to complete a restorative justice reflection form while waiting to meet with either the principal or the RJ facilitator. The staff referred to many of the students I saw in the main office as "frequent flyers." To paint a picture of what happens in the main office, here is what I witnessed in one thirty-minute observation period:

> I saw a boy who was sent to the office. A mother and her daughter were waiting for the principal. One teacher came in and turned in a cell phone he took from a student. Another boy sat behind an empty desk. One girl strolled into the office making a screeching noise; the school administrator told her he didn't need her making noise in the hallway. Staff spoke to students, parents, and each other in both Spanish and English. One girl seemed to be an office helper or aide. Another boy wandered in. A Spanish-speaking mother with a baby in her arms came in to ask some questions. The office was a very busy place. A lot of students who were sent to the office were waiting to speak to the principal. When things slowed down, the secretary tried to work with a student who needed to take a test. He said that he did not like the teacher so he did not want to do the work. The secretary was making him read the test out loud. She threatened to call his dad if he did not read it and finally he started.

These observations were telling. The number of students sent out of the classrooms showed that teachers were not handling behavior in their classrooms, which could also mean they were not using processes that would help them build relationships with their students. Staff in the main office were overwhelmed. This is usually when people resort to controlling, authoritarian behaviors rather than take the time to work things out—to problem solve and develop relationships. Shifting the paradigm from punitive to restorative can be very difficult, certainly when leadership changes but also when resources are as tight as they are at Grant.

▓ Reflections on Grant

As soon as I walked into Grant, I felt tension in the air. Not only was there a greater SSO presence, but I also witnessed a much more authoritarian approach to dealing with students. Although I saw students eating, laughing, and playing together, I also witnessed more students yelling and arguing each other. While Antonio and the office staff were very friendly and welcoming to me, teachers and support staff were cautious and a bit more closed. Overall, people seemed suspicious, wanting more information about who I was and why I was there. A few were openly hostile. One sixth-grade teacher questioned me in the hallway the moment I met her. After I told her about my research and asked her to participate in the focus group, she relaxed a little, but I realized that I had a lot of work to do to build trust. While sitting in Circle with the sixth-grade teachers, they opened up to me and one even invited me to attend a community building Circle in her classroom.

After a few days in the school, I understood that the tension and stress I felt were largely due to the school being so understaffed and under-resourced. Although the staff had commendable intentions, the budget and turnover left them struggling to help students who come to school every day with so many needs. The stress that Caridad described in the neighborhood had carried into the school. Whereas I felt excitement and hope at Davis, at Grant I felt compassion for these dedicated educators who were doing their best under tough circumstances.

Chart 5.1. Comparing Davis and Grant: facts and figures

		Davis MS	Grant MS
School	Grades	6-8	6-8
	# of students	807	436
	% eligible for free/reduced lunch	70%	96%
	% students reading at/above grade level	47.8%	13.2%
	Suspensions	4 (0.5%)	33 (4.7%)
	Chronic absenteeism	4.7%	7.1%
	RJ room	Yes	Yes
	Reflection room (OCR)	Yes	No, main office used
Principal	Gender	White Male	Latinx Female
	Tenure	6 years	6 years, interrupted by 6-month maternity leave
Staff	# of teachers	34	19
	Teacher/student ratio	1/24	1/23
	# RJ facilitators, race & gender	2 African American Males	1 Latinx Male
	# School security officers (SSOs), race & gender	2 African American Male & African American Female	1 African American Female
Students	% students living in immediate neighborhood who attend this school	32%	62.6%
	% students African American	30.1%	14%
	% students Latinx	20.8%	76%
	% students Asian	29.5% t	8%
	% students White	12%	<1%
	% all other ethnic groups	4.5%	<1%
	Peer mediators	Yes	No
	School uniforms	No	Yes
Parental Engagement	PTSA raises money	Yes	No
	Level of engagement	High	Low
	PBIS store (parent run)	Yes	No

Sources include personal correspondence from OUSD personnel, data from OUSD websites, National Center for Education Statistics, and descriptive information collected from observations and interviews.

Despite the stress, Grant's staff remained committed to building relationships with students, supporting them, and not suspending them. Teachers and staff had just been through a very trying, if not terrible, six months while their principal was on leave. They wanted RJE to work, but they also knew that, after the damage done during the era of "suspension madness," they had their work cut out for them. They were tired, but not without hope.

Relational Ecologies and How They Affect Change

CHAPTER 6

What Do the Schools' Relational Ecologies Look Like?

Change Has Rhythms and Cycles

How people in an organization relate with each other affects their capacity to change; more than anything, this is what I came away with from my study. These schools revealed a simple but profound lesson about implementing restorative justice in education (RJE): the change process requires that people create a common vision and work through challenging times together. Relationships need to be strong enough to endure change, so building relationships is the place to start when schools consider implementing RJE. Nurturing relationships is how a new, positive, equitable, and just relational ecology takes root. People learn to trust, listen to, and feel safe with each other. To tell the story of these middle schools, then, I have turned to two core concepts—relational ecologies and change. What I found is that each feeds the other.

Certainly, creating a restorative school involves change. Change theory suggests that schools need effective leaders who can motivate staff, but they also need a core team of teachers and staff who embrace the reform, work to implement it with fidelity, and bring others along.[1] I wanted to understand what changes occurred across the schools when the schools adopted school-wide restorative practices (SWRPs). One thing is for sure: *change is messy*, and rarely do things go as planned. Program planners may map out timelines and implementation phases, but reality finds its own path: change does not happen in a straight line; it has rhythms and cycles. John Paul Leder-ach argues that change, or transformation, is more of a circular process or sideways spiral. Figure 12 shows how the change process goes up and down, forward and backward, around and around, while ultimately, still moving forward and expanding the capacities for both positive relationships and change.

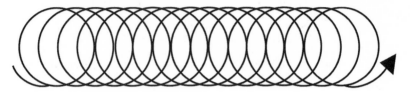

Figure 12. Circular process of change

Looking at change through this lens invites a more realistic understanding of what is involved with creating a restorative school. The steps and stages that program specialists map out serve as signposts, but actually traveling the terrain is full of surprises. Lederach offers both a language that replaces nega-tive phrases, such as "setbacks" or "backsliding," and a space to accept that things may not always go as planned or fit our timelines. As we will see, both schools experienced a circling process of change. They used times when they circled back-ward to reflect, renew, and redirect their efforts, so that over-all, they moved forward. Just because change is messy does not mean that it is not good or not having the needed effect.

■ Building Blocks of a Healthy Relational Ecology

The schools I studied, though different from each other in many ways, share an emerging relational ecology built on four factors or themes: trust between members of the school community; people being heard; a relational-based, student-centered culture; and a commitment to social justice.

To explore what goes into making the relational ecology of a restorative school, this chapter combines the qualitative and quantitative data I gathered from both schools. The four themes provide a framework, and subthemes emerged as I went along. Chart 6.1 illustrates these themes and subthemes.

Chart 6.1. The schools' relational ecologies: themes and sub-themes			
THEME 1: TRUST	THEME 2: BEING HEARD	THEME 3: RELATIONAL-BASED, STUDENT-CENTERED CULTURE	THEME 4: COMMITMENT TO SOCIAL JUSTICE
Trust among adults	Teacher voice	Physical environment	Becoming culturally competent
Trust between adults and students	Student voice	Restorative & relational-based ethos	Supporting African American male students
Trust among students			

Theme 1: Trust

"It's all about trust, it's all about love, it's all about creating the space," one teacher said to describe the relational ecology of her school. In a survey about trust, I asked staff whether they agreed or disagreed with five statements. Chart 6.2 shows the responses.

The vast majority of respondents felt that teachers, students, and parents in these schools trusted each other. These high levels of trust were less strong about familial or close feelings: 40 percent disagreed with the first statement, although 60 percent agreed. I wondered about the 40 percent: Were people keeping a safe and professional distance while still trusting each other? Perhaps they were feeling there was room to improve connectedness and attachment in the school community. Or maybe the high rates of teacher turnover inhibited teachers' ability to form close, familial connections with each other.

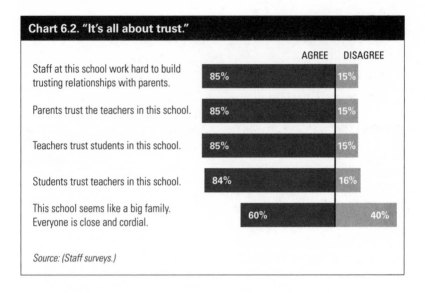

Chart 6.2. "It's all about trust."

AGREE DISAGREE

Staff at this school work hard to build trusting relationships with parents. — 85% | 15%

Parents trust the teachers in this school. — 85% | 15%

Teachers trust students in this school. — 85% | 15%

Students trust teachers in this school. — 84% | 16%

This school seems like a big family. Everyone is close and cordial. — 60% | 40%

Source: (Staff surveys.)

Trust among adults. Other survey questions focused on how much the staff trusted their principals. Chart 6.3 shows the percentage of staff who agreed or disagreed with each of six statements.

Clearly, most of the staff felt they could trust their principals and that their school leaders supported them. Successful school reform requires relationships of trust, especially with the school leader. A principal alone cannot change a school for the better.

For staff to embrace school-wide restorative practices, which involves working a different way, they need to know that their principal advocates for RJE and believes in it. In these two middle schools, they did. One survey respondent wrote:

> I think by him being firmly committed to reducing the suspensions and to really just not suspending—that commitment has opened up a space for restorative justice to be something that people can be committed to in opposition to sending kids home.

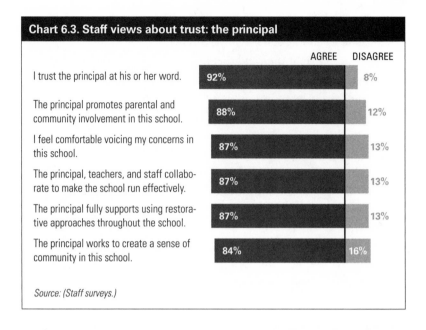

Chart 6.3. Staff views about trust: the principal

	AGREE	DISAGREE
I trust the principal at his or her word.	92%	8%
The principal promotes parental and community involvement in this school.	88%	12%
I feel comfortable voicing my concerns in this school.	87%	13%
The principal, teachers, and staff collaborate to make the school run effectively.	87%	13%
The principal fully supports using restorative approaches throughout the school.	87%	13%
The principal works to create a sense of community in this school.	84%	16%

Source: (Staff surveys.)

Although this survey question revealed that the staff trusted their principals, the principals at both schools knew they had to work to establish that trust. Elena Baez told me about several previous attempts to bring RJE to Grant and that these attempts did not go well. She reflected: "Maybe the school wasn't ready. There wasn't trust between myself and the school. I was developing trust, and not enough of it was built yet." I observed Stan Paulson tell a group of parents, "I've been able to absolutely build trust with the teachers and set really high expectations for teaching in this school." Getting staff to trust these principals and to support their initiatives took time and effort. However, once staff trusted their administrators, they more readily embraced RJE as a whole-school reform.

Trust is developed not through words but through actions. Riordin, Stan's assistant principal, told the focus group how he demonstrated trust to his teachers:

I have seen classrooms where there was some conflict or some harm was done, and the teacher decided a Circle was necessary right then and there. The content was put on the back burner so that the relationships and the harm could really be addressed. I think that's really important and I really trust the staff's judgment when it comes to doing that.

Administrators trusted staff to do their jobs and focused on supporting students, while also providing staff with additional support when needed. Trust was embedded in the schools' cultures.

Another part of the survey invited staff to reflect on the level of trust they felt with each other, including when it comes to using restorative practices.

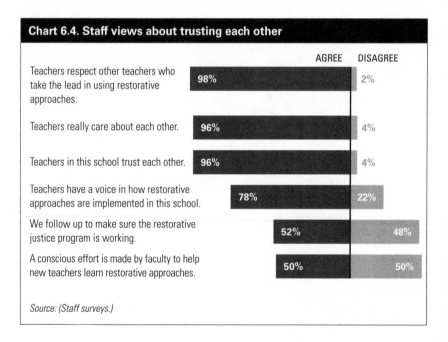

Chart 6.4. Staff views about trusting each other

	AGREE	DISAGREE
Teachers respect other teachers who take the lead in using restorative approaches.	98%	2%
Teachers really care about each other.	96%	4%
Teachers in this school trust each other.	96%	4%
Teachers have a voice in how restorative approaches are implemented in this school.	78%	22%
We follow up to make sure the restorative justice program is working.	52%	48%
A conscious effort is made by faculty to help new teachers learn restorative approaches.	50%	50%

Source: (Staff surveys.)

Teachers and staff overwhelmingly agreed with these statements, revealing a sense of caring, respect, camaraderie, and trust. The teachers clearly want to be using restorative practices and respect others who do. These qualities in relationships are essential for schools to embark on changing school culture. Teachers who trust each other and have good relationships with each other are able to rely upon, help, and support each other as they navigate the often turbulent waters of change. More important, they contribute positive vibes into the relational ecology of the school. They model healthy, supportive adult relationships for students. In turn, the students can then, according to Albert Bandura's social learning theory, adopt prosocial behaviors with adults and each other. Surely the adults' commitment to restorative practices and to using Circles among staff as well as with students and parents contributed to the high levels of trust among the adults. This created a pleasant and supportive work environment. Because staff and administrators trusted each other, students felt more inclined to trust the adults in their schools as well.

Trust between adults and students. In my focus group Circles at both schools, I asked the students if they felt they could trust the adults, especially the teachers, in their schools. Of the sixteen students who participated in the focus groups, 88 percent, or fourteen students, said they could trust *most* of the adults. As one student commented, "Overall, I think students can trust the adults. There are certain adults you kind of, like, step back a little bit." Several students explained that they trusted teachers who gave them good advice and who were not strict.

One student said, "I trust most of the teachers here except some, cuz some, they just . . . [*smiles and shakes head*] a whole 'nother world. I just don't like them because they're strict with you, like, they don't let you do nothing."

We cannot expect all students to have trusting feelings toward all their teachers. But what these students show us is that certain teacher behaviors inspire trust, while others do not. Specifically, this group of students said that they trust teachers who listen to students, who are nice, and who offer advice more than those who are strict and seem to care mostly about control. This goes back to how Brenda Morrison characterized RJE: as moving toward behaviors and practices that promote social engagement and away from those that focus on social control. A survey respondent wrote of that movement:

> Having RJ Circles with students who have had conflicts with me in class has dramatically increased my ability to form close relationships with these students that I think otherwise I would not be able to teach as well due to a breakdown in communication and trust.

When teachers listen and care, they engage their students and foster their social and emotional development. By contrast, when teachers adopt a rigid, authoritarian demeanor and focus on control, they turn students off and send the message that they do not trust students. As one student said, "I think that students can trust the adults, for the most part. But I think sometimes the adults have trouble trusting the kids." The more trust permeates a school's relational ecology, letting the ecology grow from social engagement, the less need there is for hard-line controlling measures and disciplining behaviors that erode trust. When students can trust adults and feel trusted by adults, they can more easily form trusting relationships with each other.

Trust among students. Cameron, the RJ facilitator at Davis, explained that "[i]n order to be a peer mediator, it is important that students are able to keep their mouths shut and also have

Figure 13. Peer mediators during a trust-building training exercise

the respect of their teachers." In other words, students need to know they can trust peer mediators to keep their confidence. Figure 13 is a photograph of one trust-building exercise, during which blindfolded students had to follow each other when only the first person in the "train" could see. In this exercise, students had to rely on others to keep themselves and others safe.

Teachers in both schools held community building Circles during advisory periods and some classes. These Circles provided safe spaces for students to build trust with each other. Miss Zang, a sixth-grade teacher at Grant, held community building Circles in her class every Friday, and she invited me to participate in one. She and her students were adept at listening and speaking in Circle because they did it frequently. The day before this scheduled Circle, Miss Zang had to hold a very intense Circle to repair harm in her class. She asked me not to attend that Circle because I would be a distraction and she needed that time with her students to resolve a problem. But on Friday, she and her students were excited and happy to be in this community building Circle, because they had resolved their problems the day before. Her students had settled on three prompts to talk about when they received the talking piece. One of the prompts invited Circle members to share something about their country of origin or birthplace. As they passed the piece around the Circle, I learned that this one class had students from more than six countries. Here is one story from that Circle:

> One boy shared that he and his brother, who sat next to him and did not speak when he received the piece, were "from a country [Nepal] where there was a lot of violence and where people were kidnapped a lot." As soon as he said that, students quieted down and tuned in to the petite, smiling, dark-haired boy holding the talking piece. He talked about how they lived in houses made of mud, not cement, and that they only had dirt roads and outhouses. Some students, especially those who were born in Oakland, could not imagine living in a place that did not have indoor plumbing and giggled. Others, who also came from poor countries, nodded their heads, relating to the boys' prior living conditions. The boy explained how they lived near the jungle where there were wild animals and elephants, and how their mother was almost bitten by a green mamba [a large and highly venomous snake]. Students who lived in the dangerous neighborhoods around the school identified with this boy and his brother, even though he painted a very different picture of an unsafe environment. Many of the kids in the Circle knew what it felt like to live in danger.

Miss Zang and her class had worked hard to build trust and community with each other and dedicated time each week to doing this work. They solved problems together, and they spent time in Circle getting to know more about each other. The Circle was a safe space for this boy to be open, honest, and vulnerable and to tell his personal story to twenty-eight squirming sixth-graders who listened to him with respect and compassion. He and his brother were part of a caring and safe classroom community, which they needed, especially considering the dangers he had been exposed to as a young child in his homeland. Stories like this illustrate the need for trauma-informed practices in schools. A growing body of evidence supports RJE and Circles in particular as one such trauma-informed practice.

One of the ways to build trust is to create time and space for people to share and listen to each other. In these two schools, people could trust each other because they felt heard, which is the second component that builds a positive relational ecology in restorative schools.

Theme 2: Being Heard

The fact that "being heard" became one of the four components essential to making these schools' relational ecologies positive was no surprise to me, as restorative processes intentionally create spaces for people to speak and be heard. I developed a survey to measure, in the staff's view, how much different groups in the school listened to each other. Chart 6.5 shows that, of the staff who responded, which varied from thirty-nine to fifty-three staff members for each statement, a very high percent believed a listening culture had taken root within and between these groups.

These responses are stunning. Overwhelmingly, the administrators and staff who responded felt that they were heard

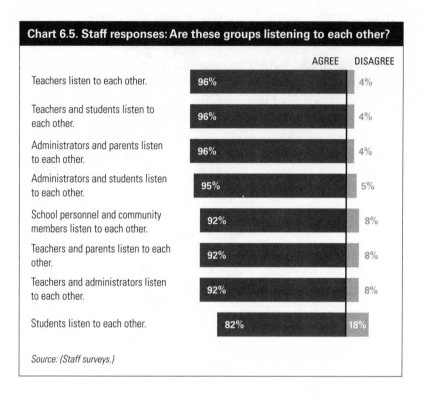

Chart 6.5. Staff responses: Are these groups listening to each other?

	AGREE	DISAGREE
Teachers listen to each other.	96%	4%
Teachers and students listen to each other.	96%	4%
Administrators and parents listen to each other.	96%	4%
Administrators and students listen to each other.	95%	5%
School personnel and community members listen to each other.	92%	8%
Teachers and parents listen to each other.	92%	8%
Teachers and administrators listen to each other.	92%	8%
Students listen to each other.	82%	18%

Source: (Staff surveys.)

and that people in the schools really listened to each other. One of the teachers in a focus group used the term "listening culture" to describe her school's culture. A survey respondent explained why a listening culture is so important:

> RJ has supported and reminded me why we all must make time to listen to everyone's stories, 'cause we all have one. There is always a reason why people behave a certain way, may say something a certain way, or react a certain way. We have to take time to ask questions, truly listen to one another, and make time to really heal together. RJ has definitely reminded me to listen to staff and not just our students.

In a listening culture, people's voices are heard, and people feel heard. Restorative processes create time and space for people to find their voice and express it. In their book *When Blood & Bones Cry Out*, John Paul Lederach and Angela Lederach explain that voice is essential for both healing and empowerment. Yet in many schools, teachers and students often feel they have no voice. Teachers are silenced when districts roll out one new program after another without engaging teachers in the decision-making on these programs or in finding out how the last one went. Students are silenced not only by zero tolerance discipline policies but also by a teacher-centered model of instruction that views students as passive recipients of other people's knowledge. I wanted to explore teacher and student voice in restorative schools to see if these frequently disenfranchised and marginalized groups felt heard in this environment.

Teacher voice. The leadership styles of the principals, the structure of the schools, and the use of SWRPs intermingled in these restorative schools to create space for teachers to express themselves and be heard. The principals actively and regularly solicited input from teachers and staff. As Stan Paulson explained: "We really solicit intentional feedback around what's working and what's not working. Teachers do a lot of innovation here, too. It is really kind of collectivistic. It's not a top-down environment." This invitation for input was not limited to using restorative practices but also included feedback on curriculum, schedules, and structure. When I asked teachers in the focus group how decisions were made in the school, one teacher said:

> We have a culture team that meets once a month, and teachers can opt into that culture team. We have teacher leadership at a lot of levels. We have family heads and we

have department heads, so there are different platforms
for teachers to get their voices heard, related to initiatives
and this [RJE] initiative in particular.

The principals and administrators at both schools appreciated and encouraged teacher-led initiatives, which empowered
teachers to actively contribute to their schools. As one teacher
said, "This is a school full of strong teachers who speak up
and who make trouble [*laughs*]. I think the school has rightly,
carefully said, 'We want things to come from the teachers.'"
Another teacher described how, because of restorative justice,
teachers could make a case for not suspending students, even
when district policy required suspension. She said,

> Now we can go to the principal or whoever's going to deal
> with this discipline issue and advocate for a child and
> know that there's this whole system that we can rely on to
> help them [the children] stay here because we don't want
> them to leave.

At Grant, two teachers approached principal Elena Baez
about the opportunity to hold Circles with their students.
As Elena explained, "Both women said, 'We want to have our
own weekly Circle, and we are elective teachers, so we don't
have a core—we don't have advisory classes.' We changed that.
Everybody has advisory now." Yet another teacher said that
her school "is a wonderful place to be around a lot of really
caring and compassionate people. I think when the staff comes
together here, we make really amazing things happen."

How do restorative schools facilitate the kinds of conversations between teachers and administrators so that "amazing things" can happen? Mainly by participating in Circles.
At these schools, teachers and administrators spoke with and
listened to each other in Circles on a regular basis. I observed

one Circle at a faculty meeting at Davis: the principal and RJ facilitator asked teachers what they felt they needed in order to improve their skills at using restorative practices in their classrooms. The RJ facilitators then used this feedback from the Circle to plan ways to provide the requested support.

Student voice. Both Davis and Grant had a variety of structures and processes in place for students to speak and be heard. At a parent meeting, Stan Paulson described how the student members were involved in what happens at Davis.

Even daily communication methods affirmed the listening and being heard culture. For example, both schools used "academic discourse" in their classrooms to engage students, promote critical thinking, and spur active listening. Stan defined academic discourse as a form of communication based on respect: students acknowledge what they heard from another student before they themselves speak. I observed students using academic discourse at a parent meeting: one student said, "[Charlie], I'd like to build on what you had to say," and then continued speaking. Classroom bulletin boards emphasized academic discourse and constructive conversation skills along with the values that support these processes.

That said, only 72 percent of the forty-seven staff who responded to my survey agreed with the statement "Students are encouraged to say how they feel about restorative approaches" (see chart 6.6). Following up with students in my focus group Circles, I asked whether they felt they had input or some say about what happened in their school. Half of the sixteen students said that through Circles, student councils, and by working with individual teachers, they did. Six students did not answer the question, and two said they were not heard because they did not get what they wanted or because things did not change.

One student explained how he and his peers contributed

to changing one of the school's core Panther P.R.I.D.E. values at Davis:

> I don't think we get to make big money choices and stuff like that, but, for example, we changed the "E" in "P.R.I.D.E." [from "Empowerment"] to "Empathy," and students got to take a—well, students and teachers—we got to take a poll of who thought the "E" should change or stay the same.

All students in the schools participated in community building Circles where, according to one staff member, "Students are better trained on how to use a talking piece and how to listen in a Circle." A student in the focus group stated, "There are a lot of chances for us to put input in [*laughs*]. And I feel like this Circle place, right here, is where we put the most input in." Teachers in both the survey and focus groups spoke about how participating in Circles has helped everyone, teachers and students alike, to become better listeners. As one survey respondent said, "I feel I am more willing to listen before reacting to what they [students] are doing." Additionally, 93 percent of the fifty-five staff who responded to the survey agreed with the statement "I allow all students to share their perspectives even if I don't agree more frequently."

Because the two schools avoided using suspension as punishment except in the most egregious situations, both teachers and students smiled when I asked them about behavior issues, saying, "We just have to talk about it," or "There is no suspension. It's just like you have to sit down and have a conversation." Even though teachers and students sometimes made light of this response, in reality, conversation and dialogue were at the heart of the schools' relational ecologies. I frequently observed adults taking the time to "just talk to" students who were in trouble. "While we are consistently still getting referrals, students are still needing to engage in restorative conversations," said Elena Baez, Grant's principal. As I walked throughout the schools, I saw adults speaking with and listening to students across all school environments. Teachers, SSOs, counselors, administrators, behavioral intervention specialists, and even school secretaries were engaged in conversations with individual students, trying to understand the students' circumstances and current needs.

■ Theme 3: Relational-Based, Student-Centered Culture

A third theme that emerged was that, through using restorative practices, the schools were able to develop a relational-based, student-centered culture. Students were actively involved with implementing restorative practices and were empowered by doing so. I posed some positive statements about students' role in implementing SWRPs, and most of the teachers and support staff agreed with them. Chart 6.6 shows the five statements, and the percent of those who agreed or disagreed with each.

Again, overwhelmingly, staff believed that students benefitted greatly from being in a restorative school. One staff member responded to a question by reiterating how SWRPs have prevented students from "being eliminated from the equation," saying, "There have been multiple occasions where using RJ has helped students who have made severe mistakes stay in our school community and work to repair harm rather than be sent to another place."

Administrators, teachers, and support staff spoke unabashedly about what an important role positive, healthy relationships with their students and each other played in their schools. They wrote as well as spoke about how restorative processes helped them better relate to each other and to their students. For example, one teacher described her school's philosophy about students as follows:

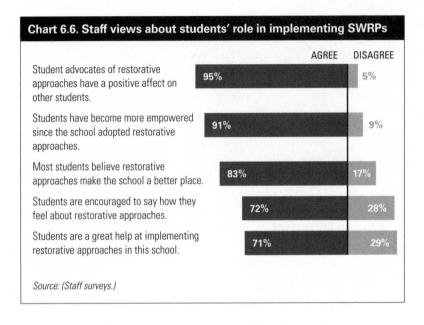

Chart 6.6. Staff views about students' role in implementing SWRPs

	AGREE	DISAGREE
Student advocates of restorative approaches have a positive affect on other students.	95%	5%
Students have become more empowered since the school adopted restorative approaches.	91%	9%
Most students believe restorative approaches make the school a better place.	83%	17%
Students are encouraged to say how they feel about restorative approaches.	72%	28%
Students are a great help at implementing restorative approaches in this school.	71%	29%

Source: (Staff surveys.)

We are going to acknowledge that this is a struggle and humanize you [the student] and use a humanizing process to support you in making better decisions. And when you mess up again, you are not deleted from the equation again. We are going to sit down and have another conversation, and another adult is going to have a conversation. I think it's telling that a number of adults know students in different grades, whether or not that adult had them, because we are a relational school. So you can count on somebody who you didn't necessarily have as a teacher.

A teacher at Grant said that her school was "a lot more relational-based than any school I have interned in before or just visited, which is part of the reason why I love teaching at this school." Her colleague agreed, saying, "I'd say 95-98 percent of the adults really put a lot of emphasis on relationships with students and at times relationships with others as well." Caridad described the deep feelings of support for students that a relational-based school fosters:

> You, as a young person, will feel that the adults here love you, and you will be able to explicitly say the different ways that they are willing to support you. And so I think in that way . . . our students have experienced a lot of support and love and benefit from us being a relational school, which is the foundation of the restorative justice process.

"Students are the center of school," Stan Paulson told me as we walked through the hallways of Davis. Though I could not interview everyone in these schools, the staff and students who did share their views with me agreed with this relational and restorative ethos.

Physical environment. The physical environment reflected this culture. Both Davis and Grant were open, inviting, and hospitable buildings that lacked fortress tactics—no locked gates or metal detectors. Student artwork and posters promoting restorative values and behavioral expectations hung throughout both schools, as in figure 14.

Inside the classrooms, positive messages appeared on bulletin boards and walls. Teachers displayed student work, and some had "shout out" walls to commend their students for academic and behavioral achievements. More than 75 percent of the twenty classrooms I visited were arranged either so that students could sit with a partner at a table or with three other students in a grouping of desks.

Teachers frequently placed their technology stations on a cart in the center of the room, close to their students, while the teachers used the computer and projected lessons onto the screen. Most of the teachers I observed were in constant motion, moving around the room to answer individual

Figure 14. Poster promoting a restorative value

students' questions or to monitor their work in progress. Very few of them sat or stood at their desks. The open environment, positive visuals and displays of student work, teacher proximity, and student seating arrangements in the classrooms communicated in physical terms that students were at the center of the schools' culture.

Restorative and relational ethos. Belinda Hopkins frequently writes about the ethos in restorative schools. "Ethos" can be defined as the spirit of the schools and describes what I *felt* each time I visited a restorative school. One of my main goals was to learn if teachers and staff believed that restorative approaches and practices had helped to facilitate more positive interactions within the school community. To find out, I developed a set of four survey statements, and chart 6.7 shows the staff's responses.

Clearly, these teachers and support staff believed that restorative approaches helped people interact, relate to, and work with each other in positive ways, so much so that 98 percent of them said they would rather work in a restorative

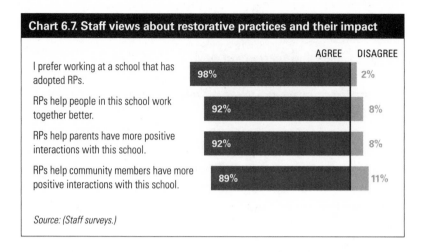

Chart 6.7. Staff views about restorative practices and their impact

	AGREE	DISAGREE
I prefer working at a school that has adopted RPs.	98%	2%
RPs help people in this school work together better.	92%	8%
RPs help parents have more positive interactions with this school.	92%	8%
RPs help community members have more positive interactions with this school.	89%	11%

Source: (Staff surveys.)

school than in a school that does not practice RJE. As one person reflected in the survey, "I like it here because I feel safer when people assume positive intent. I like interactions based on compassion." The schools' restorative and relational ethos also helped to support teachers as they embraced new initiatives. One teacher said, "It's a huge community, we support each other, but it's also a place where we are pushing each other a lot."

I consistently observed that teachers, administrators, SSOs, and support staff maintained a relaxed demeanor. The adults in the school made eye contact with students when they spoke to them, showing genuine interest and care. I watched adults spend time with students in the courtyards or cafeterias talking casually, laughing, listening, and just being there for them, being present with them. For example, after escorting me to the teacher's lounge so I could eat my lunch, the band teacher told me that he was going back to his classroom to eat with his students, a practice that he felt all the teachers should adopt. Most of the adults in these schools seemed to truly enjoy being with their students, and it seemed natural for most of them to let students know they were cared for, safe, and supported.

Principals and teachers at both Davis and Grant told me that this ethos was already present in their schools before they adopted restorative practices. In fact, one reason the leaders and faculty readily embraced SWRPs was because they cared deeply about the students, particularly those who were being suspended; they wanted to find better ways to help these youths. Stan Paulson talked about having a relational-based, positive orientation, and different people in the schools repeated these words and phrases. One teacher told me:

> We are a school where the adults look to make relationships with kids, so the mind-set in most classrooms with most adults when they are having interactions with students, it's about making a relationship so that they can figure out the needs. And that seems to be the mind-set with just about every adult that I can think of in the building.

I participated in one after-school Circle with eight sixth-grade boys. The Circle's aim was to discover what the boys needed from the teacher and each other to practice more respect in their class. The teacher sat in Circle and asked students to come up with their own solutions for making their afterschool experience better. Many of the boys admitted that they did not behave respectfully all the time, even though they knew better. The teacher also asked the boys what they needed from him in order to feel more respected. As the boys passed the talking piece, they worked as a group to determine how they could treat each other and the teacher with more respect. A few spoke about what they needed from the teacher in order to do so, but most of the boys could not tell the teacher what they needed from him.

I asked the principals, Stan and Elena, if they purposely hired teachers who were familiar with RJE or aligned with its values. Both said they tried to hire teachers and other staff who had a relational-based, positive orientation. One teacher described this approach as "the way you talk, the positivity, the way you don't attack, the way you don't label things." Elena described how she determined the relational orientation of potential new hires:

> One of the [interview] questions that we had was, "If a student is caught smoking marijuana on campus, what do you believe should be the consequence? What do you believe should happen? How should a school respond?" Because I think lots of times people will answer with what they know, and what they know is usually, "Well, they get suspended and they should get kicked out." So that's what I always ask . . . to get an insight as far as whether they are open to [RJ] or not.

Stan said he looked for teachers whose relational orientation was in line with the question "We are getting kids who are the best their moms and dads and guardians can do. What can we do to effect positive [change] in their lives?" He went on to say that this orientation "feels like it's so dependent on a person's mental health, like their emotional range, their interchangeability, their kind of social, emotional strength, if you will." Elena agreed, saying:

> I think we are student-centered from top to the bottom, and if a teacher doesn't like kids and is orientated against kids, it's just not going to work here. Their bosses aren't going to be okay with it, kids aren't going to be okay with it. It's the culture [here].

Five people spoke of how RJ "is resonating with people" because many teachers' "practices already had a restorative bent." Several of the peer mediators in one student focus group expressed their own relational-based, positive orientation as something that drew them to becoming peer mediators. One boy said, "I think I've been naturally a peacekeeper," while another said, "I really didn't, like, put people down or put people up. Like, everyone's equal to me."

What this information tells us is that a relational ethos where students are the heart of a school greatly contributes to a healthy school culture. This culture makes a school ripe to adopt RJE. When teachers and administrators already have a positive, relational-based orientation, they more readily reject punitive discipline and embrace the values and practices of RJE. After learning this, I wondered, "What do you do with teachers who do not naturally have this orientation? How can we foster this orientation?" Chapters 7 and 11 take up this issue: chapter 7 explores how to engage skeptics; chapter 11 offers recommendations for training teachers in RJE.

The three components that emerged as essential to a positive relational ecology in these two schools—trust, being heard, and a relational-based, student-centered culture—were no surprise to me. What did surprise me, however, was the fourth theme that emerged: a deep commitment to social justice.

■ Theme 4: Commitment to Social Justice

The restorative schools in this study were located in an urban center with a long history of social justice and political activism embedded in its culture. Oakland was the birthplace of the Black Panthers, and their legacy of striving for racial justice and equality lives on today. It makes sense, then, that teachers and administrators in these Oakland schools were committed to the principles of social justice. Two related sub-themes emerged as well: becoming culturally competent and confronting racial biases and how they harm African American students, especially males. As one person explained:

> Our school's mission is to interrupt inequity despite societal inequities, and while we are not solely responsible for the inequity existing, we take responsibility for how we interrupt that. I think we still have work to do—personally, like what am I doing that's treating kids [unfairly]? What am I doing that's within my class? And that's me personally—I've got to change some practices. I have different colleagues and resources and people to go to, to help me be reflective of our practice and what I have to do to shift things. But then as a school, I think we still have work to do there.

Grant's mission became obvious to me when I noticed the social justice theme in one of the student art exhibits. The week before I arrived, the art class had taken a field trip to Alcatraz to see an exhibit on political prisoners designed by Chinese artist and political prisoner Ai Weiwei. I had just seen this exhibit myself and was interested in learning how the students felt about it—it blew me away. Based on the students' artwork, the exhibit had a huge impact on them. The art teacher created a unit called "Art as Activism," where students learned about the plight of political prisoners around the world through the exhibit at Alcatraz. Students then drew posters about social issues that they felt passionate about (see figure 15). Their posters reflected concerns close to home, including police brutality, animal cruelty, racism, and anti-immigration policies.

Stan Paulson, Davis's principal, was frustrated, however, with federal and state expectations that schools close the academic achievement gap between richer and poorer students

Figure 15. "Art as Activism" posters

and between students of color and White students, when inequities continue to exist in society. Schools can do a lot to close the gaps, he believed, but they cannot do everything. They alone cannot compensate for or offset the inequities, injustices, and imbalances in society. He said:

> Poverty is heavy lifting. . . . To say to a school, completely
> have no gaps—have the same, have poor kids on par with
> kids from the Hills on academic achievement—seems
> really unfair to me. To just say, your school is inherently
> racist because these gaps are persisting in your school, I
> find that insulting. On the other hand, if we need to help
> underserved kids have a shot, then I want to lean into,
> what are we doing? How can we improve? So it's not that I
> am rejecting being culturally responsive and being equity
> focused and social justice orientated, I am on board with all
> of that. . . . We really care about closing gaps and serving
> underserved kids.

In the survey, I also asked the staff to share any experiences about the relationship between restorative justice and social justice. According to their responses, restorative justice appears to have raised teachers' consciousness about racial biases and inequities and contributed to the sense that they are making a positive difference. "Our commitment to restorative approaches is one way in which we are trying to do good on our mission to interrupt inequities," wrote one survey respondent. Another said, "What I most appreciate is we are not a revolving door for students who might be considered challenging. We do our best to work with all students and now [we] have something [RJE] to ensure equitable processes." Another teacher reflected:

> Being so diverse—wow! It's such a challenge to get young people and adults to try to find any system that will work with everyone. Because you can't find that, we find ourselves mediating between a lot of different factions and cultures at this school that other schools don't have to deal with. I find that fascinating. I find it the best thing that a school could ever have. Particularly in this day.

Principals, teachers, staff, and students were acutely aware of different forms of injustice, and they reported that adopting RJE was one way their schools could be more just and equitable. Additionally, staff expressed an awareness that they needed to be introspective and take a close look at anything and everything they could be doing, even unintentionally, to reinforce inequities. I created a sub-theme called "becoming culturally competent" to reflect this line of thinking.

Becoming culturally competent. Through "mediating between a lot of different cultures," the teachers at both schools became more aware of societal inequities as well as their own complicity and privilege in reinforcing power imbalances, often along racial lines. One person said:

> I think many staff members are aware of the bias they have toward Black students, especially when we do not have Black administrators and don't have many Black teachers. Despite this, I still think the data shows that Black males and females are disproportionately disciplined. I think that many Black families don't feel a strong connection to our school and are at times distrustful of the school.

Another participant commented, "African American males at [this school] are disproportionately referred out of the classroom, but I think that is a result of teachers not being culturally competent enough to communicate and build relationships." Acke, who participated in that same focus group, stated:

> We need to have an objective and subjective model of what the cultures are that we are dealing with—what the histories of these cultures are that we are dealing with, and how best do we fit ourselves to improve upon those dynamics.

On a survey, I tried to assess what kinds of training and resources staff had received and their subsequent comfort levels with understanding cultural differences. Survey respondents expressed mostly moderate to high levels of confidence in understanding cultural differences, thanks to training and resources. That said, several people expressed a need for more cultural competency training. One person wrote, "Introducing and holding PDs [professional development trainings] around culturally responsive teaching should be a huge focus at Davis to build trust among students of color." Despite receiving support and training, many teachers and administrators still felt that becoming culturally competent was the responsibility of the individual and was something that could be gained through experience and self-reflection. Riordan, Davis's assistant principal, a White man, got very emotional in the focus group when he shared this story of his interaction with an African American parent:

> I had a conversation with an African American parent today, a mother of an African American boy who's been on campus restoration for a week and a half because we have basically suspended him from attending class because he has accumulated so many referrals in the year. It's not an arbitrary decision. We are treating everybody the same way, but he has got to this point before anyone else and we actually made an exception. I made a contract and I tried to work with the family. There are many barriers for this family, and so even coming to the school is a challenge. We got to the point where that contract now requires the parent to come in and have a meeting. I had just a difficult conversation, but it clued me in to the fact—and it's not the first time I've had this, but it's always good to have a refresher—that there's so much historical distrust that I had nothing to do with and this parent had nothing to do with, but it's just there. That I have to really be aware of that—every time that she gets a little angry or rough around the edges or doesn't really want to hear what I have to say and all my warm and fuzzy solutions and suggestions. It's like—how am I going to dismantle 250 years of history? And her own experience! So I just think that if we can go forward with thinking about that, then we are in a better position to support [African American students].

Riordan's story is a reminder that, while members of the school community can strive to create fair and equitable processes and opportunities for all students, the real world does not and has not always done the same. Students and parents of color who experience daily racial injustices and harms carry their experiences into the schools. They really have no reason to expect that they will be treated any better in an educational institution than they would in any other institution.

Indeed, thanks to the legacies of White supremacy, Jim Crow, and segregation in America, White people can still live most of our lives without knowing or developing friendships with people of color. Those of us who are White miss valuable feedback from people of color about how racial biases affect our thinking, perceptions, and behavior. As Riordan observed, histories of racism and their legacies come between White staff and students and families of color. Trusting relationships are slower or less likely to form as a result. Several people identified lower comfort levels with different people as one source of the problem of disproportionate disciplining. For example, one teacher observed:

> Sometimes I see adults who don't have a lot of experience with African American people or African American communities. I don't know if it's fear or ignorance or just not having those experiences, but I don't see them making the same connections to kids.

Another teacher acknowledged her own racial conditioning, saying, "I am a human being raised in this world and raised to treat a particular group of people a certain way, and raised to communicate with people in a certain way." She understood that she must be personally aware and transform herself if she were to become culturally competent and engage all students equally. Principals, focus group participants, and survey respondents concurred. Even with the training they had received and the resulting moderate to high confidence levels they felt, they believed that cultural competency develops ultimately on a deep, personal level through reflection, opening up to experiences beyond racial comfort zones, and self-transformation. As a group, the people who participated in my study expressed a commitment to reflect on their words and behaviors and to become more aware of how racial biases and privilege can replicate oppression and reinforce racial disparities.

The following findings confirmed how right staff members were: they needed to increase school-wide awareness around race and bias. The findings gave evidence of racial biases still in play and still shaping views of discipline, at least on the part of some staff and some students. One of the best ways to support Black students, they realized, is to explore racial biases and how they affect not only discipline but also—and more fundamentally—relationships within the school.

Confronting racial biases and their impact on African American males. As I explained in the opening pages of section 2, the OUSD made a voluntary agreement with the USDOE Office for Civil Rights to reduce the disproportionate disciplining of African American males. However, David Yusem knew that, despite many Oakland schools working hard to implement RJE, it was still happening and he wanted to know why. Stan Paulson spoke to this too, noting that "teachers care about kids, but if I am an African American boy, I am not sure that all my teachers are that culturally competent in connecting with everyone." I asked focus groups if they felt the school had a shared vision for reducing the number of African American male students who experienced disciplinary actions, and this question elicited a range of responses from teachers and staff. Here, I present what students and staff told me. Their perceptions reveal a spectrum of awareness about race and racial biases and how they affect Black students' school experience.

In chapter 10, the section called "African American Males and RJE: Pushing a School's Paradigm Shift Deeper" unpacks these dynamics from an RJE perspective and explores how a restorative school can respond to them in ways that expand awareness about race and invite transformation as a school community.

"[H]istorically, if you are smart as a teacher, you know these African American boys are dealing with something else," said Acke. That something else is racism, especially longstanding institutionalized racism. One teacher reflected on her own practice: "[We have] a lot of research knowing that African American kids come in already with lower self-esteem and just, how do you focus on really building kids' self-esteem? And not in an artificial kind of way?"

"When we are talking about African American young boys, it's a dynamic that's heavy," Acke continued. This statement and others like it reveal that school personnel were acutely aware of how systemic racism, police brutality, racial biases, race-targeted poverty, and other forms of racial discrimination negatively affected their students, particularly African American males. However, even with this heightened awareness, the staff agreed that they had not gotten "there" yet in eliminating disproportionate disciplining in their schools. One Davis teacher said:

> When I think of some of the most politically minded
> individuals that I can think of on the campus, I also realize
> they are oftentimes sending out Black males. I don't think
> it's conscious—or there is a conscious effort to be like,
> "Yes, I realize this is a problem, this is why I chose to teach
> in [this district], this is why I am here." There's sometimes
> a disconnect, or sometimes they just haven't developed
> the ability yet to realize that there are skills to develop,
> particular relationships with particular kids, in order to be

most supportive. And in the right way. So yeah, you'll see some of the same kids in OCR sent out by the same teacher each time, and if you were to talk to that teacher they would say all kinds of things about how much they were in support of ending injustice, racism, discrimination, this inequity that we have, and probably not seeing their own selves as contributing to that, because they haven't yet had the skill to develop the relationship.

RJE processes are designed to help adults and students bridge these gaps, encourage self-reflection, build understanding, and connect more deeply, so I wondered about staff's attitudes toward African American students and the schools' treatment of them. After listening to various comments, I posed statements that reflected what I had heard—including outright negative stereotypes and attitudes that feed racial profiling—to see how many of the staff agreed or disagreed with the views expressed. For each statement, the number of staff who responded varied between forty-one and fifty-three. Chart 6.8 summarizes their responses.

Two of the statements explored staff biases about Black students and their behavior. Did they believe, as some staff told me, that African American students misbehaved more and were more aggressive than students of other ethnic groups? Though the great majority of staff disagreed, 33 percent and 26 percent respectively agreed. In other words, Black students faced staff who held negative views of them because of their race about a quarter to a third of the time.

The next three statements focused on the schools' patterns of disciplining students. When I posed unfair or disproportionate disciplining as a general, non-racialized statement, 60 percent said it was happening. But when I tied unfair disciplining to Black students, 76 percent and 89 percent said it was not happening to these students. Their responses puzzled me,

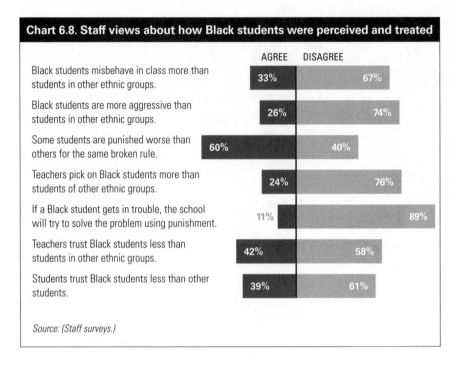

Chart 6.8. Staff views about how Black students were perceived and treated

AGREE   DISAGREE

Black students misbehave in class more than students in other ethnic groups.
33%   67%

Black students are more aggressive than students in other ethnic groups.
26%   74%

Some students are punished worse than others for the same broken rule.
60%   40%

Teachers pick on Black students more than students of other ethnic groups.
24%   76%

If a Black student gets in trouble, the school will try to solve the problem using punishment.
11%   89%

Teachers trust Black students less than students in other ethnic groups.
42%   58%

Students trust Black students less than other students.
39%   61%

Source: (Staff surveys.)

since they conflicted with what many staff members had told me about the ongoing problem their school had of disproportionately disciplining Black students.

In trying to unpack what they were saying, we might consider a few points. First, David Yusem stated that Black students were, in fact, still being disproportionately disciplined in the OUSD district, and Davis's principal and many of the staff recognized it for Davis as well, so the majority response that Black students were not being disproportionately disciplined warrants further questioning. What is going on here?

Second, Black students comprised 30 percent of Davis's student body and 14 percent of Grant's. As the previous responses indicate, almost a third of the staff believed Black students were more aggressive and misbehaved more. It would follow, at least in their view, that Black students should be disciplined more because their behavior warranted it more. They would not see the discipline as unfair, though it would be disproportionate. Yet pointing to Black students' behavior to justify disproportionate disciplining is not a restorative response.

Third, Grant's and Davis's combined staff were on average 54.5 percent White and 83.5 percent non-African American. From what we now know about implicit racial biases—that they are pervasive, involuntary, and unconscious—to what extent were implicit racial biases in play not only in disciplining Black students but also in assessing the fairness of the discipline?

Fourth, staff responses to the second and third statements of this trio may have been more about asserting the fairness of their colleagues and school than about assessing racial disparities. Perhaps they did not want to tie the disproportionate disciplining of Black students to racial biases on the part of their colleagues or schools. Yet who pays when biases go unexplored?

Each of these points could be a focus for Circle dialogues and reflection as a school community—not to lay blame but to explore, learn, build relationships, and change.

The last two statements I posed reflected other comments I had heard, namely, that some teachers and students trusted Black students less than they trusted students of other ethnic groups. About 40 percent of the staff believed this was so. (These two statements identified perceptions of race-based mistrust present in the school, not whether the respondents themselves trusted Black students less.) Given that relationships are built on trust, how might it have affected Black students to sense that many of the adults and students they encountered every day may not have trusted them as much as they trusted other students? How might it have felt to non-Black students and adults not to trust a racial group within the school? If indeed Black students were trusted less, they would have been experiencing the schools' relational ecologies differently from their non-African American peers, and this different experience of the schools' relational ecologies would have impacted their behavior.

However we interpret these responses, they indicated to me that race was a significant lens for these schools, influencing how people saw each other. Moreover, perceptions of race were shaping dynamics that were working against the kind of relational ecology that the schools were looking for. They were looking to increase trust as a basis for relationships, for example, but racial biases were undermining trust.

So I asked staff a follow-up question: "Do you have any comments on the experiences of African American male students in this school?" To analyze their responses to this open-ended question, I grouped their comments into themes and then ranked the themes according to how many times each was mentioned, as shown in chart 6.9.

There is a lot going on in these responses. The majority of staff identified racial inequities as well as ways that teachers and staff could better serve African American students and their families. They said things like: "I think we have a long way to go to build trusting relationships with African American families" and "I don't feel we have systems and structures to help support them emotionally and academically." Seven of the nine themes were social justice oriented, focusing on issues such as cultural competency, systemic racism, resources, support, and equity. For example, several staff members commented:

- [I]t's obvious that they have him cuffed because he's Black. So how do we teach young Black boys that that exists? One of the problems I am seeing is from the White teachers here: [they] don't have that

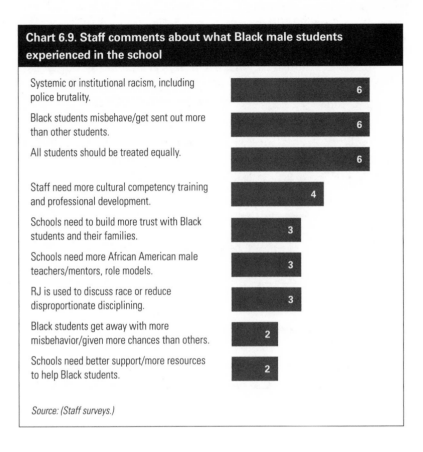

Chart 6.9. Staff comments about what Black male students experienced in the school

Systemic or institutional racism, including police brutality.	6
Black students misbehave/get sent out more than other students.	6
All students should be treated equally.	6
Staff need more cultural competency training and professional development.	4
Schools need to build more trust with Black students and their families.	3
Schools need more African American male teachers/mentors, role models.	3
RJ is used to discuss race or reduce disproportionate disciplining.	3
Black students get away with more misbehavior/given more chances than others.	2
Schools need better support/more resources to help Black students.	2

Source: (Staff surveys.)

perspective. So they don't know how to really grasp that this . . . it's just knowledge based.

- Many students, some African American and male, have PTSD from living in poverty and violence.

However, two of the themes singled out Black students as misbehaving more, getting sent out more, getting away with more, and being given second chances more. Black students were, again, being characterized negatively. Some of the staff recognized that adults' and peers' lack of trust with Black students and their families might be contributing to negative dynamics. Because of lower trust, the African American students' relationships with teachers, peers, and the school as a whole would not be as strong or as positive.

Students struggled with issues of race and racial biases as well. In a focus group, students' comments about race revealed feelings of unfairness, either of Black students being treated unfairly or of White and non-Black students being denied breaks that they perceived Black students as receiving:

> *Girl 1:* The people that act out a lot get treated differently but sometimes they get treated better because they're allowed to walk around. When I'm having troubles, I can't walk around. . . .

> *Martha*: How do you know who those people are?
> *Boy 1:* They're loud.

> *Boy 2:* Sometimes African Americans or people of color will get possibly treated differently than White people.

Their comments indicated to me that racial biases were present and seeding resentments. Insofar as they were unaddressed, they were impairing relationships and could have easily led to conflicts, both in the classroom and outside of it.

These responses showed that staff and students were aware of the struggles African American students face. They also gave evidence that greater awareness of racial biases, implicit and explicit, and how they affect attitudes and relationships could benefit not only African American students but also everyone in the school.

To be clear, most staff tried to create just and equitable spaces in their schools and classrooms. However, like the rest of us who live in a society that struggles with acknowledging systemic racism and White supremacy and that has yet to repair race-based harms and practice equity, staff and students struggled as well. Young Black males struggle in schools all the more as a result. With millions of Black lives on the line, the question is pressing: What do Black male students—and all students of color—need from their schools so they can feel a sense of belonging in their school community and thrive?

If this means recognizing our own racial biases, countering negative stereotypes, and naming microaggressions, then we must find ways of doing that. If this means recruiting more Black male teachers so that young Black males have strong educator role models, then we must do that. If this means establishing mentoring Circles where young Black males can talk about what it means to be a Black man, then let us create those partnerships and invite mentors into the schools. If this means increasing cultural competency through workshops on White privilege and anti-racism, then we need to invest in them and make them part of every educator's professional development and preparation programs. If this means allying with students of color as they struggle for social justice, then let us engage parents and the community in anti-racism and reparative initiatives.

RJE is powerful: I know this is true. However, we cannot expect RJE to be "a quick fix" for people who have been wounded by centuries of racism, economic oppression, racial terrorism, police brutality, and all manner of injustices. Society at large is far from being on board with racial and reparative justice. RJE can, though, provide spaces and processes for people to come together to do this work and to prepare new generations to take it up going into the future. Schools can contribute to repairing long-standing, multigenerational mass harms. As big as the job is, it starts with ourselves and how we are with each other in schools, so we can better respect and nurture all the children in our care.

▮ Summary: Relational Ecologies and Change

To summarize, four themes shaped the relational ecologies of these two middle schools: trust among members of the school community; people feeling heard; a relational-based, student-centered culture; and a commitment to social justice.

Trust. Trust has a very high and very positive impact on the relational ecology of schools. When trust pervades relationships, the school's atmosphere is positive and the school community has a positive foundation on which to build when challenges inevitably arise. RPs are all about building a base of trust for relationships in a school and its overall relational ecology.

Being heard. We feel trust when we feel heard. Across groups—students, teachers, staff, principals, and parents—people felt they had a chance to speak and that their voices were heard. Being heard has a positive impact on a school's relational ecology, and RPs are all about creating a listening culture in a school as well.

Culture: relational-based and student-centered. Both schools had developed a student-centered and relational-based culture. This priority was reflected not only in a restorative and relational ethos but in their physical environments and school schedules as well. Teachers and support staff agreed that students benefited from participating in restorative practices and that adopting restorative practices was good to do because it best served the students.

Social justice. Social justice principles mattered to the people in these schools, both adults and students. They were aware of historical and systemic racism and injustice, and they wanted to do the personal and school-wide work required to become more culturally competent, so their schools would be fair, equitable, and just. They knew that African American students, males in particular, faced racial injustices on a daily basis, and they were dedicated to getting better at supporting these students by confronting their own racial biases.

None of the themes exist independently of the others; they are interrelated. Trust allows people to be heard, while people listening to each other builds trust. Focusing on students and building trusting relationships creates spaces for people to wrestle openly with issues of bias, structural racism, cultural competency, police brutality, and injustice. The combined presence of these four elements developed the relational ecologies that the schools needed to change, so that they could function restoratively.

CHAPTER 7

Changes in the Schools' Structures

> We were starting to really shift how we do things towards restorative justice, and I think it's always helpful when Antonio says it's not a program. Because lots of people try to do it as a program. Like "Oooo, reduce suspensions—throw restorative justice at it." You know, that's not what it's about. Right? And so we started shifting how we do things, how we resolve problems, in a more relational way.

This Grant teacher is describing the school's experience of change: people chose to shift how they thought about things and did them. They started looking beyond seemingly simple solutions to complex problems. The people in Davis and Grant realized not only that zero tolerance policies were not working for anyone but also that they were hungry to find a new way to "do school." School-wide restorative practices (SWRPs) gave them the means to create relational-based, student-centered schools at the tier 1, school-wide level. They did not confine restorative processes to tiers 2 and 3 simply to reduce suspensions.

Section 2 described the structural changes the schools had to make when they adopted restorative justice in education (RJE)—in particular, their use of space, personnel, schedules, and budget. Both schools hired at least one RJ facilitator, identified at least one room as the RJ room, and dedicated time in the school schedule for all teachers to hold Circles with their students. Since creating a restorative school calls for many changes, I wanted to explore what the changes looked and felt like as well as what made change more difficult for these two schools. Change theory (see appendix 1) and implementation science (see the introduction) can help educators negotiate the changes involved with whole-school reform. Both provide a framework for understanding what makes change happen in a school—including discipline policy revisions, leadership, capacity building, and reflective action.

◼ Discipline Policy Revisions

In 2012, the Oakland Unified School District (OUSD) voluntarily resolved with the United States Department of Education Office for Civil Rights (USDOE OCR) to change how the district handles discipline problems, specifically to reduce the number of African American males who were being suspended or expelled. The OUSD adopted less punitive disciplinary measures and required all schools in the district to follow suit. Both Davis and Grant radically changed their school's discipline policies and adopted RJE to reduce the disproportionate disciplining, thereby formalizing their decision to become restorative schools. I asked principal Stan Paulson what changed in the discipline policy at Davis:

> Fighting is not a suspension. Marijuana smoking is not a suspension. So we've kind of undone some of the automatic suspensions. . . . When I first got here, fighting was an automatic suspension. Immediately. And it [suspension] doesn't curtail fighting; it keeps happening.

When I asked students if they felt that RJE made their school a better place to be, one of the girls said:

> I agree that the school has gotten more better, less violence. *It's better because, instead of just suspending them, they actually talk to them* [emphasis mine]. They help them with

the problem, not just like, suspension it. 'Cuz like last year, they only would suspend. They wouldn't talk to them and now they talk to them about the problem. It's better now.

If students, who do not read research, understand that suspensions cause problems rather than solve them, then why is it so hard to convince adults of the same?

For restorative discipline policies to work, all school staff must know about the new approach and the proper procedures for dealing with challenging student behavior. The school's leader is responsible for this task. Policies need to be clear and well-documented, and procedures and processes must be in place to support the new policy and motivate faculty members to embrace the change. Not only should all the adults in the school be trained in the new way, but they should also receive regular trainings, which improve fidelity of practice. Schools need to support these trainings by providing the necessary time and funding. *If teachers and other staff do not know what to do when discipline policies change, they will resort to doing what they used to do under the former policies.*

Grant principal Elena Baez reflected on this. Although RJE was in their school handbook, she said, "We are not really clear. Maybe it's not written down, maybe it's not posted. Maybe it's not really ingrained in our system here that that's the way we do things here. We are an RJ school." While the revised discipline code documented the policy in the handbook, other processes and procedures were not so clearly established. Grant was still finding its way through the changes, and people in the school needed clearer communication on the new discipline procedures. When any policy is written and implemented, the very next step is to develop procedures for administering the policy. Neither school in this study took the time to do this, and that created problems and tension.

Explaining changes to the discipline policies is critical,

because these changes motivate the staff, at least externally, to buy into SWRPs, even if they have not yet embraced RJE internally. Policy changes can propel teachers to think differently not only about school discipline but also about the relationships within the school.

Decreased conflict. Even though people in the schools were finding their way through the changes, circling forward and back and reflecting on what they needed, they were nonetheless making positive changes. Conflict and fighting in the schools was decreasing, perhaps as a result of the decision to stop suspending and expelling students. In their report *Restorative Justice in Oakland Schools: Implementation and Impact,* Dr. Sonia Jain and her colleagues provide preliminary evidence that schools using restorative approaches reduced suspensions.

Likewise, I wanted to know if staff members at Grant and Davis felt that RJE had helped to reduce conflict between different groups:

- Teachers and students
- Racial/ethnic groups
- Teachers
- Administrators and teachers
- School personnel and parents

Through a survey question and in focus groups, I asked staff, "Have conflicts between these groups decreased?" Of those who agreed or disagreed, most agreed that conflicts had decreased, but a significant number said they didn't know. In fact, people chose "Don't know" for this question more than for any other. This choice is interesting in and of itself. We also have to keep in mind that Grant was just a few weeks into getting back on RJE after six months of "suspension madness."

For those who did respond, about one-third reported that

conflicts between different groups had not decreased, while about two-thirds indicated that conflicts had gone down. Respondents perceived that the greatest decreases in conflict occurred between ethnic/racial groups, between teachers and students, and among teachers themselves. One teacher said, "Within adult Circles, both community building and working through conflicts, we grow our relationships with each other." It also appeared that people at the schools had more work to do when it came to reducing conflict between teachers and administrators and between teachers and parents.

On the other hand, all sixteen of the students in the focus groups said there were fewer conflicts and fights in their schools. As one student said, "There is even less conflicts this year. I think there've been two fights so far this year." Another stated:

> I've noticed that we have less conflicts and stuff than other schools. My friend goes to another school out of the district and they don't have RJ, and they have way more issues and way more problems and stuff, because there's nobody working it out with them. They just get suspended and come back mad and stuff like that.

Again, we see students naming suspensions as one of the causes of fighting. Another student thought that just the act of having to talk about conflict was a deterrent to fighting:

> It [RJ] is worse than having a suspension because you have to see the person that you harmed or has harmed you, and you're talking to them face-to-face. So I think it has changed this school because the kids don't want to be in that case where they have to know the feelings of other people and be face-to-face with them.

While critics believe that RJE is too "soft" and not punitive enough, students feel that having to actually face the people they have harmed is much harder than being suspended.

Another student admitted that, although students still tend to resort to violence and fighting as an initial response, different things happen to prevent or curtail the fights.

While SWRPs have not eliminated fighting altogether, it appears that the school-wide restorative practices have helped to decrease both the frequency and intensity of the fights that do happen in these two middle schools. One survey respondent offered an explanation for this:

> Restorative approaches have lowered the number of students having minor squabbles with teachers and peers. I believe that this is due to the incorporation of the philosophy of taking responsibility for one's actions, which is permeating our school since the incorporation of RJ. I think that it works prophylactically as well as reactively. Additionally, it gives the students and staff a language to speak regarding conflict other than "she did this or that."

Another survey respondent wrote:

> Before RJ, I often felt that the staff did not have enough training to help the students navigate their conflicts/feelings and that the staff was often overwhelmed by the large amount of age-appropriate middle school drama. I feel now that the teachers have more tools and a language to address these conflicts. I also feel that the Circles allow the students to know each other better and for the teachers to know them better, which promotes greater understanding and less conflict.

So even though conflicts still occur—they are a natural and valuable part of human relationships—conflicts between various groups decrease in schools that practice restorative justice. That much is clear from the OUSD's evaluation report, evidence from this study, and many other studies and evaluations on RJE. Forward movement is happening, just in non-linear, organic ways.

The lens of change theory helps us examine other changes—organizational ones—in these schools. It provides a road map for implementing school-wide reforms with fidelity and also allows us to identify problems that arise when RJE is not implemented with fidelity. We start with leadership.

Leadership

Leadership styles. A school leader may or may not be the one to initiate a whole-school reform effort, such as RJE. But for the initiative to succeed, schools need a leader who believes in the initiative and motivates staff to adopt the change.[1] This means that the principal must do more than allow the reform initiative to take place: he or she must support it.

The principals at Davis and Grant were polar opposites in terms of personality and leadership styles. Stan Paulson described himself this way: "I am like a heavy tough guy. I am really compassionate and I am a caring person but I don't wear it as much as my urgency. . . . I've always been a caring, socially-emotionally sophisticated person. But... I've not infused that in my leadership to the degree that this school has taught me is necessary."

Stan said, "I run a tight ship. I like good communication, and I am a stickler." He is also a staunch supporter of restorative justice and believes in its philosophy and processes. As principal, Stan is comfortable sharing power with staff, students, and parents in order to create a school community in which everybody thrives. But he was not always like this. Over his six years at the school, Stan said his leadership style has shifted:

> I think I really learned how to do shared leadership here
> because I didn't come in really strong at it. . . . I think you
> suspend your ego and you deeply believe in the collective.
> It's not about who's right, it's about all of us. Let's do the
> right thing together, no matter who gets to take credit for it.

He went on to explain that "I think we try to engender an adult community where adults have a voice to say, 'Hey, this is awesome, this sucks, this isn't working, this isn't fair." In the focus group, one teacher described Stan as a leader who "finds people who have strengths where he has weaknesses to be on his team. . . . He knows what he is not good at, and he will find somebody else who is good at that."

Stan came to Davis with strong leadership abilities, but he grew into his relational capacity by working in a school that prioritized relationships. He benefitted from working with a capable staff who could offer strengths where he was weak. Further, because he was a stickler for communication, he had the processes in place that enabled him to share power with staff. He and the teachers at Davis worked effectively as a team, even when they disagreed.

Very different in personality, Elena Baez is a quiet, thoughtful, and heart-led principal who believes in RJE and cares deeply about her students and staff. Here's how Elena described her leadership style:

> There are a lot of different challenges, but that's usually
> when I find myself having to talk through things with
> people. Kind of like reminding them that we don't have
> control over that, but we are still going to keep working
> through our system and our process. . . .
>
> I will name a gap in my leadership—accountability. Like
> holding staff accountable to "We said we are going to do this,
> now we need to make sure to do this." Even with restorative

practices . . . I want to have a shared responsibility with at least one other person, which would by my admin.

Capacity to inspire, motivate, and empower others. School leaders who seek to reform their schools must both demonstrate courage and command the respect of teacher-leaders, who will then be motivated to actually do the work of change. Elena wanted to share power with her staff, but teacher and administrator turnover, lack of communication, and ill-defined processes prevented this from happening. It is not enough for principals to hold the restorative vision, nor is it enough to define RJ as the disciplinary method of choice in the school's handbook.

Restructuring urban schools requires many things, but three factors stand out as necessary for making the change:

1. Effective, visionary leadership
2. Flexible schedules to allow for collaboration and professional development
3. A democratic form of governance, expressed in shared decision making and teacher leadership

Leaders who drive successful reforms empower and motivate others to respond to challenges constructively, build capacity, reflect on the change process, and persist despite problems. Without the support of others who can hold the vision and engage the restorative processes, initiatives can fail or struggle despite the leader's best intentions.[2] Staff at both schools respected their principals for upholding their commitment to SWRPs despite the challenges.

Changes in leadership and the impact on RJE initiatives. Stan and Elena were strong advocates of RJE. They helped facilitate the changes these schools made—or were in the process of making—by providing funding for RJ facilitators and making the structural and scheduling changes needed for whole-school reform. However, the reform initiative took a hit when the leadership changed, even temporarily, at Grant. Why were Grant's core team of teachers unable to uphold RJE and keep the restorative processes in place when a punitive interim principal came on board? The hierarchical structure at this school, like so many others, is the obvious reason. The interim assistant principal was too strong and too autocratic to allow other voices to be heard. She believed in suspensions and punishments—social control instead of social engagement.[3] While some teachers continued to hold Circles to address harms in their own classrooms, others let the RJ facilitator or the principal handle challenging student behaviors. These responses ushered in the era referred to as "suspension madness!" When Elena returned to work after her maternity leave, she found RJE at her school in a very different state from when she left it. It was hanging by a thread. Davis's staff had not been tested in this way.

Stan Paulson believed in RJE. The staff trusted him as a leader, and there were no interruptions to his leadership. As a result, staff members felt safe to invest their energy in the change. As Stan shared:

> In the organization, you need people who know how to do their job well—accountability, and support, and trust, and training. . . . The initiative or the strategy is important, and it's important for a school community to implement strategies [with] fidelity. But I think also important is the quality of staff, the quality of leadership, the alignment of the staff, the partnership with parents, [and] trust.

Ability to balance conflicting priorities. A principal's job is never easy, and pressure comes from all sides: district administrators, teachers, parents, students, and community leaders. It is extremely political.

In addition to balancing the skills, needs, and agendas of all the stakeholders in a school, the leader must also contend with directives and mandates from the school district. Sometimes, newer district initiatives force RJE into the background and negatively affect the fidelity of its implementation. Elena Baez expressed her frustration with trying to meet the needs of her school while contending with the demands of district higher-ups. She said:

> One person has to hold that preparation and facilitation with all the variables involved. How much fidelity can we do for the restorative justice program when there are these essential pieces that are not there? And there's just the reality of, like—we are a school that now has like an extra four weeks of testing!

Keeping RJE a school-wide priority. One of the teachers described how important it was that her school leader stood behind RJE:

> I definitely think that she [Elena] has been a very strong advocate and supporter for restorative justice, other-wise we would not have had Antonio [restorative justice facilitator at Grant]. I do know that there has been a fight to keep him and [to keep] believing in having an RJ facilitator. I think the crazy year was when we didn't have an AP [assistant principal] because we still needed the person to be receiving the kids, checking with them, the whole paperwork. The RJ facilitator is to do the prep work specifically for Circle; [when] that was taken away, we felt that. . . . Elena has always been a very strong believer in RJ. No doubt in my mind. How you could actually bring the

staff, though, to really understand it and love it and believe in it is another thing. . . . So . . . if you are really a believer and when you bring people on, new staff, it's like: "This is the program that we do, this is why we do it." I think that needs to be a little bit more felt and conveyed when new folks come onto our campus.

As one teacher said, "Since we've become an RJ school, I've seen a tremendous change in our whole philosophy around discipline." Another teacher explained how Elena motivated staff and students alike to push forward with SWRPs:

She doesn't come across like she is in charge and everyone answers to her. I mean, you debate as to whether that's effective or not, but when it comes to restorative [justice], I think that helps. Because it allows for more talking, and it doesn't automatically make the student or the teacher feel that they are necessarily wrong either way. There's going to be some talking about it, and there's going to be some ownership on both parties.

Core teams. Even though their leadership styles and personalities were very different, both Stan and Elena kept the priority on creating a restorative school. Their leadership empowered the teaching staff to do the work of change, confident that it would make a difference and bring change that endured. Both principals established trust levels that allowed teachers to share power, express themselves, and take ownership for the implementation of SWRPs in their schools. The core teams worked in partnership with the principals to provide consistency and momentum for the change effort. They also provided essential support to their principals as they dealt with resistance from other staff and parents.

At Davis and Grant, the leadership teams comprised the principal, assistant principals, teachers, instructional coaches, and other interested or relevant staff, such as RJ facilitators. In addition to dealing with curriculum issues, these teams took on the primary responsibility for implementing any change or new initiative at the schools, such as PBIS or RJE. One teacher explained:

> There's a set of teachers that presents the vision to any-body who comes in new and who reminds people of that vision and who scramble when that is in threat, scramble to sort of find a way to gather people.

These team members were powerful voices for change in their schools. A teacher explained, "When Elena came on [as principal], we took a full stand to say, 'Let's get a restorative justice facilitator and actually try to have this be something that we really believe in.'"

Skepticism: An opportunity to listen. Of course, not every-one believes in RJE or at least not to the same degree. Some teachers may be burned out after experiencing so many "next big things" over the course of their teaching career. They may not understand RJE at first or know how to practice it. This is especially true if the school community has not taken enough time in the "Exploration" phase of implementation. Accord-ing to many staff I spoke with, some teachers and parents did not feel that restorative practices were sufficient consequence or punishment, and some teachers felt ill-equipped to use restorative practices to deal effectively with challenging stu-dent behavior in their classrooms. These are honest concerns.

Teachers at both schools admitted that they were initially skeptical of RJE when their principals returned students to their classes after a fight, or worse, when the returning student continued behaving in disruptive ways. One teacher described how she reacted the first time students were not suspended for fighting—even though when I met her, she was a fierce advocate for RJE:

> He [Stan] got pushback from us as a staff. Those first few vicious fights, and there were no suspensions, and people were like, "What the hell is going on? That kid just beat the shit out of that other kid and he is back in class?" That was a big shift. Even for me.

This teacher's reaction is not surprising coming out of decades of zero tolerance thinking. RJE calls for a change in how we think. Elena Baez faced similar concerns and pushback from Grant's staff.

Newer teachers in particular seemed to struggle with this new method of holding students accountable for their actions without punishing them in the traditional sense. Two teachers emphasized that their teacher training programs, whether Teach for America or university colleges of education, did not prepare them for restorative practices.

I met with a core team member to talk more about why some members of her school community had difficulty buying into RJE at her school. An ardent RJ supporter and practitioner, she speculated about the causes of their skepticism:

> So there has been some noise about restorative justice. But I always have to ask myself, does this work for more students? There's always gonna be students and teachers who do not have positive relationships [with each other]. That is just the reality of things. So if you're a teacher who feels like your relationship with certain kids is antagonistic— that you and the kid are against each other in some way— then restorative justice has not felt good for those people

because it doesn't [*animatedly pounds the table*] make the
kid own [the consequences].

This same teacher continued explaining that Stan Paulson
had to deal "with serious pushback from some parents who
felt . . . like the kid didn't get enough punishment! Or this kid
poked my kid and then they just got talked to!"

Leaders and core team members also heard from teachers
who were not sure how much time they wanted to invest in
doing SWRPs. One teacher explained the dilemma of feeling
torn between spending time doing SWRPs and teaching content:

> Sometimes you have to have a talk day. Sometimes things
> come up that aren't in your curriculum, that aren't in the
> textbook. They are just a lived experience that you have to
> let kids talk about and let kids talk through. And I don't see
> a willingness on teachers' parts to do that. I think there is a
> strong desire to get through the curriculum. I see teaching
> as curriculum, but also, there is a human side. There is
> a love side. There is a connection to kids, helping them
> develop connections with each other's side. I don't know
> that everybody is willing to do that quite yet because they
> want to get through their curriculum.

Indeed, every teacher feels tremendous pressure to teach the
required standards, cover certain material, and prepare students for high-stakes tests by which they and their schools will
be judged—harshly and punitively. For thirty years, the zero
tolerance mentality has allowed teachers to make challenging
student behavior someone else's problem by excluding them
from class. So when a school adopts RJE and essentially says to
teachers, "In addition to teaching, you now also have to resolve
conflicts, hold Circles, and keep disruptive students in your
classroom," RJE can appear to be a less-than-teacher-friendly

initiative, especially if teachers are not adequately trained. Stan explained that his staff would say things like, "I don't know what I am doing, I am not a therapist, I can't run a community building Circle, this is awkward, I am a math teacher."

Such comments illustrate the real and honest concerns that arose in both schools, and for good reason. Neither of these schools had yet built the capacity of all teachers to feel comfortable using restorative practices in their classrooms, nor had all teachers been adequately trained and mentored in SWRPs. Likewise, as implementation science suggests, neither school took the time to fully explore how they wanted RJE to function in their schools: what would RJE look like and how would it respond to situations differently? They had no procedures to guide them, and this left staff feeling unsure and doubtful.

Creating a restorative school begins with the adults, who must first become comfortable with practicing a new way of being together and working out differences among themselves in good ways. This is why it is so important that the adults in schools take one to two years to lay the groundwork together, establish the guidelines, define roles, embrace restorative values, and spend time in Circle with each other. To proceed with school-wide implementation before all the adults are comfortable committing to tier 1 restorative practices is to jeopardize the entire initiative.

Implementation Challenges and Their Impact on Program Fidelity

Along with examining the changes these schools experienced when they adopted SWRPs, I also explored the challenges in implementing RJE with fidelity without adequate support, time, and training. Building capacity in these two middle schools was difficult due to budgetary and time constraints, limited resources, turnover, and insufficient training.

Capacity building: money and personnel. Teachers at Davis and Grant believed they knew what they needed in order to advance to the next level of implementing restorative practices or to improve program fidelity. However, these schools differed widely in terms of their access to the financial resources necessary to meet these needs—that is, to maintain and expand SWRPs. Davis was a well-resourced school with a large number of middle-class students whose parents, via the PTSA, raised money for the school; Grant was an under-resourced, under-staffed, high-poverty school with little to no outside financial support.

Caridad, the family engagement coordinator at Grant, expressed concern that the resources needed to support RJE were not always readily available:

> Our capacity to run RJ with fidelity holds us back; whether that capacity is affected by money or staffing, I don't believe it's affected by philosophy. I think leadership buys into it and leadership wants it. But the people who work at a school aren't necessarily the people who run the school or make the plan for the school.

High and competing demands, limited staff and time, and real needs unmet. Elena Baez expressed empathy for her staff who had to juggle supporting high-needs students, implementing restorative practices, and dealing with heightened demands from the district to increase testing and raise academic achievement. She simply said, "Where are the limits? The capacity of the staff to contend with all that?"

The RJ facilitators at both schools had multiple responsibilities. Responding to challenging students was not their only concern; they were also responsible for training and supporting staff. At a faculty Circle at Davis, Cameron asked teachers what they needed in order to increase their RJ skills in their classrooms. The following list summarizes what teachers said:

- Because restorative discipline is a different process from everyday relationship building, teachers need help connecting the dots between social and emotional learning (SEL), academic work, and restorative discipline.
- Teachers need a designated time to repair harm in class and a protocol for engaging this process.
- When do repairing-harm Circles happen? "A process is lacking. It's a total mystery."
- Teachers want a regular, protected hour for Circle to develop skills, so that they have consistent practice as a Circle keeper.
- "As a proactive measure, it's awesome. As a reactive measure, we don't get it."

As these responses reveal, teachers reported having much to learn about RJE and they wanted to get better at their practice, but they did not feel they had enough information, training, or mentored experience—or time.

Indeed, even teachers who had the tools, comfort level, and desire to incorporate restorative practices into instruction still struggled with finding the time for Circles. A teacher summarized the issue:

> I think the struggle is structure, and it's always going to be structure. We have competing interests from what the district forces the principal to do and what we would like to spend our time doing. . . . Like, people have to have time to be in Circle, and that means training for staff, and that

means opportunity to be in Circle with each other, and that means more than just community building Circles with each other.

Confidence levels. Teachers' limited experience and knowledge impeded capacity building at these schools, which took a toll on confidence levels. "We would love [to say] that we felt like we've got this down, but we don't feel like we have this down," said Elena. A teacher concurred, saying, "I think it's just an experience thing. Because it can get uncomfortable." Core team teachers believed that new teachers struggled the most with integrating restorative practices into their work. One teacher said, "I would say that new teachers are not really incorporating it at all."

Very few teacher credentialing programs in the United States prepare teachers for how to deal with discipline restoratively or how to build community in their classrooms. Regarding her experience with "new teacher orientation, but especially with RJ," one teacher said, "I think I just kind of learned as I went along what RJ was. But being as it's so important at this school, there should be a training."

On a survey, I asked teachers what kind of training and support they had received and how confident they felt using different restorative approaches. They rated their confidence levels along a spectrum from most to some to least confident. Not surprisingly, the more sophisticated the restorative process, the less confident teachers were in using it—a pattern that indicates where more training is needed.

Staff had the most or some confidence in using RPs to build community (over 90 percent). They felt positively confident about asking restorative questions (80 percent claimed most or some confidence) as well as in using RPs to de-escalate conflict (over 80 percent claimed most or some confidence). A majority said they had most or some confidence in using

Circles for instruction (65 percent) and in using Circles after a harm (58 percent). They were least confident about facilitating conferences (over 60 percent said they were least confident here).

These are very promising responses. Nonetheless, having some confidence in using RPs is different from feeling solidly confident. For example, under 30 percent said they felt high confidence in using Circles for instruction and just over 20 percent reported high confidence in using Circles after a harm. Training would definitely boost staff's confidence in these cases. However, the schools faced limited resources for personnel and training, competing demands, and limited experience with or knowledge of restorative practices, all of which inhibited their ability to build capacity for RJE.

Teacher and staff turnover. One systemic challenge in building RJE capacity is the high rate of teacher and staff turnover. At a meeting for parents of prospective students at Davis, principal Stan Paulson spoke bluntly about teacher turnover:

> It's brutal! We have the best teaching staff in Oakland. I love our school and I love our teachers. We have an excellent staff. The negative of this is we have a high turnover rate of teachers. I take personal responsibility for that, even though OUSD pays its teachers 15 percent less than neighboring districts. I try to create a positive work environment. I'm trying to keep teachers here, but it's demoralizing. Right now, I've lost three teachers for next year that are not coming back in September. So we have a lot of turnover here, but I'm really proud of what we accomplish in spite of teacher turnover.

To determine how much turnover Davis had, particularly since the school adopted SWRPs, I asked survey participants,

"Were you already working at this school when the decision was made to adopt restorative approaches here?" Only 58 percent of teachers and staff who responded were at the school when it adopted SWRPs; the rest (42 percent) came on board after SWRPs had been instituted, which means they missed many of the initial trainings.

The high rates of turnover, and thus need for additional training in SWRPs, placed great stress on the schools' abilities to implement RJE with integrity and to sustain it consistently and with fidelity.

During our interview, Elena described how losing administrative and support staff affected the restorative justice initiative at Grant:

> *Elena:* I think at the beginning of the year [2014], we were doing pretty good with our restorative practice, at least repairing the harm, those pieces. But I went out pregnant and on maternity leave and I wasn't really up here while I was pregnant. I think we lost some of that traction. And then the other part of it was, I didn't have an assistant principal last year. And our clinical case manager left in December and our admin assistant was put on leave in January.
>
> *Martha:* That's a lot of personnel change.
>
> *Elena:* Yeah! Or no personnel!

Both Elena and Antonio told me that the clinical case manager and the administrative assistant were both strong advocates of restorative justice and provided support to the students, the staff, and the RJ facilitator. Losing all of these key personnel in one year caused significant damage to the fidelity of restorative justice at Grant, leaving Antonio little time for preventive, community building measures, training new teachers, or conducting harm Circles. Instead of increasing staff capacity to build community and repair harm, Antonio was constantly reacting to behavioral incidents and dealing with students one-on-one. What this means in RJE terms is that the tier 1 and tier 2 practices that might have given his tier 3 interventions their power—strong relationships and the bonds of community—were not in place or functioning.

Leadership turnover. During the 2013–2014 school year, Elena was out on a six-month maternity leave. As I explained earlier, the interim assistant principal replaced restorative discipline with traditional punitive discipline. Grant's suspension rate increased 20 percent, and the bulk of these suspensions were for "defiance." Indeed, this school suffered tremendous setbacks when the interim principal did not hold the RJ vision.

Initial and ongoing training. Clearly, training is essential. Although the OUSD district RJ facilitator and school-level restorative justice facilitators are responsible for training teachers and support staff, teachers and staff did not always receive the initial and ongoing training they wanted and needed. When I asked Stan Paulson if he thought his staff were getting enough ongoing training and support, he said, "I would say no. I would say we should do more. It's a pretty new initiative, so I think trying to figure out how to train people to do it is still something that's maybe being figured out."

Determining how to meet the needs for staff training was a challenge for the RJ facilitators at both schools. When I asked staff on the survey if there was enough follow-up to ensure the program was working, only 42 percent reported there was. Staff agreed that new teachers in particular were unsure about how to use SWRPs in their classroom. Indeed, only a small number of all teachers really understood how to do this. Survey respondents were divided on whether the school made a conscious effort to help new teachers learn restorative approaches. One first-year teacher stated that he was unclear about what should be happening in his classroom. He wondered, for example, if he was asking students the right restorative questions. New teachers reported experiencing a "high learning curve" and said they were frustrated that they did not receive any training that year.

Veteran teachers more familiar with SWRPs faced a different problem: they wanted more advanced training to improve their skill level. One teacher who was trained in SWRPs said:

> I see the awesome potential in the RJ system, but I feel like I have been on level 0.5 for a year and a half, and the teachers are the ones with the most face-to-face time with the kids, so we are the ones that need these skills the most.

Because training of both new and veteran teachers at these schools was inadequate, teachers frequently had to learn SWRPs as they went along. In change theory, this is known as "learning in context."

Learning in context. Principals, RJ facilitators, and RJE experienced teachers often encouraged others to learn more about SWRPs by participating in Circles, observing more experienced teachers, being mentored by them, and then trying it out for themselves. Elena Baez said, regarding the professional development calendar, "You always make [sacrifices]. . . . If you are doing training on holding Circles, that means you are not engaging in PLCs [professional learning communities] on the assessment." School leaders must constantly make decisions about how to best use limited time to address multiple initiatives, including district- and state-mandated assessments. Core teams of teachers more experienced with using SWRPs understood the dilemma and attempted to fill the training gap themselves. Elena said she expected new and inexperienced teachers to let someone know if they needed help. If that did not happen, then administrators should be more proactive about identifying individuals in need of additional training.

Elena envisioned a more personalized approach to training. Stan Paulson also questioned what teachers really needed— more training or more personal guidance on how to conduct SWRPs. Several new teachers told me they had no training in SWRPs. That said, of the twenty teachers I observed, 95 percent of them used some form of positive discipline or relational-based pedagogy, including academic discourse and PBIS, even if they did not know how to ask restorative questions or effectively use Circles in their classrooms. All relational-based, student-centered instructional practices promote listening, community, cooperation, respect, and positive behavior. However, I observed one first-year teacher who, it seemed, had not been trained in SWRPs or any other relational-based practice. She relied wholly upon traditional punitive and authoritarian classroom management methods. I wrote down my observations while sitting in her class for forty-five minutes. My observations provide an opportunity to sharply contrast traditional authoritarian, high-control, teacher-centered teaching with a more relational-based, student-centered culture. Here is what I wrote:

> This observation is of a seventh-grade, female, first-year teacher. This teacher did not display any evidence of being trained in PBIS or RJE. She spoke harshly and gave commands: "Move! Be quiet! Move to the back!" She never said please or thank you, nor did she recognize students who were following instructions. I witnessed the kids constantly pushing back against their disrespectful and frustrated teacher. She focused only on her lesson, not on her students. . . . The students were not engaged in the lesson at all. As the class went on, they just got more playful,

more disruptive, and more off task. Two boys near where I was seated talked constantly to each other in their native language, not on task at all. The teacher was in a state of constantly reacting to different student behaviors, and she did this by issuing direct commands or by moving students to other seats. On the board, she listed names of students who had received lunch detentions, which is a form of public punishment. One boy removed himself from the group and came and sat in the back near me.

A girl and boy were disrupting the class with loud banter. The teacher got very angry and took the girl outside in the hallway. I could hear their voices, and the conversation sounded argumentative. The teacher sent the girl to the OCR room; then she called security for the boy because he took the girl's backpack and ran off. The girl came back and tattled, and the teacher wrote a referral. It was total chaos.

Clearly, this teacher needed training and coaching in how to build relationships with her students and how to respond restoratively when they acted out. Every single one of her actions escalated the problems.

In cases like this, it is important not to judge teachers harshly or blame them for doing what they may have been taught to do. This teacher did not receive the training and support she needed, and it is not fair to expect that all new teachers can learn about RJE just by being in a school that practices it. Schools adopting SWRPs simply cannot rely solely upon teachers' ability to learn in context from a few core team members who are comfortable using SWRPs.

The majority of study participants in these restorative schools wanted to improve their skills, acknowledging the need for more procedures, training, and processes to help them integrate SWRPs into their teaching practices and to learn how to repair harm. They recognized not only where they lacked confidence but also where their abilities to build capacity and to learn in context were limited, given the time and resources available.

Reflective action and persistence. Leaders and staff in both schools wanted to implement RJE with fidelity and often talked about what they needed and how they could improve. Reflecting upon successes and challenges is essential to the change process and lies at the very heart of implementation science. Here, the staff openly reflected upon their experiences and sought ways to improve. Elena told me, "We are not where we need to be because [RJ] is not [yet] a system; it's just how individuals are doing things. Maybe it's not clear enough that this is how we function [as a school]." This circling back to reflect helps everyone persist by allowing time and space for people to regroup, rethink, and renew.

I was pleasantly surprised when four teachers approached me to thank me for conducting the study because my questions gave them pause to think about things. They considered the time they spent with me in Circle or answering questions on my survey as time well spent.

The staff's ability to persist was evident at both schools. I learned that RJE had gone through several iterations and that the first attempt to implement SWRPs did not get the schools where they wanted to be. However, teachers and administrators did not give up; instead, they continually worked together to find solutions to the problems and improve their practices. Teachers who believed in RJE stood by their principals' commitment to the initiative. A deep commitment to students motivated teachers to stay the course even with all the structural and budgetary challenges. The teachers I spoke with said it was a successful method for supporting students and keeping them in school. However, despite administrators and staff being persistent, reflective, and willing to learn in context, several key factors ruptured program fidelity: the lack of initial and ongoing training; teacher and administrator turnover; and the absence of clear policies and procedures, specifically about holding Circles during advisory period.

Advisory period. In the daily schedule, if teachers were not conducting their classes in Circle, they could still spend time practicing RJE during advisory period, when they could conduct community building Circles and facilitate discussions with students. Both middle school principals asked their staff to hold Circles during advisory period, because, in addition to building relationships and trust with their students, the process allowed them to practice and develop their skills in conducting Circles, learning in context, and familiarizing students with the Circle process. One of the hopes was that teachers would then transfer these skills and practices into their academic instruction. Unfortunately, this was not happening when I was there.

Both schools had an advisory period that included approximately twenty students in each class; however, the structure of advisory period was different at each school. At Davis, students were graded on goal setting and Circle participation in their Wednesday morning advisory class called PACT (see chapter 4). In the previous school year, this hour-long class was a dedicated time for community building Circles with teachers and students. During 2014–2015, PACT became a time for teachers to distribute and collect weekly progress reports, assist students with homework, *and* conduct Circles. Neither teachers nor students were happy with splitting the PACT class between homework and Circles. They didn't think it allowed enough time for a Circle or for teachers to really get to know their students. Additionally, some teachers allowed the Circles in their advisory classes to devolve into processes that the students perceived as less effective, such as simple community-building activities or even study halls.

Grant held advisory every morning during the first period, but the Wednesday advisory period was dedicated to community building Circles. Unlike at Davis, this advisory class was not graded. Elena Baez confessed that "We have had troubles with advisory in general. Just what is the curriculum? The accountability of staff—they feel like it's a different prep. The kids also feel like it's not a graded classroom." Most classrooms I observed one Wednesday were set up for Circle, and all four of the sixth-grade classrooms held Circles. But again, due to turnover, lack of training, and competition for professional development time, not every teacher really understood how to hold Circles or was comfortable with the process. Elena explained:

> [RJ is] not in a place where we said, school-wide every-
> body opens every morning with a Circle. I think that's
> what we say, but I can't say that's really in practice. And I
> think the challenge is when you are not used to that, or it
> doesn't come natural to you, it's a challenge to change that
> dynamic. But again our expectation is that we begin the
> morning in a Circle with advisory this year.

The inconsistent use of Circles during advisory periods threatened program fidelity. New teachers were struggling with using Circles in advisory because most did not receive any formal training and were not confident enough to use them. Given that advisory class was the best opportunity for teachers and students to build community through Circle, the RJE momentum was blunted when some teachers chose not to hold them or substituted non-restorative processes for Circle discussions. While Circle during advisory period was required in both schools, follow-through was needed. If teachers were not holding Circles, why? Staff needed at least a Circle and better yet a training to deepen their understanding, so that they understood why holding Circles during advisory period was so important and valuable.

When it stops being RJ. Some disciplinary processes and actions considered to be restorative actually fell outside the realm of restorative discipline. Even used with the best of intentions, these practices undermined the culture change and pulled the climate—the ecology of relationships—back toward the coercive, punitive approach.

As more people hear about restorative justice, there is a real danger of using the term as an umbrella to represent all things good, all things rehabilitative, or all things new. In authentic restorative practices, restorative values lie at the heart of every process. Every effort is made for all voices to be heard. Processes for repairing harm include the person(s) harmed and reparations to hold accountable the person(s) who did the harm. Above all, the emphasis is on building, maintaining, and repairing relationships.

These are essential components of RJE that differentiate it from other positive disciplinary processes. It is very easy in a restorative school for every conversation to be construed as restorative, even when it is not. During my month in the two schools, I discovered several threats to program fidelity. While I was analyzing my data, I created a code called *Not RJ* to describe processes that were intended to be restorative but that had been modified to the point where they no longer met the criteria of being so. Some of the basic tenets of restorative justice processes (see chapter 3) mark the difference between RJ and *Not RJ*.

For example, most important to repairing harm, a restorative process should include all stakeholders. Without this, relationships cannot be built or repaired. However, in the schools I observed, the person(s) harmed was frequently omitted from the restorative process, especially when the person was a teacher. In fact, one school used the phrase "restore the referral," instead of "restore the relationship" (a referral is a "write-up" of an offense that then requires acting upon). In RJE, there is no such thing as "restoring a referral." Does the student repair the harm done in the classroom with the teacher and classmates? Or does the student serve time in OCR or detention—forms of punishment based on exclusion?

From what I gathered from listening to teachers, students were not held accountable for repairing harm when they behaved in ways that led to a teacher-initiated referral. One teacher explained, "So do they come back and actually correct the harm or restore the harm in the classroom? Not often." If RJE were implemented with fidelity, each time a student committed a harm, a Circle, victim-offender mediation (VOM), or a family group conference (FCG) would be scheduled (depending on the harm). Those who were harmed would be able to say what they needed for the harm to be repaired. People in the Circle or conference would support the person who committed the harm while naming the behavior as unacceptable and holding him or her accountable for making things right. Instead, different kinds of quasi-restorative/semi-punitive processes took place.

For example, a teacher at Grant described a process that allowed students to reflect on their behavior and repair harm but did not specify how the process ultimately involved the person(s) harmed:

> I think teachers have been very willing and appreciative
> of being introduced to the [restorative] structures, so it
> changed from years of having a dean of discipline who we
> sent kids to, to teachers setting up chill corners or those
> places where they [the students] actually fill out a reflection
> that gets them to think about whatever's going on. And then
> come up with solutions to repair whatever is happening.

At Grant, at least when I was there, the standard operating procedure was that students who were sent to the office completed a Restorative Justice Reflection Form before speaking with the principal or RJ facilitator. While Ron and Roxanne Claassen, authors of *Discipline That Restores,* promote this as one step in the restorative process, it is not the only step nor the last step. However, in most of the cases I observed, the student was sent back to class after filling out the form and having a conversation about what happened. The RJ facilitator was then responsible for following up with that student to see if he or she was upholding any verbal or written behavioral contracts. RJE at Grant was very one-on-one; adults talked with students but did not regularly engage them in Circles or other restorative processes that would allow other voices to be heard. As we know, this was primarily because staff were spread too thin due to turnover and vacancies.

Due to the sheer numbers of high-needs students, the stress in the school was palpable. The number of staff vacancies at Grant contributed to the stress and negatively affected the capacity of staff to deal with behavior problems restoratively. Under these circumstances it is very difficult to conduct restorative processes for each incident. It is, however, critical that everyone is clear that the response is not in fact a restorative process but is hopefully a step toward getting to restorative responses as a routine. I asked Elena Baez about what happens in the main office. She said she preferred that students who were struggling with their behavior be sent to the RJ room rather than the office.

It is quite possible that the reason so many students were sent to the office was still due to the breakdown of restorative processes that occurred when Elena was on leave. Antonio could not just sit in the RJ room waiting for students to come to him, because he was busy responding to calls from teachers. RJE in Grant was hanging by a thread when I arrived there, or was, as Elena described, "hit and miss." Caridad referred to the sixth-grade teachers who were committed to restorative processes and values as the "Dream Team." However, the number of students school-wide who were sent out of class showed clearly that the breakdown of RJE began in the classrooms.

The teachers at Davis also expressed frustration with the process at their school, saying that "teachers are not part of restoring a referral" and "students don't know what restoring is. . . . They don't understand that the restoration needs to equal the act." Not only did teachers want to learn more about RJE, but they also felt that "some kids clearly don't care" or that "the pre-requisite for RJ should be that students understand the consequences." This problem was exacerbated by the common use of the phrase "restoring the referral." The role of relationships—the bonds of community, mutual understanding, and empathy—in repairing harm got lost. This suggests that teachers were still thinking about punishment instead of restorative opportunities, in which the teachers and the class could voice what they needed, and students could repair the relationships that had been broken by their behavior.

Teachers and administrators said that if they wanted to know how restoration was occurring, they had to "chase the students down." In reality, they wanted students to understand that being accountable meant taking on responsibility for approaching the teacher to restore the harm. Yet there were no clearly established processes describing how this should be done. Again, organizational change requires not only a change in policy, but also clear procedures that support the policy's implementation. Certainly, not every harm in a classroom calls for a Circle or conference, but harms do call for a conversation where everyone has a say in how things will be made right, and that conversation should include the teacher.

■ Summary of Changes in the Schools' Structures

The school leaders' decisions to modify their discipline policies and adopt RJE drove structural changes that created space for RJ rooms and RJ facilitators. They also brought ecological changes: conflicts were perceived as decreasing among various groups in the schools. Even when processes were interrupted by leadership changes or teacher turnover, school leaders and committed core teams kept the process of change alive in these restorative schools—albeit on life support during principal Elena Baez's leave. They worked together to build capacity and to learn as they went along, with or without adequate resources and training. They reflected on their progress and challenges and verbalized what they needed to persist.

However, the schools also faced challenges that had yet to be addressed. For example, the lack of clear processes for repairing harm threatened program fidelity. Their time management lacked sufficient space and flexibility to hold not only the tier 3 "intervention" processes but also the tiers 1 and 2 processes that would make tier 3 processes effective and less needed. In other words, the foundation in relationships and community was not being laid on a daily basis. Finally, high teacher turnover, leadership changes, and lack of training affected these schools' ability to implement RJE with fidelity.

CHAPTER 8

Changes in the People

Grant and Davis underwent many organizational changes after they adopted school-wide restorative practices (SWRPs), and, like all schools implementing restorative justice in education (RJE), they are still changing as they continue to improve the fidelity of the initiative. We know that restorative justice (RJ) has the power to change people too, not just organizations, so I wanted to see if and how SWRPs changed the principals, teachers and staff, and students at these two middle schools. Research on restorative justice shows that RJ has the potential to change attitudes, leading to more positive behaviors and improved relationships. Given RJ's proven effectiveness in this area, we need to better understand why restorative practices may not always produce these desired changes in individuals. I began by asking Elena Baez and Stan Paulson, the two principals, if they had experienced personal changes.

Personal Changes in the Principals

Elena, Grant's principal, already had a relational-based, positive orientation when she came into her position. She was in many ways predisposed to restorative values and philosophy, so understanding and advocating for SWRPs was an easy task for her to take on. It did not require her to make any major shifts in her thinking or leadership approach.

Stan, on the other hand, admitted that he did not have a relational-based, positive orientation when he first arrived as principal of Davis. He attributed two events to his personal growth and change: becoming a principal in a relational-based school and becoming a father. He told me:

> I did turnaround work before I got here, so I worked in two really upside-down, screwed-up schools. I came in here "Mr. Turnaround Heavy, I've got all the right answers." The school definitely let me know that this is not the right leadership style in this school. I didn't differentiate my leadership; I just used the one leadership strategy I had used in the two previous screwed-up schools, and I didn't make sure that it fit this context. . . . The school also changed me in terms of helping me understand the power of positive reinforcement.

Because Davis had strong teachers who did not hesitate to use their voice, it did not take long for Stan to understand that he needed to change to be a successful principal there. Teachers appeared to enjoy reflecting on how Stan had changed over the years and how becoming a father contributed to his transformation. One teacher commented:

> I've known Stan since he started being a principal. I was teaching for him on his very first day of his very first year. That has been a fascinating transformation, now that I think about it in the long context. Since I've been at Davis, I feel with restorative justice, I did feel like it was sort of a data-driven initiative at the beginning. It was like, "Our numbers are bad, we have these ultra-terrible suspension rates, let's look at the data, let's look at the data, let's do something, let's do RJ!" But I do feel like that transition from him has been a very genuine transition from "let's change these numbers" to like, "wow, let's keep doing this thing that is working" and that people have bought into.

Elena embodied a restorative ethos as a person. Stan transformed from being "Mr. Turnaround Heavy" to really embracing restorative justice and positive reinforcement on a personal level. What mattered to staff at both schools was that their principals were committed to the *values* and *philosophy* behind RJE as well as to the goal of reducing suspensions and the disproportionate disciplining of African American male students.

Personal Changes in the Teachers

In the survey, I asked teachers and staff, "Has your experience with restorative approaches changed you in any way? In other words, do you think differently about your schools, your colleagues, your students? Do you behave differently?" Like Elena Baez, six of the teachers who responded described themselves as already having a relational-based, positive orientation before they started teaching at the schools. This group did not feel that they changed much. Other teachers reported that they did change as a result of working in a restorative school. To make sense of the responses, I again grouped comments that had similar themes and ranked them according to the number of times the theme was mentioned, as Chart 8.1 displays.

Of the forty-two teachers and support staff who responded to my general questions, 86 percent said SWRPs had facilitated positive personal change in them in one way or another. Here are some of their comments:

- "I think that I do have better tools for dealing with conflicts that come up between kids, and I think the kids are more apt to talk because they are used to this format [Circles]."
- "I think I am a better listener and pay more attention to what may be hiding beneath the surface."

Chart 8.1. Staff comments: Has using restorative practices changed you? If so, how?

	AGREE	DISAGREE
Conflicts between teachers have decreased.	73%	27%
Conflicts between teachers and students have decreased.	71%	29%
Conflicts between racial/ethnic groups have decreased.	69%	31%
Conflicts between school personnel and parents have decreased.	60%	40%
Conflicts between administrators and teachers have decreased.	59%	41%

Source: (Staff surveys.)

- "I think about the school, colleagues, and students more as people with social and emotional influences rather than one big system."
- "My practice as a teacher has opened up to include much more student voice."
- "I have a better understanding of middle school-age youth, what they are experiencing, and how adults have a different role to develop youth competencies."
- "I think I am more thoughtful about what I say and allow my students to say. I think that being mindful of words helps the learning community."
- "I try to have more patience and I try to understand both sides of the situation."
- "I put problem solving on the students rather than act as an authoritarian."

The remaining 14 percent reported no change because they believed their behavior and instructional practices were already aligned with restorative values and practices.

Clearly, RJE was helping principals and staff become more compassionate, caring people, and they were aware of how they changed through using RJ principles in the classroom. The changes that the adults in the schools experienced had an effect on the students. This is critical. So often, policy makers want to use restorative practices to change only student behavior. Again, they miss the point that RJE trainers and researchers like Belinda Hopkins, Rita Renjitham Alfred, Kathy Evans, Dorothy Vaandering, and Nancy Riestenberg stress: adult change must come *before* student change. Albert Bandura's work on social learning theory teaches us that young people learn from watching and listening to each other *and* to the adults in their lives. So the way teachers talk with each other and their students sets an example for how students will talk to others. Whole-school reform means exactly that. According to one teacher, "Students change as a result of having a school community that listens to them. They change because we change."

▓ Personal Changes in the Students

The third group of school community members I was curious about was, of course, the students themselves. I posed four statements and asked staff whether they agreed or disagreed with them.

Chart 8.2 (page 186) shows their responses.

Most staff felt that SWRPs had undoubtedly changed students for the better. Over 80 percent said that students solved problems without violence and worked more cooperatively in groups. When it came to showing respect toward adults and each other, more than 60 percent of staff saw improvement

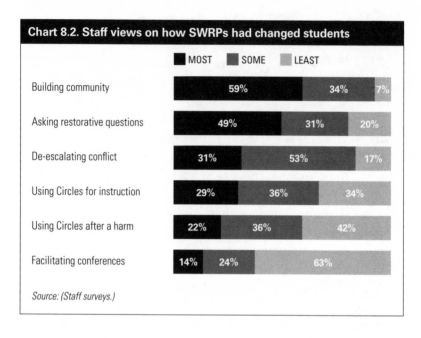

Chart 8.2. Staff views on how SWRPs had changed students

	MOST	SOME	LEAST
Building community	59%	34%	7%
Asking restorative questions	49%	31%	20%
De-escalating conflict	31%	53%	17%
Using Circles for instruction	29%	36%	34%
Using Circles after a harm	22%	36%	42%
Facilitating conferences	14%	24%	63%

Source: (Staff surveys.)

here as well, though some staff felt students still had room to improve. Their responses supported my own observations: while most students were respectful, polite, and well-mannered, some students acted disrespectfully toward their teachers and peers. Still, of the roughly thirty staff who responded, 67 percent said students were behaving more respectfully in school—not bad!

I also asked staff if they thought students changed as a result of participating in restorative approaches. Once again, I grouped their comments into themes and ranked them according to how often a theme was mentioned. Chart 8.3 shows the results.

Of the fifty-two responses, 73 percent agreed that students had changed for the better as a result of restorative approaches. They said:

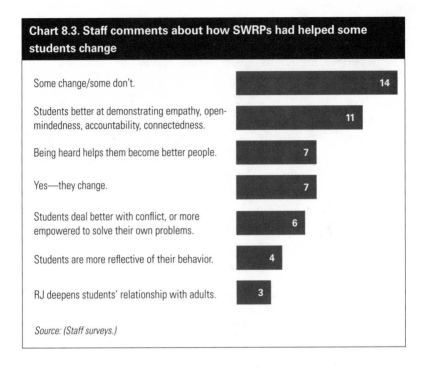

Chart 8.3. Staff comments about how SWRPs had helped some students change

Comment	Value
Some change/some don't.	14
Students better at demonstrating empathy, open-mindedness, accountability, connectedness.	11
Being heard helps them become better people.	7
Yes—they change.	7
Students deal better with conflict, or more empowered to solve their own problems.	6
Students are more reflective of their behavior.	4
RJ deepens students' relationship with adults.	3

Source: (Staff surveys.)

- "Restorative approaches make students honest, accountable, community-minded, thoughtful, and resilient."
- "They also come to expect and appreciate the community Circles, because they have a place where they can be heard."
- "It empowers them to take on the issues and handle them with the help of students."
- "It forces them to be reflective about their behavior."
- "Using a restorative approach to address discipline issues has resulted in greater personal accountability on the part of those involved and a deepening of relationships between students and adults."

However, 27 percent believed that some students did not change at all or were using restorative justice to get away with bad behavior. Elena referred to this population of "frequent flyers" as "students who we don't really know how to support," or, as one teacher described, "a small cluster, and we usually know their names very well." As I walked through the schools, I, too, saw the same faces day after day in the hallways, main office, or OCR. Youth who were in high need of support received one-on-one interventions repeatedly, over and over and over again, day after day. This is the 5 percent of a school population that requires tier 3 interventions. One of the teachers reflected on this:

> Yeah, the conversations that I have with teachers, we do spend a lot of time talking about the same students causing the same problems. You know, the same students [are] being sent back. When I had this talk with my [advisory] class today, eighth graders, they know what restorative justice is, and they know that it's about fixing the problem, solving the problem. But what they notice in class is that it's the same kids—the same four or five kids being sent out on a consistent basis. So the results of restorative justice are not really seen in the classrooms as much as we would like.

Another person echoed these comments, writing, "I think it is a very slow process, and we have yet to see a lot of change in the student body as a whole." In such a situation, the RJE response is to up the use of tier 1 (whole-school) as well as tier 2 (issue focused) restorative practices.

Students themselves had other insights. Davis's RJ peer mediators reported that being in that role made them more confident, better leaders, better students, and more empathetic. Plus, it gave them hope. Students at Grant who were not peer mediators said that SWRPs helped them make better decisions, take their education more seriously, and behave better in school. The sixteen students I spoke with reported that RJE did help them change for the better. These same students were also aware that some of their peers did not respond to the interventions, as practiced, in ways that produced positive behavioral changes. On the tier 3 level, students received numerous supports and intensive interventions, and the hope was to see some change. So, even though students in my focus groups said SWRPs had helped them change, they didn't see the same level of change in some of their peers. Everyone was aware of the "frequent flyers," and students talked about them with a certain level of disdain.

One girl said, "I haven't really seen any kids change from it, though. I haven't really seen it." Others reflected on students they knew and on the circumstances they thought might cause students not to change their behavior.

Staff and students agreed that some students changed and some did not. They acknowledged that RJE cannot meet all the needs or address all the issues that students bring with them to school.

Given these comments, let's step back and get our RJE bearings. For RJE practitioners, the term "frequent flyers" and expressions of disdain for other students raise red flags. They call for Circle space and time for people to listen, talk, and find out what is going on in each other's lives, so they can break through stereotypes, biases, and disdainful attitudes about other community members. If one group holds negative feelings about another, the targeted group is going to sense it, and the relational ecology of the school as a whole will be weaker. If some students feel alienated and targeted, especially along racial lines, they may have a hard time behaving as the school expects them to. This feedback speaks more about the need for intensifying restorative practices for all students than about "problem" students or their lack of change.

That said, we also need to listen to these perceptions, because they will come up as schools go through the transition process. Not all students respond to restorative practices at the same rate. Students with stronger and more positive relationships with the school, such as peer mediators, will likely respond positively to restorative practices faster than students who have more tenuous relations with the school community. These students need the fullest experience of restorative practices with the greatest fidelity. The varying degrees of student change that teachers and students reported makes sense when you think about it through the RJE lens. But it calls for a different response: rather than taking the perceptions at face value, which easily lead to negative judgments of students and their families, we, the adults in the school, can interpret these perceptions as calls to go deeper into our own understanding and practice of RJE.

How Much Can RJE Do?

Of course, many factors shape students' capacities to change, ranging from brain development, nutrition, family, and history. RJE is not the only player in student change, and respondents were well aware of these factors. They raised issues of development and social environments in particular to explain why some students did not change as readily. They also talked about what RJE can do for students to promote positive change, given the challenges these factors pose.

Age/Development. "Every child is not going to have the same development or the same delivery of a system or process," said one teacher. Teachers, administrators, and even students were very aware of the developmental stages that middle school students go through as they move from grades six through eight. One student commented that RJ helped him grow up and prepare for the outside world.

Teachers and administrators tried to create a relational ecology that allowed students to be who they were, and they felt that RJ helped them in this effort. As one teacher stated:

> I like the idea of dealing with pre-teen and "teen brain" behavior in a way that doesn't set students on the path of having a record. Most grow up, settle down, and get focused. Most of what happens is normal pubescent testing of boundaries.

Other teachers believed that certain aspects of RJ were not a good fit for the developmental level of middle school students, who they felt were "not able to go deep into issues" and were "unable to have the depth of conversation and understanding required." A teacher in Circle said that he was having "trouble with eighth-graders. Many of them are checked out and tend to show no empathy."

Yet, the sixteen students I spoke with in these two Oakland middle schools displayed extremely profound and deep thinking, even though I saw them acting like typical middle schoolers as they went through their school day. I remember laughing as I thought about the amazingly brilliant things they would say in Circle and then watch them act goofy in other situations!

Speaking of the challenge of using RJ with this age group, one teacher thought that "part of it is cognitive, but I also think the other part of it could be the factors that we don't have any control over, or also just trust, like, 'I just don't trust you and we don't have a relationship.'" This teacher brought up two very important points: factors teachers cannot control, like a young person's living situation, and trust, a factor that they *can* do something about. We see once again that building authentic relationships and establishing trust with students are absolutely critical for RJE to succeed in schools, perhaps especially so for middle school students. It is unreasonable to expect high-needs youth to change the way they act simply because they had a conversation with an RJ facilitator, when we, their teachers and administrators, have not invested the time and effort into building caring, trusting relationships with them.

I know this is easier said than done. Some young people behave in ways that make them very hard to like. But as educators, it is our *job* to love them, whether we like their behavior or not. For students who have high needs, love from teachers could save their lives. This is a lot to ask of teachers, though, which is where RJE comes in. RJE brings processes that support teachers in building positive, caring relationships not only with individual students but also within the class. Building relationships with students and among students does not all hang on the personality or will of the teacher. Circles in particular create a space where understanding and compassion can grow organically among all participants. Circles convey a loving atmosphere by their very structure, and Circle practices build feelings of love and care for each other as human beings. Children of all ages respond to the Circle space, especially when they are going through developmental stages they do not understand. They feel the support of their peers.

Home, community, social environments, and trauma. The home, community, and social environments present another set of forces that stress youth and cause them to struggle. We live in a wealthy country where 40 percent of all children grow up in poverty. In these two middle schools, many of the children's families struggled with the traumatizing legacies of historical harms and racial, economic, and political injustices and inequalities. Many of the teachers, support staff, and administrators recognized this and acknowledged that some of their students had "crazy lives." One teacher noted:

Within the community, there's also a lot of trauma and struggle, and so a lot of our families face that, too. Some [are] really resilient, and some are really struggling, and that impacts our students. As I look back, year after year, I think I can notice patterns [regarding] students I struggle with the most. It's generally the students who are oftentimes facing a lot of difficulty, a lot of trauma, a lot of different things. It comes out in different ways in class.

Only recently have educators been learning how trauma affects students and their capacities to learn. Some progressive school districts, like the OUSD, are implementing trauma-informed practices through professional development workshops. In 2016, OUSD's RJ facilitators received training in trauma-informed practices. But while educators and schools are in the process of learning about how to support students with trauma, thousands of young people are living with it every day, and very few of them are getting the help and support they need. Most teachers are not equipped to deal with trauma or even trained to recognize the signs. Many teachers are busy wrestling with the demons of their own unhealed traumas and do not realize how this affects their own lives. Many of us do not get out of childhood intact and undamaged, and unresolved trauma creates emotional scripts and biological responses that can be triggered by various events.

Educators are learning much about how trauma affects their own and their students' behaviors and reactions. Whatever trauma levels we and our students carry, we can create safe spaces in our classrooms. Learning about trauma and how it affects the school and their classrooms is one way educators can support struggling students.

Restorative processes, especially Circle, are trauma-informed processes that we can all use. The experience of being listened

to respectfully and treated with dignity supports trauma healing, as does the opportunity to express one's voice. Trauma
healing strategies are organic in RJE.

While dysfunctional families, poverty, violence, and police
brutality are by no means confined to Oakland, both Grant
and Davis are situated in this city where all of these challenges
exist. So it makes sense that a teacher would say the following,
when asked if students changed as a result of SWRPs:

> I think it depends on the student. If they have a back-
> ground of support at the home, outside of school, and just
> happened to get caught in peer pressure, then I'd say yes.
> However, if there's a lack of support at home, then it's
> likely that the *student won't change unless everything and
> everyone around them has* [emphasis mine].

For the second time in this study, a teacher stressed that the
adults around a student must change before we can expect the
students to change. Nonetheless, RJE can still provide spaces
of support in school. Even if parents and neighbors stay the
same, RJE can give students opportunities for developing loving and caring relationships with the people in their schools—
adults and youth—and through these healthy relationships
begin to heal from the pain and trauma in their lives.

On my very first day at Grant, for example, I walked into
the main lobby where a fight was just about to break out. I
heard a girl shouting at a boy, and teachers and the SSO had
separated the two students. The girl was extremely agitated
and yelling that she was ready to fight the boy. While teachers
herded the rest of the students to class, the principal, Elena
Baez, calmly stood beside the girl, speaking to her in low, kind
tones. Students did not try to escalate, encourage, or video
the fight, as I had seen happen many times in the urban mid-

dle school where I once taught. Instead, the students went on their way to class, and in a matter of minutes, the incident was over. Elena continued to stand near the girl while she called her mother on her cell phone. The girl paced back and forth and talked in a loud voice. After a few minutes, when the girl had begun to calm down, Elena gently put her hand on her shoulder and escorted her into the main office to wait for her mother.

Later that day, I mentioned the incident to Antonio, the RJ facilitator, as we walked through the courtyard and athletic fields during lunch. I noticed that the girl was hanging out with her friends and commented that, despite almost starting a fight, she had not been sent home. Antonio told me that the girl's mother had recently been released from prison and that she needed a high level of support. When I later spoke to the SSO, she explained that this student had a "hair trigger" and that these outbursts were common for her (hair triggers and rage are common symptoms of trauma and shame). Any punishment a school would inflict on a student like this will only add to the pain, trauma, and rage. I began to understand why the SSO and the principal acted as they did. After a conference with the student's mother, the principal integrated the girl back into the school community where she could be around the friends who supported her. Is it likely that this student will act out again? Yes. The hurt that this girl carries inside will take time to heal, and although she may need more help than the school is capable of providing, the staff at Grant are doing their best to support her with the resources they have.

Restorative practices have never been billed as a quick fix or panacea. But what RJE has done in this school is surround troubled students with caring adults who take the time to listen to them, both in Circle and out. This, in and of itself, is significant, transformational, and healing.

Summary of Changes in the People

Students, staff, and administrators in these two middle schools found that learning restorative values and processes helped them change in many ways. Staff reported that they had become more patient, better listeners, more open, and were placing greater emphasis on building relationships. Students said RJE helped them do better in school, take their education more seriously, mature, and develop leadership skills. Staff who had not changed said it was because they were already aligned with restorative values to begin with. Granted, some teachers did not respond to the survey and had not changed, because they did not believe in RJE. Students and staff reported that students' age or home environment contributed to the perception that some students did not change from participating in restorative processes and attending a restorative school.

We know that schools are limited in what they can do for young people who come from dysfunctional homes, violent communities, and an unequal, all too racist society. But we are also talking here about changing what we can in the school environment. We as educators can make conscious decisions about our schools' relational ecologies and how we deal with young people who are struggling. We can respond to conflicts in schools as opportunities to practice restorative values and to use RJE processes. We can build relationships, break down walls, eliminate exclusionary discipline policies, and invest in our children. If we play the long game, our schools can become places that facilitate great change in both the adults and the students at the school, and this change will then ripple out into our communities and society now and into the future.

CHAPTER 9

Changes in the Classroom

The last area of change that I explored was whether teachers at Grant and Davis middle schools changed the way they taught as a result of restorative justice in education (RJE). Specifically, I wanted to see if they incorporated restorative and relational pedagogies—teaching strategies—into their daily instruction, or if they had trouble bringing school-wide restorative practices (SWRPs) into the classroom. Teachers can use many instructional strategies to encourage students to build strong relationships with each other and their teachers, including collaborative learning activities, social and emotional learning (SEL), and Positive Behavioral Interventions and Supports (PBIS). Many of the teachers at both schools had received training in SEL and PBIS, and the new teachers used relational-based strategies that they learned in college, such as cooperative learning activities. After observing twenty classrooms in the two schools, I found that all but one teacher used PBIS strategies, restorative pedagogies, or related with their students in ways that promoted SEL competencies.

Relational Practices in the Classrooms

Teachers at both schools modeled SEL competencies for their students. In one classroom, I heard a student make a disparaging remark and the teacher calmly reinforced the expectations, saying, "If you disagree with someone's answer, you don't call out. We're not going to say it's wrong or bring anyone down.

What's important is you work at your best." Another teacher dealt with students who were talking out of turn by saying to the student who was about to speak, "Wait till you are respected by everybody—I hear some blah blah over here." These non-punitive and relational-based behavioral redirections promote self-awareness, self-regulation, and respect without alienating students, and many of the teachers I observed integrated these practices seamlessly into their instruction.

I spoke to a science teacher after observing his class working collaboratively on a project. He explained that more than 40 percent of instruction throughout the school was done using collaborative learning activities (that is, when students work in pairs or groups), which is also considered a relational pedagogy. Students appeared skilled at working with a partner or in a group and demonstrated their SEL competency. They worked independently, followed directions, and collaborated with their peers to solve problems or answer questions before consulting the teacher. Teachers encouraged students to discover the answer themselves or check with a peer before asking the teacher. This promotes student-centered learning, independence, and cooperation, and it keeps students engaged with their learning.

Students certainly did not behave perfectly all the time, yet in most instances of misbehavior in the classroom that I observed, teachers addressed students in relational-based and student-centered ways. For example, when one boy was out of his seat talking to a girl when he was supposed to be writing, the teacher calmly said, "How are you helping yourself? How is being over there helping you?" The young man smiled and walked back to his seat without further incident. This question promoted self-regulation, one of the SEL competencies.

Using relational pedagogies and strategies to teach helped create positive relational ecologies in the schools. Principal Stan Paulson believes that SEL is "on the same level, if not a higher priority than the core subject matter." Overall, teachers praised and rewarded students often for meeting expectations, used student-centered teaching practices, and gave students ample opportunities during classes to develop relationships with the curriculum, their teachers, and each other. Most of the teachers were more experienced and comfortable with SEL or PBIS than they were with using SWRPs during normal classroom instruction. At this point in their journey, they had made only a slight shift toward using restorative pedagogies in the classroom.

During our focus group Circles, I asked staff if teachers were modifying their teaching practices in the classroom to include restorative approaches. Overall, staff believed that, for tier 1 SWRPs to be implemented with integrity, most teachers needed to change their outlook and behaviors.

Acke, Davis's RJ facilitator, agreed, saying that teachers needed to trust the process as well as trust the RJ facilitators and other staff who were there to support them. He said:

> The teacher [has] to become comfortable with their discomfort, and trust the trust in a situation and what's holding them, [i.e.,] the staff that's helping them and supporting them. Trust what's being said and how they are being guided. They are going to have to let go a little bit.

Another teacher added:

> If you are a brand-new and young teacher, it can be challenging to be vulnerable like that in a group of kids that you think you are supposed to be in control of and have power over. But once you step away from that method of teaching, then you are okay with it. You can be vulnerable. You can have your own transformations. But, you know, young people, new [teachers]—they are not always ready for that.

The staff acknowledged that creating restorative classrooms means reevaluating how teachers use their authority.
The shift calls them to let go of the more rigid, controlling, and
traditional aspects of authority and embrace a more flexible
approach. When it comes to restorative practices and pedagogies, teachers inevitably come up against the traditional
instructional practices and educational theories that have
been deeply engrained in our psyches about how we are supposed to talk and act in front of our students. Acke understood
this and believed that, for teachers to learn to let go a little bit,
they needed to trust that others would be there to help them.
Once again, we see how critical relationships of trust are.

Circles in Academic Classes

I developed four statements to determine if teachers were
using Circles or other relational pedagogies in their classrooms
now more than before the school implemented SWRPs. I asked
staff whether they agreed or disagreed with the statements.
Chart 9.1 shows their responses.

Teachers said they are now using more curricula that promote awareness of others, creating more activities that allow
students to get to know each other, and giving students
more opportunities to share their perspectives. Of those who
responded, 57 percent—more than half—reported using Circles more frequently in their classrooms. However, teachers
reported that they were more comfortable promoting cultural
competency and SEL than they were with using Circles for teaching and learning. Teachers indicated that SWRPs gave them
more tools to improve their relationships with students and to
deal more effectively with conflict, but some teachers—43 percent of those surveyed—were uncertain about how to incorporate SWRPs into their teaching practices. In other words, with

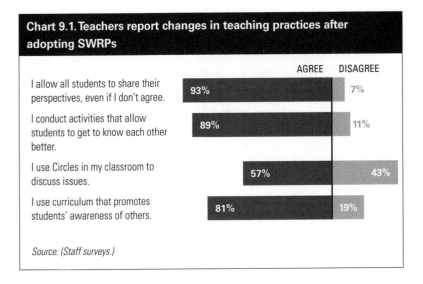

Chart 9.1. Teachers report changes in teaching practices after adopting SWRPs

	AGREE	DISAGREE
I allow all students to share their perspectives, even if I don't agree.	93%	7%
I conduct activities that allow students to get to know each other better.	89%	11%
I use Circles in my classroom to discuss issues.	57%	43%
I use curriculum that promotes students' awareness of others.	81%	19%

Source: (Staff surveys.)

more training and experience, teachers could be using Circles for teaching much more than they were doing.

Several core team members shared how they were incorporating restorative pedagogy into their classrooms:

> We have that commitment to holding Circle with them and using that as a tool in advisory and using that as a tool in our classrooms, to help them build relationships, both in getting to know each other, but also to use the Circle as a place to reflect on what's been going on in the class, on things that they would like to see improved. Because we don't believe that things are just academic; things have to be both relational and academic. Our commitment is that we are doing the work to be good teachers in the classroom, which involves a lot of relational stuff. And that's our core. And so for us, restorative justice represents that core value of relationships and that commitment to each other [and that is why] we will hold Circles in our classroom.

I observed a writing teacher using Circles during her class. She asked her students, who were seated in groups of four, to use a talking piece to share with their peers what they wrote. I noted how easily this teacher incorporated Circles and a talking piece into her small-group activities. She asked students to quickly grab anything that was close by to use as a talking piece; the piece focused students' attention on the person holding it, while they shared their writing with peers. These students were adept and comfortable using this restorative process, because their teacher had found a way to incorporate into her daily instruction what they normally did as a community building practice during advisory period. She told me, "I use a talking piece constantly." She added that it was also very natural, almost intuitive, for her to transfer SWRPs to her instructional practices. In fact, she had a box of talking pieces and a Circle space, complete with a rug and pillows, in front of her classroom that was available to her students anytime, as shown in figure 16.

The writing teacher shared this story with me:

I had this moment the other day I wish I had on tape. These two boys, they're in the corner of the room, and they had been talking for the first half of the period—whispering, clearly not paying attention. . . . Finally I said "Alright, we're gonna have a conversation about this." And I just sat down and I just looked at one kid. And he goes, "HE OWES ME MONEY!" [*she laughs*], and I just turned to the other kid, and he goes, "Well, I got your money." The first kid goes, "You owe me ten dollars." "I do not. I owe you five dollars." I sat there. I just kept looking back and forth between the two boys—they worked out the whole thing by themselves. Well, they worked it out, like, about 80 percent. They figured it all out, and then they were like, "We

Figure 16. A prepared Circle area in a classroom

need to talk to these two other kids," and I said "All right. Go sit on the rug. I got a class to teach." They grabbed these two other boys, they went and sat on the rug, they pulled a talking piece out of the talking piece box. These are four kids who goof off all the time. I mean, if you're just going to put kids in boxes and label them, these are four knuckleheads [*she laughs again*]. And they're sitting there—they found a talking piece—and they passed the talking piece around. I taught my class. They sat in the corner, passed the talking piece, they worked it out. I went over there and said, "Okay, does everyone have their money back?" And they said, "Yeah, we're done," and they haven't caused a problem since then. It was two weeks ago. That was really a cool moment for me. I was like, "Okay, they get it." It was just a hilarious moment.

Another teacher wrote this on the survey:

> Circles in class have centered student voices and our relationships with each other. It has increased student ownership of our classroom, school, and our community. Students feel more connected to each other and more responsible for and to each other. Students and I also are able to see and understand each other in different ways from our experiences in Circle.

Teachers who used restorative pedagogies in their classrooms either knew intuitively how to transfer their skills from their advisory classes to their academic classes, or they relied on the experiences of others to guide them. Based on teacher narratives and self-reported confidence levels (see table 8.2), 43 percent of teachers were unsure how to use SWRPs for instructional purposes.

Even some core team teachers in the focus groups were not comfortable using restorative practices as a pedagogy in their classrooms. One teacher said, "It is a process, and I don't think it translates immediately into how you do instruction." Whereas many teachers held Circles during their advisory periods, only a few teachers spoke of using Circles during instructional time as a way of delivering or understanding content.

I saw less change in instructional practices than I did in personal or organizational change. How to transfer the Circle skills practiced in advisory class to a regular academic class is not always obvious. This is an area where RJE advocates and trainers need to focus our efforts more intensely. Most discipline problems start in the classroom, so it makes sense that most restorative practices should occur in the classroom to build the trust and community necessary to solve problems and conflicts before they escalate—before a student is asked to leave.

Nancy Riestenberg's book *Circle in the Square* gives many examples of how different teachers have used Circles in their classrooms. Kay Pranis and Carolyn Boyes-Watson's book *Circle Forward* provides teachers with step-by-step instructions on how to use Circles for different topics and in different situations. And Belinda Hopkins's book *The Restorative Classroom* contains hundreds of activities that build community, provide opportunities for students to learn cooperatively, and prevent problem behaviors. I defer to my colleagues' work for more information on how to implement SWRPs in the classroom, but I will note that it all begins with training.

Setting Schools Up to Succeed

CHAPTER 10

Putting It All Together:
Relational Ecology and Change

So many lessons have emerged from studying restorative justice in education (RJE) at Grant and Davis middle schools. Their trials, challenges, changes, and successes are probably not unique to them. Those who talked with me or took my survey made it clear that they believed RJE is the best way to do school. They also made it clear that they needed support. And that is where this book comes in.

In the introduction, I wrote about the tendency to "throw restorative justice (RJ)" at disproportionate disciplining—to want RJE to be a "quick fix" for lowering suspension rates, particularly for students of color. After hearing all the voices in this book, we know that RJE has enormous potential to change schools—and people—for the better. We also know that RJ is not something we can just throw at systemically embedded problems—punitive thinking in schools or racism, inequality, and privilege in society.

I do not say this to discourage people from adopting RJE, but rather to paint a realistic picture of what is involved. Creating a restorative school is a paradigm shift. Nancy Riestenberg describes our work as trying to alter the course of a fleet of aircraft carriers. But big as our work is, our children need and deserve RJE—a humane, compassionate, respectful, and effective way of doing school.

◼ A School's Relational Ecology Sets Its Capacity to Change

Where do we start? To change, we need the capacity to change. This is where relational ecology comes in: the stronger the net of relationships, the more a school is capable of change.

In both these schools, positive relational ecologies supported people, so they could embrace change together. Strong relationships enabled them to reflect, acknowledge what wasn't working, make adjustments, persevere, and embark on the challenge to transform their school cultures. A positive reinforcing loop then kicked in: the restorative changes further improved the relational ecologies of the schools. Figure 17 shows this synergetic relationship.

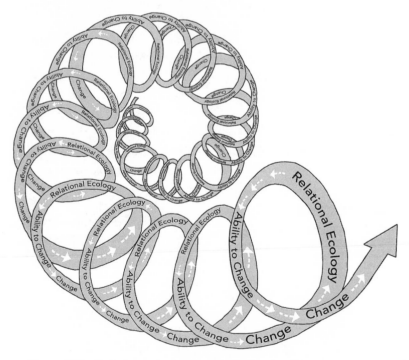

Figure 17. The interdependent relationship between relational ecology and change

Educational researchers Anthony Bryk and his colleagues write about this very dynamic between relationships and change:

> Relationships are the lifeblood of activity in a school community. The patterns and exchanges established here and the meanings that individuals draw from these inter-actions can have profound consequences on the operation of schools, especially in times that call for change.[1]

We can talk about school relationships in many ways. "School culture" has been a pivotal term in identifying the quality of relationships in a school. I find the term "relational ecology" also helpful, because it both deepens and widens my understanding of what is going on. The term takes an intimate as well as a systemic look at relationships—simultaneously.

A river provides a metaphor. A school's relational ecology is like the parts of the river we cannot see from a raft or from the banks. It represents the deep parts—the living parts—where twenty different kinds of fish and countless other organisms may live together, as well as the rocks, roots, and plants that provide food and shelter to the fish. Relational ecology represents the life of the school—the school as a living ecosystem made up of everyone. In the river metaphor, school-wide change is more like the top water of the river that we see: we can watch its flow, ripples, currents, and rapids; we can observe what it carries downstream, what dams it up, and how the river snakes and moves throughout the landscape and communities surrounding it. But what gives a school's river its life—what nourishes and sustains the school community and energizes needed changes—are the deeper currents: the relationships, namely, the school's relational ecology.

How do relational ecology and change interact in a school's journey to become restorative? The following themes, which emerged from my study of these two schools, depict different facets of this relational ecology–change interaction. This interaction is the bright red thread I see woven throughout their stories, lending insight both into what worked and what did not.

Trust Feeds School-Wide Change

Trust, a feature of relationships, and change are critical partners. At the very heart of the relational ecology of Davis and Grant was a growing sense that people could trust each other. Trust is a power source for reform: trusting relationships among the entire staff are essential for successfully implementing school-wide restorative practices (SWRPs). Whether staff feel they can trust each other depends heavily on the school's principal: is he or she both trustworthy and able to foster trust among colleagues? People need to know that their principal is committed to making RJE work, even when resources are scarce or parents get uncomfortable.

At Davis and Grant, the principals' actions, advocacy, and support helped build the trust necessary for change. Both Elena Baez and Stan Paulson underscored how important trusting relationships among staff, students, and parents are to RJE's success.

Teachers trusted, respected, and cared about each other, and they showed empathy and concern for new teachers who were struggling due to lack of training and support. Trust among the adults spread to trust between adults and students, which contributed to trust school-wide. When the staff modeled trust, the students felt safer about trusting each other. Students and staff became more skilled at communicating their needs and expectations with each other. Higher trust levels enabled teachers and students to act as change-makers together. The time spent in Circles paid off: trust took root in the relational ecologies of these two schools, and this trust enabled them to make the changes they needed to function restoratively.

▒ Making Time for Relationships

To build relationships of trust strong enough to support change, schools need to make relationships top priority. One of the best ways to do this is to set aside time to tend them.

School-wide restorative practices give everyone in a school an opportunity both to be heard and to hear others. This is especially critical when a harm has occurred or when some tension or conflict has surfaced. Listening and speaking respectfully with each other is what Circles facilitate. Students, teachers, and administrators at Davis and Grant had learned to talk and listen to each other across all school environments. Communication and conversations were priorities in these schools, because relationships were priorities, and the strength of their relationships made change doable.

The benefits of building relationships multiply. To thrive, students need a personal relationship with the people in their schools. Researchers have found that middle school students want to talk about their schools and education, and that their ability to do so positively affects their academic achievement.[2] Restorative processes create space and time for students to have conversations about things that matter to them. At Grant and Davis, these processes included check-ins, Circles, restorative conversations, peer mediations, and conferences.

While in Circle, teachers shared their personal stories and feelings with their students, thereby humanizing themselves and the process of education. The Circles gave students a chance to form positive attachments with their teachers. Many researchers have found student-teacher bonds to be important, especially for African American students.[3] Given our society's history of violent, broken relations with African Americans, the need to put extra energy into building positive bonds with Black youth makes sense.

The strength of students' ability to bond with a school

community is, in fact, a predictor of their achievement or delinquency. Humanizing a school through restorative practices creates positive school cultures. The river metaphor applies: when water, oxygen, earth, and light interact in perfectly balanced amounts, the fish, birds, plants, and animals thrive in and around the riverbed. So, too, when people in schools trust each other, listen to each other, and take on struggles together, students, staff, administrators, and parents thrive.

Visionary and Democratic Leadership Nurtures Change

Keeping relationships a priority, which expands a community's capacity to change, calls for effective, visionary leadership—leadership that will, for example, change schedules to allow time for listening and collaboration. These school leaders also share decision making and leadership with teachers and staff, so that schools can have a democratic, shared form of governance. Change theorists and researchers on effective schools agree: such leaders empower and motivate others.[4] The staffs of Davis and Grant respected their principals, Stan and Elena, for upholding their commitment to SWRPs, despite the challenges they each faced. These principals provided funding for the necessary personnel (RJ facilitators) and made the structural changes (RJ room, advisory period) needed to successfully implement RJE as a whole-school reform. They also instituted a democratic form of governance and listened to their colleagues—administrators and teachers—as well as to their students.

Restorative schools need a way of operating that is more open and inclusive. They require democratic processes that include all stakeholders and leaders—and for many reasons. For example, democratic processes draw on everyone's knowledge and creativity; they invite people to share in problem-solving; and they generate authentic buy-in of the changes. Democratic processes nurture the relational ecologies of schools, and the schools become more change-friendly and change effective as a result.

■ Creating a Positive Ethos and Atmosphere

Both schools adopted positive disciplinary methods that emphasize relationships and put students at the center of educating. The schools embodied a restorative ethos, evident in their welcoming and friendly physical environments. They were open, colorful, and clean, and most of the people in the schools were friendly, smiling, relaxed, and caring.

Teachers adapted their classrooms for collaborative-learning activities, allowing students to engage each other, their teachers, and the curriculum. Positive relationships in school benefit everyone, but particularly students of color, since they have been historically denied respectful relationships with authority figures and communities. Teachers and administrators acknowledged that most people who worked in these schools had a relational-based, positive orientation, and that principals actively sought to hire teachers and staff who had this orientation.

Circles contributed to the relational-based, student-centered culture, as did trust and the absence of fortress tactics. The strength of the schools' relational ecologies, rather than tactics of force, kept the schools safe, positive, and conducive to learning.

■ Training and Support: Keeping RJE Change on Track and Going

Two of the most critical factors in creating a restorative school are training and support, which build both the knowledge and the relationships needed for change to go forward. "Training, training, training" is a mantra for schools engaged in RJE change, from introductory and basic training to advanced training in restorative processes to opportunities for reflection and sharing what people have learned. As in the river metaphor, the shift to restorative practices goes deeper than what we see in outward policy and discipline changes. Change has to go down to our fundamental assumptions about human nature and behavior.

The two schools achieved what they did because their leaders not only motivated core teams but also supported them. These teams, in turn, implemented the restorative changes in their schools, helping peers and other stakeholders make the shift. They responded to challenges and skepticism with deeper discussions about RJE and cultural competency. And they acted as advocates as they modeled the restorative approach.

But the schools faced obstacles not of their making: high teacher turnover rates, high external stressors, limited funding, and the non-RJ functions that the RJ facilitators had to perform. These factors inhibited their capacity building for RJE and affected their program's fidelity to RJE practices.

Although I observed only one new teacher who relied on a punitive and authoritarian classroom management style, those I interviewed spoke of the struggles that new teachers faced. Without adequate RJE training and experience, they are more apt to turn to repressive and authoritarian methods of classroom management.[5] RJ facilitators and teachers alike realized that school-wide restorative practices call teachers to let go of traditional notions of authority and trust the process. But to feel safe enough to do this, teachers need training, coaching, support, mentoring, and experience with restorative practices.

With initial and continuous training, teachers and staff are less likely to let restorative practices slip away and resort to old, punitive habits. Training builds the adults' understanding of how and why RJE works as well as the entire staff's confidence in restorative practices. With such a foundation, the RJE program stays on course.

Using Class Circles Creates a Learning Community

The least amount of change, by far, occurred at the instructional level. One reason is that many staff were already using other relational pedagogical practices, which were evident in 95 percent of the classrooms I observed. By reducing the fear and stress around learning, these practices contributed to the positive relational ecologies in these schools.

But Circles offer the classroom something that other practices do not: community. With community comes mutual understanding, mutual accountability, mutual support, and capacities for self-regulation as a group. Only a few teachers reported that they had mastered the use of Circles in their classrooms; most struggled with knowing how and when to use them as an instructional practice. Further, they did not yet understand the full benefits that using Circles could bring to their classrooms, especially in preventing, reducing, and resolving problems.

Using Circles for classroom instruction brings many benefits. While sitting in Circle with their students during advisory or academic classes, for example, teachers can assess the emotional states of their students as well as what they are learning. The students and teachers who sat in Circle with me talked about their lives, their cultural backgrounds, their schoolwork, conflicts in the classroom, and issues in the community, including the Black Lives Matter movement.

Listening respectfully to each other in Circle helps both adults and students develop the five SEL competencies (see chapter 3). Further, using the Circle as a teaching and learning strategy helps students link classroom work with their lives and cultures. This connection inspires students to contribute to their school and community beyond what they do in the classroom. The energy students devote to meaningful projects in turn enhances their talents, stimulates their interests, and expands their life experiences, all of which improves their grasp of academic work. Their studies become real for them; they see how their class subjects matter and how they can use their learning.

The benefits of teaching in Circle go yet further: it turns the class into a teaching-learning community. Teaching-and-learning Circles increase understanding among students and give students an experience of community with their peers and teacher. Students experience both the learning and the teaching side of education. Often, they can help other students who are having trouble, whether academically or behaviorally, in ways a teacher cannot. The impulse to bully goes down, and cooperative, collaborate skills increase. Students begin to share accountability for how the class goes.

Learning is a change experience: it changes us. If it is true that relationships increase our capacity to change, then it makes sense that using classroom Circles, which build relationships and community, will enhance students' capacities to learn. Just think about how learning something new becomes less scary when we feel related to those around us—a teacher and other learners—who support us and help us change through the learning process.

◼ Repairing Relationships Fosters Change

Restorative practices are designed to change relationships for the better. They bring people together in a space of respect, so that positive change is possible and even likely to occur.

Restorative practices have definite components that set up these relationship–change dynamics. Accountability and repairing harm in the context of supportive relationships are key RJE factors conducive to personal change. We all need feedback to learn, and restorative practices create spaces for feedback to flow through relationships in non-threatening, non-accusatory, learning-oriented, and problem-solving ways.

How these two schools responded to harms often bypassed key RJ components, especially the relationship-repairing ones. As a result, the hoped-for changes did not follow as readily. Instead of using Circles to repair harm, for example, RJ facilitators at Grant and Davis frequently met one-on-one with students, tracked them down to check in, or supervised a kinder, gentler variety of in-school suspension. When they counseled students, they did not always involve other stakeholders in the reparative process. In other words, they did not draw on relationships as the muscle or power source for tapping students' capacities to change.

Instead, challenging students were sent out of the classroom to RJ facilitators or other administrators. By shifting the responsibility for repairing the harm to another adult, teachers essentially forfeited their role in the restorative process. Failing to involve the individuals who had been harmed or to allow them to verbalize what they needed for the harm to be repaired compromises a very fundamental part of RJE. The teacher's relationship with the student, as well as other students' relationship with their peer, went unrepaired, untransformed. Students and teachers alike were taught how to "restore a referral," instead of how to restore a broken relationship or build one in the first place, which, according to RJ, is where the impetus for change lies.

In all likelihood, these non- or quasi-restorative processes evolved from a combination of practical concerns and old habits. Should a teacher stop instruction to participate in a restorative process every time a problem arises? From an RJE view, when teachers teach in Circle, they can focus the Circle immediately on whatever issue arises. Students share how another's behavior is affecting them and why learning is important for them. Not the teacher but the Circle process builds relations within the class as a community, and students hold each other accountable. Through honest sharing, students understand each other and at least recognize the issues that each student faces. The Circle process and the community it builds hold great potential for responding to behavioral issues constructively and resolving them inside the classroom.

As these schools demonstrated, sending the students out of the classroom did not resolve the issues but led to the stereotyping of some students as "frequent flyers." Stereotypes alienate and divide; they cause stress all around. The schools were still defaulting in some situations to the mind-set that adults are the disciplinarians and individual students are the problems. Because they were not yet bringing Circles into the classrooms, they were not building the in-class community capital they needed to prevent, deescalate, or resolve problems.

Even implemented in part, though, SWRPs help many students change for the better: I heard this repeatedly from both adults and youth. Repairing relationships was happening, especially with Davis's peer mediators. Students who changed saw themselves as better leaders and better students. This shift in self-perception also contributed to a positive relational ecology in the school.

One of the takeaways from this is not that these two schools fell short in their RJE implementation. They were new and working against great odds. Rather, the SWRPs they were using revealed a great potential for positive change that would only increase the more they could bring restorative practices into their classrooms. Classroom Circles would jump their relationship building and their capacities to repair relationships to new levels. The changes they hoped for would be much more likely to follow.

African American Male Youth and RJE: Pushing a School's Paradigm Shift Deeper

And now we come to a critical discussion. Some adults and students in these two schools believed that RJ interventions did not work with some students, particularly some African American young male students. This is where the framework of relational ecologies and change pays off for understanding how and why RJE works. What can we learn here?

Interventions that did not work with some Black youth. Both teachers and students spoke about students who acted out repeatedly. Those who raised this issue believed that the students tended to be African American more than any other group: the students were not responding to "restorative interventions" in the ways the school district had hoped. The Oakland Unified School District (OUSD) had a documented problem with disproportionate disciplining of Black students, as do many school districts, and the district adopted RJE district-wide precisely to remedy this harm. So the perception that RJ was "not working for Black students" was of great concern. As I learned more, I realized the interventions were not, in fact, fully restorative. Often, they did not repair relationships and thus fell short of a restorative goal. However, this gap between RJE and what was actually being practiced was not recognized.

Also, despite their commitment to both RJE and social justice, conscious (explicit) or subconscious (implicit) biases against Black students persisted in the schools, as I discussed in chapter 6 (see charts 6.8 and 6.9). These biases appeared to be exacerbated or fueled by teachers' and students' negative experiences with certain Black students, who continued to get in trouble despite numerous interventions. In turn, the negative racial biases damaged the Black students' relationships with the schools—relationships that, when strong, help students stay on a good path.

Overall, teachers and support staff were empathetic to the fact that Black male youth have been stigmatized, judged, and targeted more than any other ethnic group and gender in this country. Yet a number of teachers and students still felt that Black male students exhibited challenging behavior more than other students and also got away with more than other students. On surveys, a substantial number of people expressed discomfort with the way Black students tended to express themselves, using racially coded language to describe them as "loud" or "most vocal." Some teachers and students felt that restorative justice allowed Black students to get away with more disruptive or disrespectful behavior than other students. Others believed that SWRPs did not work for all students, especially those with the highest needs.

RJE's response: go deeper. How does relational ecology and change speak to this experience that these schools had? In *The Little Book of Restorative Justice in Education,* Kathy Evans and Dorothy Vaandering stress that RJE theory is about relationships and their transformational power. If a student or group of students has weak ties with a school's relational ecology, then the student's or group's capacities to change in that environment will be weak as well. What does it mean to have weak ties? For example, unaddressed racial biases, which in fact showed up on staff's responses (again, see charts 6.8 and 6.9), would drive a wedge between Black students and the rest of the school community. Black students would feel they do not belong as much as non-African American students. They would not feel as welcomed or accepted. They would feel not as trusted, and they would have good reason to feel mistrusted, since 40 percent of staff reported that Black students were, in fact, not as trusted by students and adults in the schools. Not only that, but the dynamic of a group of students who feel alienated from the school would weaken the school's relational ecology as a whole. The school's capacities to change would be impaired too; it would be easy to resort to old-paradigm thinking to respond to problems, which is what happened.

The RJE response to these dynamics, which involve not only the so-called "problem" students but the whole school, is to push the paradigm shift deeper. Using processes that attend to the relationships between students and their teachers and peers is most critical where trust is lowest and disconnection greatest. Referrals to the main office and then one-on-one interventions with a third party, the RJ facilitator, did not do this. When this constituted the intervention, the process denied Black students a chance to engage face-to-face with their teachers and classmates, so they could resolve the conflict and repair or build the relationship. From the teachers' side, their commitment to the student's well-being and to being in a good relationship with the student had no forum for expression when their last-resort discipline method was to send students out of their classroom or give them referrals. The "referral" response to Black students caused the schools to miss prime opportunities for (re)weaving Black youth into the school community. It took a toll on everyone.

Historical and ongoing racial realities for Black students. Many African Americans—students and their families—have a tenuous relationship with schools for good reason. In the US, White-run society has denied African Americans an education since slavery: literacy for African Americans was illegal. White supremacist laws and policies have controlled the historical relationship between schools and Black communities. Today, substandard education in many communities of color, particularly in urban centers, continues with underfunding and mass public school closings in African American neighborhoods. Textbooks have mostly taught White perspectives and White history. Even today, K12 Black students seldom see themselves, their communities, their histories, and their own knowledge systems in their coursework. White filters shape and dominate the course content. In these and other ways, schools have historically been—and in many ways still are—racist and hostile toward Black students, conveying messages of White supremacy to the most vulnerable population: children.

The multigenerational experience of many Black families is not, therefore, inclusion in the full benefits of the US educational system but rather aggressive exclusion from it. In society, pervasive racial stereotypes, lowered expectations, and coded racial fears alienate and disconnect Black youth, dishonoring them and holding them in contempt, even to the point of killing them and their relatives with impunity. What message does this send to Black youth about the value of their lives and where they belong?

No wonder teachers and Black students still struggle, and the most persistent school failure in US schools generally is with Black youth. The very structure of schools is adapted to White cultural norms of behavior. The behavioral norms of other cultures often do not fit within the traditional Western model of schooling, which requires students to be passive, quiet, and obedient. Racial and culture clashes overlay classroom conflicts, evident, for example, when "defiance" becomes the most common reason in a school for giving Black students discipline referrals.

Dynamics outside of schools hurt Black students as well. Unrepaired histories of multigenerational violence and trauma against African Americans, White-controlled institutions structured to serve White interests but obstruct Black interests, racial terrorism, job discrimination, redlining, police harassment and violence, and the daily racism that people of color cannot escape: Black students carry all this. The result? High stress and trauma levels for youth and their families. As some staff observed, many of their students led "crazy lives" in their homes and communities. Grant and Davis were both Title I schools, meaning that the majority of students lived in poverty. Children in poverty may experience health, emotional, academic, and social problems that may not be obvious but may nevertheless take a toll on their academic ability and social interactions.

On top of this, adverse childhood experiences often associated with living in poverty—abuse, neglect, household dysfunction, and exposure to violence—are trauma stressors. They place extra loads on students' developing psyches, affecting them socially, emotionally, and cognitively, all of which affects their behavior. Parents living in poverty often experience the same symptoms, making them less capable of attending to the physical, emotional, educational, and social needs of their children.[6]

Whatever trauma or burdens students carry with them into the school, the school's job is to help them learn, stay in school, have a positive experience, and graduate. To do that, RJE weaves relationships into a net—a whole-school positive ecology—that can carry the weight of supporting youth in managing whatever is going on in their lives. The teachers in both schools were acutely aware of the home and community lives of their students and sought to build trust, create a safe learning environment, listen to students, and provide social and emotional support. Yet that weight is too great for individual teachers or counselors to carry alone. Both the students and the adults caring for them need a broader base of support, which is what RJE gives.

Those with tenuous bonds need the fullest RJE practices. Relationships within a community are, once again, the key to RJE's effectiveness. Kay Pranis explains,

> Those with the most tenuous relationship with the school or those most in struggle with racial realities need the most relationship building, hence the fullest and most complete practice of RJE. RJE theory does not predict that a string of one-on-one counseling interventions will bring about positive change.[7]

What she is stating goes to the heart of this book and RJE's theory of relational ecologies. Namely, it is the net of relationships—not just one-on-one relationships but the whole relational ecology of the school—that supports long-term, meaningful transformation. (See chapter 11, recommendation 17.) RJE, as a way of life for a school, engages problems as opportunities to make the school's overall relational ecology stronger.[8]

Was "the problem" with individuals, either teachers or students? In the old paradigm of meritocracy and American individualism, expectations land on the person, independent from and unaffected by structure. Some staff believed, for example, that teachers who struggled with African American male students in their classrooms had not tried hard enough to understand Black culture or had failed to build trusting and caring relationships with Black students. At the same time, they acknowledged that the dynamic surrounding African American males was "heavy" and that they needed to make an extra effort to help Black youth, especially those in middle school, succeed in schools.

These comments seem fully well-intentioned, and both students and staff made them. Yet the views cast individual teachers or students as the problem, rather than examining the relational nature of the school as a whole and how restorative processes can shift it. From an RJE perspective, everyone has a role in making the relational ecology of the school positive, and that includes turning things around for individuals—teachers and students—when they struggle. The job of turning the tide is shared, because everyone contributes to a school's relational ecology, and everyone has an interest in conflicts being resolved in ways that make relationships better out the other side. What happens in any classroom affects the whole school, whether on the playground or cafeteria or in grades to come.

For example, though the first view suggests that the people were thinking about relationships, the job of making teacher-student relationships positive began and ended with the teacher. Teachers are human and make mistakes; they have implicit racial biases like everyone else in our society, founded as it is on racial privilege and oppression. If a teacher is struggling and his or her relationship with a class is strained, then the teacher needs support, first from colleagues and then, for example, through relationship-building Circles with students and support colleagues, like an RJ facilitator, to get to the root of issues and build trusting relations.

The second comment about the dynamics around African American males feeling heavy shows that these two schools still struggled with viewing African American males as "the problem." Making an extra effort to support those facing greater challenges is right and good, of course, and yet relational ecology also calls us to look at our own contributions to what is going on. Viewing one person or group as "the problem" that needs fixing only further alienates the person or group. Building relationships from a place of mutuality, respect, and shared accountability is more likely to be transformative all around.

RJE is holistic and considers not only what the students

bring into the school but what the adults bring in as well. We the adults are subject to the same society-wide programming as youth are, and we must address our own biases through training and Circles. Otherwise, racial and other biases come out as microaggressions that damage our teacher-student relationships—the most vital relationship for student achievement.

RJE offers processes for sharing the job of making positive change. The entire job does not fall to the teachers or other adults. In-class Circles give students a chance to help each other and provide support and understanding in ways a teacher cannot. Youth learn how to step out of the bystander role and contribute to the well-being of their class and everyone in it. The shift from individual to community begins.

RJE as an ongoing, self-reflective practice. These schools were only at the start of making a paradigm shift to RJE. Teacher and leader turnover kept them in "start-up" mode, rather than allowing them to deepen their restorative practices. As a result, the schools' relational ecologies were not yet working for some male Black students, who demonstrated this disconnect through their behavior. In response, the school continued to make "daily interventions," even though they realized this approach was "not working" either.

At such times, self-examination and self-reflection can realign us with an RJE, relational-ecology perspective. For example, how did these interventions feel to the Black students? What self-image did it build for them? In the name of doing "restorative interventions," the schools may have been further isolating and disconnecting these students, though granted, not as much as suspending them would have done. A hard lesson in RJE is that just because we intend an action to be restorative does not mean it is; we could end up doing unintended harm. Feedback loops help us recognize when outcomes are out of sync with our RJE intentions.

A self-reflective RJE process might involve people coming together in Circle to ask questions like the following:

- How might each member of the school community be contributing to the pattern we are witnessing?
- Are we practicing RJE or have we slipped into old habits?
- Does everyone involved feel treated with respect?
- What do students in struggle and their families need?
- What do the teachers need?
- How might other students take part in shifting the dynamics by strengthening their relationships with their peers, in this case, with African American students?
- How might the school as a community better support Black youth, their families, and the teachers?
- What changes could the school community make to meet everyone's needs to engage the learning process in respectful, positive ways?
- Would it be helpful for the school to seek more training, both in RJE and in becoming more aware of our own biases?

The two Oakland restorative schools have made enormous changes based on the relationships they have built through school-wide restorative practices, and much more change is possible as they tap the full power and potential of RJE. Other researchers in Oakland and practitioners all over the country have witnessed the profoundly transformational effects that trusting relationships with class and school communities have had on African American students who were struggling in school.[9] These practitioners use restorative practices to save the lives and futures of the Black youth in their care every day. They prove what I truly believe, that, yes, restorative practices do work for African American students—they work for everybody. Restorative practices must, however, be engaged with consistency, fidelity, and continuity. If schools fall short of this, then authentic relationships are less likely to form, relationships are not as strong, and Black youth are not fooled. They see through the disciplinary-only uses of restorative practices as just another form of social control and not as a genuine commitment from the adults to be in relationship with them.

As I have said from the start, treating restorative practices as a kinder, gentler way to punish students—or merely to suspend Black male students less often—does not work, because the approach does not change the underlying, often racist assumptions about Black students. Nor does it build the relationships and community that are the power source for restorative change.

The issue, then, is not "Does RJE or do SWRPs 'work' for all students?" but "How can schools deepen their understanding and practice of RJE so that authentic relationships do form and restorative practices prove transformative for all students, indeed, for the school community?" In these middle schools, Black students were pushing them to dig deeper.

Two Currents Shaping Our RJE Work

The experiences these schools had with African American youth illustrate two concepts that I have done my utmost to emphasize throughout this book. These are like two currents in the river of RJE work: one is about the actual practice of RJE; the other is about the larger society in which we practice it.

First, program fidelity: no program or initiative, no matter what it is, will ever produce the desired outcomes or changes unless it is implemented with fidelity. Schools cannot choose from a menu of change items, do a few of them, and then say they are doing RJE. These same schools will soon find themselves believing that RJE does not "work." RJE, when implemented incompletely, will not produce the outcomes and changes that it is capable of producing. Will some things improve? Yes. But for the entire system to change and for the people within the system to change, RJE must be given the resources, time, energy, and personnel it needs to be implemented with fidelity.

Second, RJE, even when implemented *with* fidelity, operates within a much larger unjust, unfair, and discriminatory economic, political, and social arena. We cannot expect schools doing RJE to perform miracles when the institutions, communities, people, and systems surrounding them embrace methods and philosophies that create systemic and ongoing harm. Students come through the door bearing the effects of a racially unjust society, including poverty, trauma, and PTSD. RJE helps schools share the job of making positive change, not only among adults but also with youth. But it will take even more work to transform our world—inside and out—into a just and equitable river that holds up each of us and enables us to thrive.

■ RJE Helps Schools Achieve Social Justice

Social justice was a significant value for many of the people I interviewed in these two schools. They realized that our society's structural racism and violence against people of color puts an extra burden on youth of color—in Oakland, that meant Black youth in particular. They also realized that schools share society's responsibility to acknowledge this and to ally with these youth in working to dismantle structural racism. A school's strong support for social justice sends the message to its students of color and other marginalized groups that they do not have to cope with society's racism and biases alone.

These two middle schools took the social justice challenge seriously. Being committed to social justice does not mean they had no issues or no further work to do in this area. Given our racialized and economically polarized society, it is fair to assume that every person and institution has work to do, within and without, to advance social justice. These schools' open and honest acknowledgment of their failure to support some of their Black students showed how serious they were about social justice: what they witnessed in disproportionate disciplining was not okay with them. They may not yet have been clear about why or how to change their RJE practices, but at least they named disproportionate disciplining and rejected it as an acceptable norm.

Indeed, social justice framed their RJE work, which they saw as including the need to educate students on social justice issues generally. Most of the adults were very aware of social inequities and harms. They were committed to meeting the needs of all students by becoming more culturally competent. The impacts of structural and systemic racism were not lost on the teachers and students in these schools either. Their empathy for and understanding of the unique challenges that Black males face was evident in their efforts to shift the relational ecology of the schools, especially around race.

Teachers used Circles to create safe spaces for students to talk about racism, social inequities, police brutality, and the challenges of living in poverty and crime-stricken neighborhoods. I participated in one Circle during an advisory period where the teacher invited students to talk about stereotypes and the Black Lives Matter movement. Both students and faculty had participated in actions inspired by this movement. Davis had a designated day when everyone wore black clothing to stand in solidarity with Black Lives Matter. They demonstrated engagement in what Paulo Freire called "praxis," defined as "the action and reflection of people upon their world in order to transform it."[10] The majority of teachers in my study believed that being culturally competent, building strong relationships with their students, and making sure their classrooms were welcoming, just, and fair to all students, particularly African American males, was the best way to interrupt inequities and put an end to disproportionate disciplining.

Brenda Morrison and Dorothy Vaandering assert that RJE helps schools achieve social justice.[11] Educating for social justice explores the pervasiveness of oppression—its multiple forms, institutions, and intersections. Social justice education also examines the interplay between individual and systemic change, aiming both to improve academic achievement and to raise social consciousness and action. Restorative processes in the schools I studied created spaces for students and teachers to talk about tough issues, like racism and police brutality. Through compassionate listening to individual narratives shared in Circle, students and teachers found their voices. Their dialogues about oppression and injustice broke down racial barriers and deepened their journey to create more just schools.

▨ Tending the Paradigm Shift, Outer and Inner

RJE is far more complex than the zero tolerance model. Because RJE is rooted in a very different philosophy, it cannot be grafted on top of a punishment-minded system that uses exclusion to control student behavior. If this philosophy shift is not solid in a school, then the practice will be a jumble of mixed messages, and positive changes will be limited. For RJE to "work," it has to go deep in both philosophy and practice.

These two schools were beginning the fourth year of their shift to becoming restorative and had faced many obstacles and setbacks with persistent commitment. Sometimes only the surface of the river had changed, and sometimes not even that. Under these circumstances, it is hard to draw conclusions about RJE's effectiveness. When schools experience RJE as not working, most likely the problem is not "out there" in the students but in the adults' own practice of RJE. This is good news, because the adults can deepen their RJE practices.

An effective, whole-school, restorative practices initiative requires that as many people as possible within the school community be on board with the shift. This means giving people opportunities to examine their values and belief systems about relationships and discipline. It also means educating them about restorative justice not as a technique but as a philosophy and way of life. At Davis, for example, one principal and most teachers changed after receiving training in restorative practices, even though they had previously accepted the punitive model. At both schools, personal changes included the sense of people becoming better listeners, being more open, placing more importance on relationships, having more empathy for students, increasing dialogue with students, being more patient, and having more tools to solve problems and conflicts. These positive changes—signs of the paradigm shift happening—not only affected administrative practices, leadership styles, and classroom instruction, but also contributed positively to the relational ecology—the living river—of the schools.

■ The Journey Continues

We have learned so much from the educators and students in this case study. Even as this book was going to press, the Oakland Unified School District was expanding its restorative justice initiative, hiring more RJ facilitators to work in more schools, adding more support and training staff, and implementing a new program regarding trauma-informed practices.

They continue to evaluate their programs so that they and other school districts can learn from the Oakland experience. For all of this, we are grateful.

The story does not end here, however. I invite you to continue the journey with me as we explore what creating restorative schools looks like and what it inspires for K12 schooling and education as a whole.

CHAPTER 11

Mapping the Shift to a Restorative School

Throughout my research and study, I worked toward developing a list of issues or actions that I believe would be helpful for schools and community members to consider when they decide to create a restorative school.

Building a Restorative Community Base

1. Develop an RJE Community Base

A restorative school starts with visionary individuals who slowly form a community. Restorative justice has endless entry points, so whoever, why-ever, and however people come to the work, a restorative justice in education (RJE) community emerges. The first recommendation is that these people find each other and self-develop into a community that can provide a base of support for restorative learning and change. Holding Circles with a meal before or after is one way to both build community and ground a core group in the Circle philosophy and process. Spending time together in a Circle training allows people to be together in an egalitarian, respectful, listening, trustful, and safe way. Enrolling as a group in online or face-to-face restorative justice courses or reading books, such as this one, also provides a foundation in restorative justice (RJ) theory and research that can inform a community's work and decisions. When people step out of their roles, form bonds of mutual understanding and care, and embrace a relationship-centered approach to educating, they lay the groundwork for creating a restorative school.

The more people learn about and experience restorative practices together, the more they can help a school implement RJE with fidelity. As implementation science shows us, the exploration stage is where a newly formed RJ community starts: learning, planning, and building a strong foundation for advocacy and eventually implementing RJE. Since creating a restorative school is not about applying a new technique within an existing system but rather involves whole-school change, a growing restorative community provides a safe place for people to work out the problems that inevitably arise. The community also carries the vision forward for how a school can move toward practicing RJE in a fuller, more complete way. The community cultivates a pool of people who can mentor teachers and perhaps offer trainings as well as build support in the surrounding communities. Such a community can also provide stability amid changes in personnel.

Many books and online resources are available on RJ; however, face-to-face training can be more difficult to come by. I recommend joining the National Association of Community and Restorative Justice (www.nacrj.org) and also searching the Internet for training opportunities near you. The Living Justice Press website maintains a list of trainers in each state and internationally, but given how fast RJE is growing, no list will ever be exhaustive or completely up-to-date.

■ 2. Build Relationships with Local Leaders

As a school's or district's RJE community grows, the group can reach out to decision makers in school and government institutions. Advocacy is essential, since funding and policy are at stake. Again, this involves educating people about RJE and inviting them into the movement. The wider the net of support for bringing restorative practices into schools, the better. School board members, district superintendents, and principals need a deep understanding of RJE, and this comes from actually sitting in Circle. Cultivating the support of those at upper levels takes time; we cannot expect those who have supported and enforced zero tolerance discipline policies to suddenly reverse course. The paradigm shift happens the more people personally experience the Circle's power—the "magic" of a space where people can be who they are, listen and speak from their hearts, and develop understanding, empathy, and care for each other.

Local educational policy makers also need to know that the RJ community will stand with them through the messiness of change. School leaders need the steadiness of support that comes from being in relationship with the RJE community. Otherwise, they might default to the safety zone of being "tough on crime" and no longer back RJE. Knowing the arguments against RJE, we have to educate decision makers with counterarguments, so they understand what RJE requires to be effective.

The Oakland Unified School District (OUSD) did not ignore its district officials. Although it took time, OUSD school board members eventually sat in Circle with RJ program staff. In May 2015, the school board and the superintendent sat in a student-led community building Circle. Even the newly elected mayor of Oakland sat in Circle! We have to make it safe for leaders to change, and this safety comes through relationships.

For Schools and Districts Making the Shift

Schools and school districts, of course, hold great power to change how we do school. Here are some ideas on how to move our school and neighborhood communities in a restorative direction and create restorative schools. This list is not in order of importance; each recommendation deserves equal consideration.

▨ 3. Create a Structure of Support for RJE

Schools do not and cannot operate in a vacuum. Restorative schools need support not only from the community but also from district and state policy makers, since RJE requires policy changes, funding, resources, and organizational change. The state of Minnesota and the OUSD have such structures in place. Because change happens in a circular pattern as schools flow through various stages of implementation, these structures ensure that RJE is sustainable. An RJE structure like the one in figure 18 provides the long-term support needed for schools to completely transform from being punitive to restorative.

▨ 4. Develop a Strategic Implementation Plan

The RJ community base must be smart, diligent, and strategic. We need to approach systems reform by working with school district officials to develop a strategic plan. Such a plan would evolve as schools move from the "Exploration" stage into the "Installation" stage (see the introduction). An RJE strategic plan supports sustainability—as personnel come and go, the strategic plan offers a way to understand the changes under way. People can see what needs to be done as well as the resources allocated to keep the momentum going and to make it work. A strategic plan also helps different segments of the school community be on the same page with the RJE work—recognizing its stages and how to meet its challenges.

Research is essential to strategic planning: research into the strategic planning process itself and research into how other schools are implementing RJE. While strategic planning

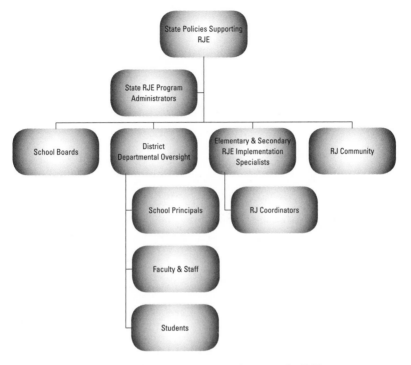

Figure 18. Create a structure of support for RJE

processes have familiar components—such as vision, mission, objectives, challenges, outcomes, evaluations, and funding— restorative approaches to planning also incorporate restorative values. The value of inclusivity, for example, encourages those engaged in planning to make sure all segments of the school community are represented in the process. By being inclusive and hence more democratic, the strategic planning group ensures greater buy-in of the RJE plan that emerges.

Those planning to create a restorative school can learn from the experiences of other restorative schools. The recommendations in this book, based on OUSD's experiences, can offer a foundation for developing a strategic RJE plan. A number of other schools and districts have put their experiences into guides that can be helpful as well.[1] The four stages of restorative implementation, described in the introduction, also give a practical frame for RJE strategic planning. Finally, educational consultants can often provide technical help and facilitate the process of developing a strategic plan.

5. Preparation: Assess the School Ecology for Trust and Listening

Within a district, implementing RJE begins with helping schools prepare for the change, and that means nurturing positive relationships within the school. As other studies affirm as well, trust and being heard are vital components for creating a positive relational ecology.[2] Schools build trust when they provide a way for people to speak and listen to each other— openly, respectfully, and safely. Circles are designed to hold such a space.

Schools may want to assess their levels of trust and listening before embracing restorative practices as a school-wide reform. An initial survey or other kind of assessment, like a readiness checklist, provides a baseline. It helps a school determine if its relational ecology is healthy enough to support change. The same survey or assessment can be used later to evaluate improvements that result from using SWRPs.

Schools with low levels of trust and listening can prepare by strengthening their relationships. A school community may be stuck in unhealthy and dysfunctional patterns that, unaddressed, would sabotage their efforts to change. They may need to do internal healing and restructuring before taking on a major organizational-change effort. School faculties that already have high levels of trust may also choose to spend time nurturing relationships before implementing school-wide restorative practices.

6. Examine Existing Discipline Policies and End Suspensions, Especially for Defiance/Willful Defiance

Restorative schools aim to end student suspensions altogether. An essential first step is to end suspensions for defiance or willful defiance.

African American male students have been particularly affected by zero tolerance discipline policies and are suspended for defiance or willful defiance more than any other group of students.[3] To rectify this wrong, school districts must remove defiance as a suspendable offense, as the OUSD and several other districts across the country have done.

In this step, leadership teams composed of administrators, teachers, *and* students examine the school's discipline policy to better understand who is being punished, for what reasons, and how.

By examining their school's discipline data, a leadership team may discover that, like many schools, theirs is disproportionately disciplining certain groups of students and may conclude that this is not acceptable. Staff members may need to discuss their philosophies and attitudes toward each other and students, and they may also seek professional development in cultural competence and awareness of racial biases, White privilege, and microaggressions.

7. Recruit and Hire Relational-Oriented Principals and Staff

School districts already committed to RJE must choose carefully whom they hire and retain as principals as well as staff. Administrators who hold traditional, authoritative, and punitive beliefs and who do not share power with their staff can derail the implementation of school-wide restorative practices (SWRPs). Before placing a principal or other administrator in a restorative school, the district should determine whether the candidate has a relational-based, positive orientation. Administrators without prior exposure to RJE should be well trained in SWRPs and RJE theory before first working in a restorative school. Those who hired the principal might also monitor how things are going through surveys, since it is so easy to slip into old habits under stress or when problems arise. Principals need feedback and support to succeed in making such a major paradigm shift in how they run a school.

Schools that are not practicing RJE but want to do so need a leader who is open to restorative values and processes and who will support implementation and training. Proper recruitment, hiring, and placement of principals is a critical component of district-wide, scale-up efforts. The principals must then recruit and hire teachers who are already aligned with restorative values and who display a relational-based, positive orientation toward students.

■ 8. Make Necessary Organizational Changes

When a school decides to implement SWRPs, some things need to change in how the school operates. The school's schedule needs to make time for staff training and development and for consistent, protected community building Circles. Other things (such as homework and progress reports) should not infringe on dedicated Circle time. Elementary schools can start and end their days in Circle. High schools may have a greater challenge creating dedicated time for community building Circles, but it can be done.

Teachers' schedules also need time and space for Circles or conferences when a harm has occurred, so that relationships, not referrals, are restored. Schools can use advisory time for all of these purposes. RJ facilitators and other administrators and support staff can help teachers with the Circle to repair harm by preparing for the Circle, contacting all stakeholders, setting the place and time, and keeping the Circle. Other teachers could support their peers by allowing students not involved in the harm-repairing Circle to attend community building Circles in other rooms. In this way, two kinds of Circles, to repair harm and to build community, can occur at the same time within the normal schedule.

Additionally, schools need to create an RJ room where students can go for support. Any school that currently has an in-school suspension room has an RJ room waiting to happen.

9. Address Leader and Teacher Turnover

Despite the most careful attention to personnel, turnover remains a challenge for schools, including restorative ones, and this can affect a school's relational ecology. Trusting relationships that took time to develop suddenly disappear, and relationship building has to start all over again.

Some districts place principals in high-needs schools and then remove them when they have not turned the school around within the first two years. Principals need time to make changes in schools. Research on whole-school reform indicates that most initiatives take at least three, and more like five, years to take hold and succeed.

Knowing that personnel turnover is inevitable, restorative schools can put in place RJE stabilizers: regular training programs for staff and students, regular staff Circles, regular Circles with parents and the community, and regular Circles with and among students. The RJ community base can also provide a stabilizing presence. The deeper and wider the school community's roots in RJE, the less likely that changes in personnel will topple the tree.

10. Establish, Publish, Teach, and Revisit RJE Procedures

When schools adopt RJE, they need to create procedures for teachers, administrators, and RJ facilitators to follow not only when discipline issues arise but even more as school-wide, daily practices. These procedures can be framed in simple and clear steps. Core team members, RJ facilitators, and administrators should work together with the RJE community base to create procedures unique to their school. While some procedures might be the same for all the schools in a district, individual schools may also have their own procedures designed to meet the needs of their students and staff. District administrators should allow such flexibility.

Along with developing procedures comes the need for teachers and staff to follow them. If they do not, then it is time to devote a Circle to the issue.

The key is to regularly revisit the philosophy and principles of RJE, so that everyone—staff and students—understands what they are doing and why. Tier 1 restorative practices lay the foundation in relationship building. Without this foundation, tiers 2 and 3 practices are much less effective and may not "work" at all.

11. Make the School Campus Warm and Welcoming

Attending to people's needs and to the quality of shared spaces is important to RJE, as this expresses respect and positive appreciation for those who come into those spaces. Circle keepers, for example, are mindful of participants' needs in the physical space. So it is for restorative schools. Tending to the physical environment and making it positive and welcoming are very important to creating a restorative school. Researchers in the United Kingdom, for example, found that the layout of classrooms, access to natural lighting, eliminating noise, good air quality, and other environmental factors contribute to student learning.[4]

School districts should also strongly consider moving away from using criminal justice technologies in the school environment. They should disarm school police, train school resource officers in de-escalation techniques and restorative practices, and reorganize spaces within the schools and classrooms to allow for greater collaboration and community building. This shift will increase student and teacher safety, because strong relationships within schools secure safety most effectively. Creating a peaceful and welcoming school environment reduces tension across the entire school ecology. It fosters trust and a sense of community both within and beyond its walls.

Allowing students downtime, for example, in fifteen-minute breaks outside throughout their school day, can do wonders for building community and decreasing tension and stress. This is another way to respect everyone's physical, emotional, mental, and social needs.

12. Treat Staff Well and Respectfully: Hold Regular Staff Circles

How a school treats staff translates directly into how the staff treats students. One of the best ways to treat staff respectfully is to provide time and space for staff to listen to each other. Regular staff Circles are essential at all phases of creating and then running a restorative school. Staff Circles help adults learn RJE: they learn the Circle process and become comfortable with it; they address problems as a school community; they learn how to function collaboratively and by consensus; they develop buy-in for RJE; and they strengthen a culture of mutual listening, care, and support. The more staff interact according to Circle values and principles, the more positive the school's relational ecology will be, and the more naturally students will respond in kind and embrace restorative processes.

Kathy Evans, Dorothy Vaandering, Belinda Hopkins, Nancy Riestenberg, Kay Pranis, Rita Renjitham Alfred, Stephanie Autumn, Carolyn Boyes-Watson, Fania Davis, and others in the RJE field cannot emphasize the importance of this enough. One of the biggest lessons I learned from studying these two schools is that when the staff are inconsistent in embracing and using SWRPs, so are the students. Transformation begins with the adults—and not as a onetime act either. For the school culture to change, the adults must continue developing their practice of SWRPs in the classroom and across all school environments. Then restorative change gets real all around.

Implementation science and organizational change back up what RJE thinkers and practitioners have found; namely, how important it is for adults to work together to create a shared vision and to bring that shared vision to life. Students are powerful change agents, and they respond positively to adults who show they care enough to work toward making their schooling positive. When the adults do their part, the students support them by doing theirs.

■ 13. Implement with Respect: Voluntary Participation

This raises a fundamental issue: voluntary participation is core to Circle philosophy. Yet this principle is hard to practice in schools, especially when the goal is school-wide restorative practices.

The more that the adults who are on board with RJE engage students in restorative ways, the more they build positive, non-confrontational relationships with students, and the more students become open to restorative practices. The relational dynamic moves from adversarial to cooperative. As teachers observe the shift, they may see the value of restorative practices as a different way of being together, not merely as something to do when things go wrong. The Circle principle of voluntary participation advises that we hold spaces for teachers not to be on board. However, again, we also need to address their reasons and figure out how to meet all the needs, including the students' needs to be in Circle.

Mandating educators to engage restorative practices disrespects their autonomy and hence is not consistent with a restorative philosophy. Nor does it work.

When schools take a year to prepare for RJE by building relationships among staff and developing a deep understanding of RJE and restorative practices before teachers are invited to practice them in their classes, many of the issues that would otherwise block teacher buy-in are resolved.

Often, teachers who are hesitant or skeptical about embracing RJE just need evidence that it works. When a group of teachers really gives their all to implementing SWRPs, other teachers watching from a safe distance will start seeing changes.

When a teacher begins noticing such changes and asking questions, the time is right to invite that person to learn more about RJE. But, again, if RJE is forced upon teachers top-down, as are so many other education mandates, relationships suffer, and authentic restorative schools will not be the outcome. Kay Pranis, Barry Stuart, and Mark Wedge, the authors of *Peacemaking Circles: From Conflict to Community*, learned from Indigenous Elders the restorative principle of respect and its call for voluntary participation in Circles and other restorative processes. "Johnny Johns, an Elder of the Carcross/Tagish First Nation, said, 'Respect is the main thing. If you don't have that, you don't have anything.'"[5]

■ 14. Provide Adequate and Ongoing Training for All School Personnel

For RJE to be successful, all staff must receive both initial and ongoing training. This means training every member of a school's staff, including custodians, cafeteria workers, teachers' assistants, and school resource officers. While doing so requires a commitment of time and money, this investment is essential to turn the school into an RJE community. These resources must be included in the initial strategic plan, allocated at the outset, and remain an essential part of a school's budget. Districts do well to develop training plans and schedules that allow all members of a school community, including parents and volunteer community members, to have the training they want and need. Districts can develop curricula for staff to gain confidence and competency with restorative practices on all three tiers, from school-wide daily practices (tier 1) to focused group practices (tier 2) to reparative interventions (tier 3).

Train staff to practice RJE together first. Again, until staff practice RJE with each other on a regular basis, students are not likely to embrace restorative practices.[6] Experienced trainers recommend that, before a school takes SWRPs to the students, the entire staff be trained and practicing them with each other. That means, for example, that staff hold faculty meetings in Circle; that department members work out conflicts with each other in Circle or via a conference; that staff and administrators reach decisions by consensus; and that schools conduct parent-teacher conferences using restorative language and processes.

New teachers. All new teachers need to be trained in RJE before their first day of school. This is a must. It may mean that new teachers' pre-service schedules differ from those of veteran teachers. Learning about RJE is essential if they are to teach at a school already practicing SWRPs. We know that most new teachers learn nothing about RJE in their teacher preparation programs—step 25 recommends changing this.

Tier 1 training for all staff. All members of the school community need training in tier 1 restorative practices: asking restorative questions, holding a Circle, and redirecting student behavior in ways that do not punish or stigmatize. Training helps people understand RJE and learn how to practice SWRPs in their own sphere. In turn, everyone's capacity to care for students and to make a difference in their lives is recognized and valued.

Teachers already comfortable with using SWRPs in their classrooms can share with other teachers how they have successfully integrated Circles and other restorative pedagogies into their classes. Modeling and sharing can also occur in district-level professional development workshops. Video-recording teachers as they use restorative pedagogies in their classrooms and putting them on YouTube and school-district websites are other ways to help teachers see what restorative practices look like.

Circle (tier 1) and peer mediation (tier 2) training for students. Some schools include students in Circle trainings. Many students take to Circles naturally. In schools with established Circle practices, students often serve as Circle keepers. Other schools train students in peer mediation as well: peer mediators facilitate restorative processes when a conflict or problem arises between students. In both instances, the more students take lead roles in restorative practices, the more the student body internalizes the restorative philosophy and practice.

Tiers 2 and 3 training for select staff. Teachers, counselors, support staff, and core team members who have received tier 1 training may desire more advanced training. I recommend that schools survey their staff, as I did in this study, to assess their confidence in using various RPs and other relational-based practices. Schools can then tailor the training program accordingly. Districts can explore ways to combine training in RJE with professional development in culturally competent teaching, critical discourse, social and emotional learning (SEL), and Positive Behavioral Interventions and Support (PBIS) in order to streamline training. The idea is to implement a single culture of relational-based, student-centered teaching across the district. The coordinated training should show how each initiative complements the others, how the skills and concepts associated with each program or initiative are interrelated, and how the core values of restorative justice tie all of the initiatives together.

Because SEL, PBIS, and SWRPs all operate within the three-tiered framework, have shared values, and complement each other, some school districts have begun to implement them alongside each other. The state of Minnesota, the state of Illinois, the OUSD, and the Santa Clara Unified School District, to name a few, have developed training curricula that incorporate multiple initiatives and programs—each in their own way and to varying degrees. This practice needs further research, but combining various approaches to whole-school culture change shows promise. Randy Compton, lead trainer of Restorative Solutions in Colorado, writes, "Restorative practices can enhance PBIS and SEL programs. In fact, many PBIS and SEL programs have certain gaps that can be filled by restorative practices when it comes to dealing with harm and wrongdoing."[7] Nancy Riestenberg and Debra Price-Ellingstad, both with the Minnesota Department of Education, wrote that "not one approach can provide everything a school needs for a safe climate"; rather, schools should "consider mental health services, social and emotional learning, and equity efforts through the tiered levels of support, in addition to PBIS and restorative practices."[8]

Integrate trauma-informed practices. A multipronged approach may better support students dealing with trauma. Barbara Oehlberg, a child development and educational specialist and child trauma consultant, states, "Becoming a trauma informed school goes beyond identifying and referring students with traumatic stress to outside services.... [It] requires [that] educators examine the cross-disciplinary research of neuro-biological research and traumatology."[9] In other words, we need to understand trauma better by keeping up with the research on what trauma does to the brain.

Because many students have experienced trauma, teachers often inadvertently trigger a child, and the child then has a trauma-related response. Knowing this, in 2015 the OUSD Behavioral Health unit began offering the following:

> a trauma informed care work-group that identifies best practices and offers PD [professional development] at school sites at the request of leadership or teachers. This PD occurs on-site with all staff and focuses on brain science, prevention and de-escalation strategies to develop trauma informed classrooms and conditions for learning.[10]

Circles are, in fact, a trauma-sensitive practice. They naturally instill the social and emotional competencies that youth with post-traumatic stress disorder (PTSD) or complex post-traumatic stress disorder (C-PTSD) need to recover. In Circles, traumatized youth bond with peers who are also dealing with trauma in ways they simply cannot do with an adult, expert, or therapist. In many ways, Circles offer traumatized youth a space where healing experiences can happen and strong, transformative bonds can form.

15. Clearly Define the Roles and Responsibilities of RJ Coordinators/Facilitators

To build capacity, implement SWRPs with fidelity, and improve outcomes, restorative schools should clearly define the RJ coordinator's job, while remaining flexible enough to adapt the job to the needs of the school. The RJ coordinator prepares for Circles and conferences that involve all stakeholders, including teachers, parents, and community members. Organizing and preparing for Circles takes time. Given the scope of an RJ coordinator's responsibilities, the size of the school, and the needs of students, one or two RJ coordinators per school may not be sufficient. Schools should carefully assess the needs of the staff and students and then budget accordingly.

In addition to clearly defining the RJ coordinators' job, restorative districts ensure that training and implementation at the school level are done with fidelity and aligned with the district's goals. The point is not to find out what people are doing wrong but rather to support schools in improving their restorative practices. Greater fidelity and more complete use of restorative practices yield greater effectiveness.

To continually improve implementation and widen the practice, schools and/or school districts can establish a training and learning community schedule that each RJ coordinator can follow, knowing that the support in resources and scheduling is in place. Ultimately, teachers' skills evolve through ongoing training and by learning in context. As more teachers become confident in using restorative practices, the RJ coordinator can focus more on staff training and handling tier 2 and tier 3 restorative processes.

16. Make Learning Meaningful: Relational Pedagogies Based on Respect

When students connect with what they are studying, they engage, become passionate about learning, and take the lead in their own academic development. Further, when students learn together, learning is more fun. Why not engage these natural human impulses to connect, both to meaningful learning and to other students, as assets for learning? Brené Brown's research consistently shows that humans have a strong need to feel they belong.[11] Why not teach in ways that foster belonging in the classroom?

Relational pedagogies do precisely that. Creating restorative schools includes restoring the joy and passion in learning by putting relationships back into the process. Restorative schools build on how we are built: they use relationships to help students learn. Because RJE is all about relationships and nurturing them, it enhances and protects this essential environment for learning.

The more students learn from and with each other, the more meaningful their learning experiences are likely to be. RJE goes beyond a disciplinary response to the core of how schools function as places of learning. For meaningful learning to flourish, respecting students is just as important as respecting teachers. Relational pedagogies turn classrooms into respectful, positive spaces where students want to learn and can engage enthusiastically with learning. (Recommendation 27 talks more about relational pedagogies and how teacher education programs can teach them.)

17. Respond to Repeated Interventions and Racial Tension by Intensifying Tier 1 Practices

Some students receive repeated tier 3 interventions yet continue acting in ways that harm others and interfere with their learning. But relying on interventions at the tier 3 level is a sign for the school to expand its work on tier 1 SWRPs and to increase fidelity in its RJE practices. The more Circles become a mainstay of school life, particularly in the classroom, the more adults and youth continually strengthen their relationships. Students who are connected to their peers and teachers tend to commit harm much less than students who feel disconnected.

When a school gives a student or group of students repeated interventions with little positive effect, the temptation is to blame the student or to start deficit profiling a group of students. In this study, we saw this happen to African American male students. This response is not helpful and is a misdirect because it is just plain wrong. Worse, it leads to treating students of color unjustly, harming them for life. Without question, RJE *does* work for Black male students. I've not only seen it, but I have also met many Black students, male and female, who are peer mediators, RJ facilitators, and RJE advocates. These young people often take leadership roles in their schools and contribute enormously to changing the school culture and helping other students. Videos about RJE on YouTube provide ample evidence: time and time again, Black youth are *leading* the transformational efforts in their schools and communities.

Instead of blaming students or making them the problem, then, we, the adults, need to reflect on our own biases and practices: How are *we* being called to change? What are *we* doing? And how can our school practice RJE more fully—consistently, with fidelity and continuity, and compassionately?

Self-reflection, critical self-awareness, and self-assessment are essential to a school's progress in implementing RJE. Repeated interventions give a school critical feedback precisely so the school can improve its restorative practices and meet its responsibilities to high-needs students.

That said, RJE cannot "fix" overnight the structural and institutional racism in US society that students of color face every day. The hope is that intense restorative work at the tier 1 level can bring systemic change school by school, generation by generation. In the meantime, RJE can help students of color today manage the added weight they carry by building relationships of care and understanding, protection from racial attacks, and support. With RJE's positive and race-aware relational ecology to support them, students of color can go to school, be safe from being racially targeted, stay in school, find meaning in their studies and relationships, blossom, and graduate.

18. Follow Tier 3 Interventions with Tier 2 Reintegration Processes

In a tier 3 conference or Circle for a student, the consensus may be that human services should be called in. Human services may be one of many remedies that members of a Circle or conference might deem useful. The RJE framework allows schools to stay focused on the supportive net of relationships, and this relational context tends to make human services or other remedies more effective. The RJE Circle or conference can help monitor the services, troubleshoot and problem solve, and find other options as needed. Human and social services do not displace RJE; they offer additional support to meet students' needs—and perhaps the needs of students' families as well. RJE's net of caring, trusting relationships stays in place as the constant in supporting students and families.

When students have messed up and then worked through

whatever happened in a restorative way, their efforts need to be acknowledged as valuable to the class and school community. They need to be welcomed back and appreciated. If they have missed classes, teachers and students need an opportunity to say they missed them and are happy to see them again—that the class learns better when they are present and that what they have to offer is valuable. Reintegration processes clear away any stigma the students might be carrying and conveys that they have every right to be in the class and the school—that messing up never means they no longer belong. Belonging in the class and school is a constant, and all the students need to know that. Powerful for building relationships and community, reintegration processes create the time and space for students to be assured that just because they might have done a bad thing, they are not a bad person. Brené Brown's research shows us how this can move students out of the painful, paralyzing place of shame to feeling guilt instead. In the restorative framework, "guilt" translates into accountability, where students have an obligation and an opportunity to make things right again.

19. Celebrate RJE Achievements and Milestones—and Publicize Them!

In community-oriented societies, celebrations play a critical role. In whatever size and form they take, celebrations create time and space to reflect on where we have been and where we are going and to appreciate the collective journey. Celebrations are also a time to honor community members for their achievements and contributions to a shared goal. Creating a restorative school is seldom a smooth transition. Celebrations bring joy to the work and are a time to revisit values and priorities. Celebrations are not a frill; they more than carry their weight in creating a positive school community and affirming the vision, values, and principles of restorative practices.

Celebrating milestones and achievements is important not only to those doing the daily work of creating a restorative school, but also to the community at large and to policy makers, who need to know about good things happening in schools. Too many times, we hear only about incidents of school violence. We can shift the media's and the public's perception of schools by publicizing when *peace* happens in schools. Write press releases. Invite the media, policy makers, neighbors, parents, and community members to your celebrations. Let everyone see and experience your restorative schools, your work in progress, your pride and joy. If we truly seek to shift the paradigm from punitive to restorative, people in the schools and outside of the schools need to see what RJE looks like. And that is worth celebrating!

20. Tell the School's Story: Document RJE Progress

Telling our stories—particularly in Circles—is central to restorative practices. In the journey to create a restorative school, sharing stories also serves as an evaluation process, albeit a more experiential, relational, open-ended, and community building one. It holds a space for those involved—the members of the school community themselves—to decide what issues need to be raised, what questions asked, and what experiences stand out as instructive.

Telling the story of a school's journey to create a restorative school brings many benefits. When the telling process is inclusive, this in itself is community building. People feel that what they have to say about the school matters. Documenting the school's story can also help with turnovers in personnel. Newcomers learn how members of the school community think and feel about the school's commitment to restorative practices. Storytelling also reveals the actual practices—essential for assessing RJE fidelity and seeing how to practice RJE more fully. If people are struggling with the shift, giving them an opportunity to tell their story facilitates dialogue about why and what might be needed. If the school is willing to document and share these stories, whether informally in YouTube videos or in more formal assessment reports, the experiences can be instructive for other schools as well as those doing research in RJE. Telling the school's story is a narrative form of feedback and assessment.

An RJE consultant or researcher can help the school develop a plan for documenting and sharing the school's story, as well as address issues of confidentiality. Feedback and self-awareness raise the RJE game: they increase a school's capacity to implement RJE with intention and fidelity.

21. Research and Evaluation: Seeking Meaningful Feedback on a School's RJE Progress

Feedback through evaluation is critical to human learning and development. When moving through the stages of implementation, data gathered by core team members can provide such feedback. Restorative schools use many methods of evaluation to gain the feedback they need to make course adjustments, and plans for evaluating RJE should be built into the implementation schedule at the outset. The evaluation approach might begin with asking: How can a school assess its relational ecology? This is the starting point, because, as a school adopts SWRPs, its relational ecology can either facilitate or hinder positive change.

Here again, professional evaluators and researchers can assist schools in designing and implementing RJE evaluations. Typical evaluations focus on outcomes that can be measured quantitatively: suspensions, expulsions, fights, numbers of harm-repairing Circles, dropout rates and graduation rates, and so on. Mixed methods research incorporates both quantitative and qualitative information, so that the nuances of change are captured through storytelling. The experiences of people in the schools may support or challenge the quantitative data findings.

In *Imagining Success for a Restorative Approach to Justice: Implications for Measurement and Evaluation,* Jennifer Llewellyn, a law professor at Dalhousie University in Canada, and her colleagues propose that we look beyond traditional research designs that track only outcomes, such as decreased suspensions or fighting, and instead focus on what restorative justice is all about at its core. Indeed, we learn so much more of value to the RJE work by looking at relationships. They write:

> Proponents and opponents of restorative justice claim
> to know what it is and make varying assertions about
> whether it "works." Whether restorative justice is "success-
> ful," or not, is a complex question. To answer this question,
> one must think carefully about what it is one is studying,
> about what one wishes to achieve, and whether or how it
> might be measured, about what might serve as indicators
> of success, and then about ways to collect data.[12]

These scholars call us to ground our evaluations in *relational theory,* because relationships lie at the very heart of RJE's "success." How much time and energies are we putting into restorative practices that build relationships? How are relationships changing? And how are a school's systems changing because relationships and the school's priority on them have changed? Pondering these questions gives a school a meaningful progress report on creating a restorative school. Doing so acts as a kind of formative assessment, which is designed to answer the question "How are we doing?" This is an enormous paradigm shift for those of us trained to think only in terms of traditional evaluation methods and outcomes.

Is it important that we track disproportional disciplining? Suspensions? Fights? Graduation and dropout rates? Yes. All of these factors are important. But Llewellyn takes us behind the numbers. She and her colleagues invite us to seek a better understanding of how deeper, more meaningful connections help students and staff: they reduce challenging behavior and improve learning for students, and they help staff address their own racial biases and need for greater cultural competencies.

When I was still young in my graduate program, I chatted with Nancy Riestenberg about researching RJE. She said, "Martha, imagine if you just went into a school and counted smiles." I thought to myself, "Nancy, you have lost your mind. Nobody counts smiles. That would just be dumb. Geez." Yet as I spent time studying the relational ecologies of Grant and Davis, I started to notice that an awful lot of people were smiling. I noticed this because I had taught in schools where I saw nothing but long faces all day long. And I remember standing in a hallway thinking, "Gosh darn it, Nancy. You were right. I should be counting smiles."

Actions for Policy Makers

State and federal policy makers have a role to play in bringing RJE to schools as well. Policy decisions at these levels should be informed by research-based evidence, critical thinking, and stakeholder wisdom, all of which support these two recommendations.

22. Repeal Zero Tolerance Discipline Policies

Many states and school districts have backed away from zero tolerance discipline policies, replacing them with positive discipline strategies, such as PBIS and RJE. Our challenge remains to educate more legislators and the public on RJE, so that, where they still exist, zero tolerance and other damaging policies are repealed. This cannot happen soon enough.

23. Fund RJE

When policy makers consider how to improve schools, they need to understand that a school's ability to change depends on its having a positive relational ecology: trust; a listening and relational-based, student-centered culture; and cultural competence. The US Department of Education (DOE) and US Department of Justice (DOJ) have taken steps in this direction. Positive as the school discipline guidance package is, though, the federal government has yet to provide school districts with adequate funding to make the transition from punitive to restorative schools.

Funding is critical. As schools and districts develop strategic plans with budgets that detail what it involves to create a restorative school, decision makers can work to provide the funding. At the same time, the RJE community can engage the local media to educate the public, so that they urge their legislators and other decision makers to support RJE with adequate funding. Part of this public education can document the human and social costs of the punitive model. Suspensions and expulsions send many youth—disproportionately youth of color—straight into prison, the repercussions of which are devastating for life and affect all of us. College is less expensive than prisons, and prison terms are often for more than four years. More than losing money, though, society loses the creativity, energies, knowledge, and gifts of those sucked into the school-to-prison pipeline. RJE is not only a bargain; it blazes a path to putting school-perpetrated wrongs right.

Putting RJE into Teacher and Leader Education Programs

▨ 24. Include RJE in Teacher and Leader Preparation Programs

RJE's call for organizational and paradigm change sends a message to teacher and leader education programs as well. The teachers in this study reported that their training programs, whether Teach for America or colleges of education, did not prepare them to work in a school practicing RJE. New educators need to understand how relational pedagogies and healthier school cultures increase academic achievement and create safer schools. Their pre-service education curricula can be taught in ways that promote relationships. By modeling relational pedagogies, teacher education programs can give teachers-to-be the experience of relationship-based learning that they will take with them into their classrooms, especially if they teach in a restorative school. At the very least, education programs can show how SEL competencies, which students and staff practice naturally in the Circle process, are instilled and nurtured through restorative practices.

RJE is currently a niche area and a nascent field. Because of its newness, courses in it are scarce, yet teachers and school leaders can still learn from books, literature, and online videos. They can also take online courses and attend trainings and workshops. Education programs interested in developing RJE courses must turn to those doing the RJE work to help them integrate RJE into their curricula. Education programs in regions where RJE is fast taking root should be the first to make this curricular change. Moreover, teacher and leader education programs can create partnerships with restorative districts, so that future teachers and leaders can intern or complete their field experiences in restorative schools. Education programs in California, New York, Massachusetts, Colorado,

Connecticut, Oregon, Maryland, Minnesota, Virginia, Wisconsin, Pennsylvania, Georgia, Kentucky, and Texas should all be preparing teachers and leaders to work in the growing number of restorative schools and districts nearby.

Education programs need to get up to RJE speed quickly. Changes in the field have outpaced changes in how teachers and school leaders are taught. Schools are quickly moving away from a classroom management model based on social control to an ecological model based on social engagement. New teachers and leaders need, at the very least, a fundamental knowledge of restorative justice theory, values, and practices. Given the large number of school districts already transitioning to RJE, teachers and leaders need to start their jobs equipped to work in restorative schools.

RJE in teacher education is a brand-new field, and only a few universities in the United States and Canada are on board. Eastern Mennonite University (EMU) was the first US university to integrate RJE into its curricula. The RJE track at EMU provides a model that other education programs can use. EMU also has a graduate program in RJE for educators. Simon Fraser University's Continuing Studies Department offers an online certificate program in Restorative Justice to adult learners world-wide and includes a course on RJ in Educational Settings. As more universities develop courses in RJE, it will be easier for other universities to envision how they can incorporate RJE into teacher and leader preparation programs.

RJE curricula in higher education should also help teachers and leaders examine White privilege and power; critical awareness about race needs to be an ongoing practice for those working in schools. They should also learn to critically examine how old-style schooling—behavioristic, authoritarian, and high-control classroom-management strategies—perpetuate power abuses and privilege and continue to marginalize or alienate students of color and other minority groups. Dorothy

Vaandering, Brenda Morrison, and Kathy Evans are teacher educators who have shown that RJE is firmly grounded in educational theories, including but not limited to critical theory and critical race theory.

Dorothy Vaandering teaches RJE courses at Memorial University in Newfoundland, as does Brenda Morrison at Simon Fraser University in British Columbia. I teach RJE courses in the Continuing Studies department at Simon Fraser, and educators and youth workers in schools make up almost 25 percent of my online students. But compared to the hundreds of schools across the country that are using SWRPs, the teacher-education programs that include RJE are few and far between. The sooner we close this gap, the sooner the supply of teachers and leaders competent in restorative practices can meet the demand.

25. Recruit Future Teachers/Leaders with a Relational-Based Orientation

Not every pre-service or graduate-level teacher or school leader naturally embodies a relational-based, positive orientation. Given the ingrained habit of isolating "problem" individuals and punishing them, the notions of building community and responding to harm restoratively may not come easily to everyone. This is not how most of us have been raised. However, these qualities are important for teachers and leaders to bring to restorative schools, and they can be cultivated.

In addition to building a robust RJE curriculum, education programs can also take steps to produce teachers and leaders whose mind-set fits with a restorative school. First, admission processes can screen applicants to determine if they have a relational-based, positive orientation. How might they respond to a student discipline scenario? What is their philosophy on discipline? Second, RJE is grounded in both values—

caring, respect, honesty, openness, and so on—and social and emotional learning theory. Given RJE's rootedness in what is essential to human beings and human societies, even teachers and leaders who may not have had a relational-based, positive orientation can still resonate with the approach and learn how to bring their core values and emotional literacies into their work in schools.

26. Increase Teacher/Leader Diversity and Capacity for Teaching in Diverse Schools

RJE thinking frames a school as a community where students feel really safe and accepted; who the adults are in the school contribute greatly to this. Experience matters. Students are likely to feel safe around teachers who look like them and who have had experiences similar to theirs. Given a national teaching force that is more than 80 percent White and given a society built largely on racially unjust mind-sets, institutions, and structures, students of color are the ones most likely not to feel safe or accepted in school. They are the ones most in need of teachers who look like them. Teachers and leaders of color know through personal experiences and family histories what students of color face in school and society. African American male youth in particular need to see people who look like them—Black male teachers and leaders. As of 2016, though, only 2 percent of US teachers were Black men.[13]

Many top teacher education programs are working to correct this. Linda Darling-Hammond's landmark book *Powerful Teacher Education: Lessons from Exemplary Programs* gives many examples of teacher education programs that purposely recruit students who look like the students in the schools where they will most likely teach. These programs form relationships with local school districts and teachers to partner pre-service teachers with expert teachers in diverse classrooms. By focusing on diversity, social justice, and equitable teaching methods, curricula in these education programs prepare graduates to be successful teachers in racially and ethnically diverse schools.

27. Focus on Relational and Restorative Instructional Strategies

Since teacher education programs help teachers learn how to teach, these programs need to teach the relational pedagogies that restorative schools use. Relational pedagogies are easily incorporated into daily instruction, no matter the subject or content. We know that students' relationships with their teachers affect their learning, so restorative and relational instructional practices help teachers build trusting relationships with their students. Using relational pedagogies, teachers model and instill prosocial behaviors and promote healthy classroom relationships while they teach their lessons.

In her book *The Restorative Classroom*, Belinda Hopkins explains that relational pedagogies build on the interactions between students and teachers. What is taught (curriculum) and how it is taught (instruction) reflect a consistent approach (teaching strategy) based on developing relationships in many directions: between teachers and students, among students, and with the curriculum. Students see themselves not only in the teacher but also in their subjects. Education professors Russell Skiba and Reece Peterson state that children are developmentally incomplete and will "always require socialization, instruction, and correction to shape fundamentally egocentric behavior into interpersonal skills that make our children capable of interacting successfully."[14] Rather than having students take separate units on "character education" or "citizenship," schools incorporate relational and restorative pedagogies into their instructional practices, so that students learn social and emotional competencies alongside their class content. The approach to teaching and learning is holistic. Shared governance or democracy, for example, is not just an abstract concept; it comes alive in students' experiences in Circles.

Restorative pedagogies can be adapted to any age in any subject area. The point is that teaching is student-centered, students are empowered and engaged, and they are interacting positively with each other and their teachers as they learn. Whether they are out of their seats, working together on a project with a partner, or in Circle, they are in relationship with each other, their teacher, and the curriculum.

In Closing

Children's lives are on the line with what we do in schools, and racial justice—our capacity to function as a just society—is on the line too. Thirty years of zero tolerance policies have harmed healthy child development and done violence to communities of color, robbing families of their children and young people of their futures. Zero tolerance has made our schools not more but less safe. We now know that punishment increases shame, anger, and trauma and does not bring positive change in either students or the classroom. Police do not make schools safe; relationships do. Whereas imprisoning youth causes lifelong harm, schooling them unlocks their potential.

So, do restorative practices work? Do they work for African American students, males in particular? Of course they do: this is my wholehearted conviction. Restorative schools across the country are saving the lives of African American students every day. Beyond school walls, RJ is working in hundreds of communities in the United States and is often initiated and led by people of color who are sick and tired of the racist injustice meted out by courts and law enforcement. These people believe that RJ offers a better way because they see it work. For them, RJ is not a program but a way of life. People of all genders and ethnicities are learning about and practicing RJ in their schools, courts, workplaces, college campuses, and communities globally. I know this because I teach online courses in RJ to a diverse group of adult learners from all around the world.

Schools in Oakland are no exception. But, again, RJE must be practiced with consistency, continuity, fidelity, and compassion. White educators must look deeply at our own White privilege—as I continue to do—and unpack the racist stereotypes that manifest as conscious or unconscious biases toward students of color. Compassion and empathy toward self and others are vital, as are a deep shift in philosophy and a commitment to building a school community on authentic relationships. This means having honest conversations about hard things, including racism, privilege, institutionalized White supremacy, and the harms they cause. The load that students of color carry with them into school has been piled on over centuries. This is not to cast them as victims but to acknowledge social, economic, and historical realities. Only genuine relationships can help lift that load, so that students of color can step into their power and thrive standing strong with their peers.

We all have a stake in the RJE shift. Changing our schools and closing the school-to-prison pipeline pushes us beyond the schoolyard. Each of us, in our own sphere of influence, can educate people about restorative practices and build momentum for changing how we do school. We can urge policy makers to do what it takes to heal our schools and make schools places staff and students want to be. We can be the change-makers that our young people need and deserve. With this list of what we can do, let's get to work.

Methodology

▇ Study Design

This book grew from a multisite case study of Grant and Davis Middle Schools located in the Oakland Unified School District. To address my research questions, I used mixed methods, which integrate qualitative and quantitative data and procedures. I collected qualitative data through interviews, focus groups, open-ended survey questions, and observations. I collected quantitative data through an Internet survey as well as by transforming some qualitative data into descriptive statistics.

I gathered the perceptions of people about their experiences with implementing RJE at two middle schools in a single urban school district that contains a total of 123 schools. These two schools had been working to create a restorative school for about three years, and they were still in the early stages of implementation. I engaged people across all grade levels and subject areas to obtain a holistic picture of the schools' relational ecologies. The OUSD's restorative justice program facilitator, David Yusem, and I purposely chose the schools that met several specific criteria, and each school was in different stages of implementing RJE. The two schools had different demographics and resources.

The Research Questions Guiding the Study

After a series of conversations with David Yusem, Barb McClung (David's boss), evaluator Dr. Sonia Jain, and my dissertation advisor, Dr. Gail Burnaford, we agreed that the overall research question for this study would be twofold:

> "What is the relational ecology of urban middle schools adopting school-wide restorative practices (SWRPs), and what changes occur throughout the schools as a result of the reform implementation process?"

Here is how we elaborated on these research questions:

1. What does the relational ecology of an urban middle school that has adopted restorative practices look like?
2. What changes occur in an urban middle school that adopts restorative practices?
   2a. What changes occur at the organizational level?
   2b. What changes occur at the individual level (students, teachers, administrators)?
   2c. changes occur at the pedagogical/ instructional level?

The study was approved by my university's Institutional Review Board and the OUSD.

The Theoretical Framework

Five distinct theories informed my approach: critical theory; critical race theory (CRT); theories of change; social learning theory and social and emotional learning (SEL); and restorative justice/relational theory. This theoretical framework shaped the study's design, how I analyzed the data, and now how I have written this book. Chart AI.1 summarizes this framework, the tenets of each as it applies to the research, and the theorists who informed this theoretical framework.

Chart A1.1: The theoretical framework behind my study — and this book

THEORY	TENETS	THEORISTS
Critical Theory	Lens through which to view power and dominance in structures, institutions, curriculum, and pedagogy: believes that education is inherently political and that teaching students to become agents of social change is primary; seeks the perspectives of those on the margins of society; focuses on resisting the dominant power structure.	Freire, 2008 Morrison & Vaandering, 2012 Vaandering, 2010
Critical Race Theory (CRT)	Lens through which to view school reform efforts: acknowledges that racism is normal in American society and that structures and policies exist in schools to promote and maintain the oppression of people of color.	Ladson-Billings, 1998 Ladson-Billings, 2009 Zamudio et al., 2011
Change Theory	Lens through which to measure methods for change based on strategic planning, ongoing decision making, and evaluation: requires participants to be clear on long-term goals, to identify measurable indicators of success, and to formulate actions to achieve the goal of improving student learning and creating effective schools.	Bryk et al., 2010 Fullan, 2006, 2008 Hall and Hord, 2011 Levine and Lezotte, 1995
Social and emotional learning (SEL)	Lens through which to model and strengthen mental, emotional, and social well-being: nurtures self-awareness, self-management, social awareness, relationship skills, and responsible decision making, so that student achievement and behavior improve.	Bandura, 1971 CASEL, n.d. Goleman, 1995

Chart A1.1 continued on page 276

Chart A1.1 continued from page 275

Chart A1.1: The theoretical framework behind my study— and this book

THEORY	TENETS	THEORISTS
Restorative Justice/ Relational Theory	Lens through which to engage relationships as the primary focus of measurement, evaluation, and programs: encourages building connections among all people in schools; promotes healthy child development and positive relationships; creates space for people in schools to speak and be heard across all school environments, especially, but not exclusively, in instances where a harm has occurred.	Boyes-Watson, 2008* Boyes-Watson & Pranis, 2010, 2015* Evans and Vaandering, 2016** Hopkins, 2004, 2011 Llewellyn et al., 2013* Morrison, 2007 Pranis, 2005 Pranis, Stuart, and Wedge, 2003* Riestenberg, 2012* Zehr, 1990, 2002

* These sources were not used in my dissertation study but are foundational sources on Circles as a relational RJ theory and are essential to the theoretical RJE framework of this book.

** This book was published after I conducted my study but articulates the relational theory of RJE and is an invaluable resource for the restorative work in schools.

Critical Theory. Critical theory is a broad, umbrella theory that encompasses many other theories, each unique to a marginalized and oppressed population. Critical theory examines power relations according to race, class, gender, sexuality, and other differences and compares the differences in power within the White (male) dominant culture. Critical theory looks at the effects of power imbalances and challenges how teachers, administrators, and policy makers have been taught—how we have been trained in practices and ways of seeing that intensify power imbalances. In the study, critical theory interacted intimately with change theory. Had the schools changed in tangible and measurable ways that recognized the humanity of all members of the school community? If so, had marginalized students become more empowered in their school communities?

Critical Race Theory. Critical race theory (CRT) places race at the center of investigations of inequality in US schools. Indeed, CRT claims that racism has become so enmeshed in the social order, systems, and institutions in American society that it appears more normal than aberrant. The central proposition of CRT relevant to this study is that "race continues to be a significant factor in determining inequity in the United States,"[1] particularly responsible for the high failure and exclusion rates of Black and Latinx males from schools. Because ways of knowing are affected by race and gender, CRT investigates racism at both the individual and the institutional levels. Racism has an impact on the relational ecology of a school. CRT scholarship applies to all aspects of this study. I sought to determine, once again, if and how minority students were empowered (or not) as the school changed. In the schools I studied, did attitudes and beliefs about African American males shift, or did they continue to lead to the disproportionate disciplining of youth of color?

Change Theory. Theories of change identify successful strategies for education reform: how do schools carry out change? Change theories strive to answer this by outlining who is involved, all the stakeholders needed to make change happen and their roles, and how to measure the effectiveness of change at different levels. In any whole-school reform, change theory connects specific assumptions and strategies with desired outcomes. In this study, schools used SWRPs to bring about whole-school reform. The desired outcomes I measured included levels of relational trust; the health of the schools' relational ecologies; and degrees of individual, institutional, and pedagogical change. Relational trust is the social glue that enables people in schools to embrace a moral purpose, because it reduces the risks associated with change. When people feel safe and able to communicate honestly with each other, they build their capacity to reach out, launch initiatives, and see them through.

Social and Emotional Learning Theory. The major premise of social and emotional learning theory (SEL) is that emotional skills can be taught, modeled, and practiced across all school environments. SEL theorizes that, as adults and peers model the five competencies and students strengthen them, student achievement and behavior improve. SEL relies heavily on students being able to observe behaviors and responses: they get to see SEL competencies being practiced, which is how they learn them and practice them themselves. Restorative practices create intentional spaces for modeling SEL competencies. Given this study's focus on relational ecologies, I needed to understand how SWRPs worked alongside SEL and other strategies, including Positive Behavioral Interventions and Supports (PBIS).

Restorative Justice/Relational Theory. Restorative justice theory has evolved through dialogue not only with communities in struggle but also with the disciplines of sociology, psychology, and criminology, as well as philosophy and spirituality. The basic premise of restorative justice theory is that all people are connected to each other through a web of relationships. Building on this core assumption, restorative processes focus on reconnecting people, sharing inherent relational values, and emphasizing social engagement. Relational theory evaluates the success or failure of RJ by measuring the effect that restorative processes have on relationships.

Applied to schools, restorative justice and relational theories encourage building connections and community as an environment most conducive to learning. Their practices promote healthy child development and create space for people in schools to speak and be heard across all school environments, especially when a harm has occurred. RJ and relational theories have been closely tied to SEL theory in this study, because restorative practices nurture SEL competencies and make their development among students and adults natural and organic to school life.

How These Theories Guided My Study

These theories provided the framework for building my study and developing the questions I posed. Critical race theory raised the issue: Did the school-wide use of restorative practices lessen the structural racism embedded in urban schools that had been disproportionately excluding African American males? Since attitudes about race affect the relational ecology of a school, CRT also supported focus group and survey questions about how people in schools perceived Black students and African American males in particular. SEL and restorative justice/relational theories spurred me to explore how students benefit from language and processes that teach, model, and promote healthy relationships and connections. I also wanted to determine whether these practices made a positive difference to the marginalized population of students who were being fed through the school-to-prison pipeline. According to change theory, if school personnel are motivated, trained, supported, and encouraged to adopt new processes and build relational trust, they will behave differently. They will become more empowered and will adopt different beliefs. These changes are observable and contribute to a more positive, caring school climate that benefits every member of the school community. I wanted to find out whether the people in the two schools experienced these changes and how they might talk about them.

Studying What Matters to Those Making the Change

This study is significant for several reasons. First, the collaborative approach to designing the study and implementing it allowed me to fully engage with policy makers, administrators, and educators, so that I would be doing research that mattered to those involved. Second, the study's findings not only fill knowledge gaps in the research literature but also provide useful information to the OUSD, especially in view of their larger evaluation initiative. Change theorist Michael Fullan observes that very rarely do researchers get close enough to understand what teachers and leaders do to implement change on a daily basis—and even more rarely do they try. Yet how school people and relational ecologies change or not in response to changes in federal and local policies is critical for educators to know. Through the collaborative study, the district, the field in general, and of course I gained a better understanding of the change process for schools. We learned about the challenges in implementing restorative practices and how we can address them.

Who Participated

The people who participated in this study were students, teachers, support staff, and administrators at Grant and Davis. I gathered as many perspectives as possible, so I used different instruments to collect insights from different groups of people.

I spent a total of seventy-two hours collecting insights in both schools, where I spent four to six hours each day conducting observations, interviews, and focus groups and interacting with teachers and students. Because I was at each school every day for seven to nine consecutive days, I was able to develop relationships with school personnel at all levels and was frequently invited to attend community building Circles, after-school Circles, advisory Circles, and faculty meetings. While in

Chart A1.2: How I gathered data at Davis and Grant			
	DAVIS	GRANT	TOTAL
Number of staff survey participants	42	18	60
Number of adult focus group participants	8	8	16
Number of student focus group participants	8	8	16
Number of principal interviews	1	1	2
Number of walk-through observations and unstructured interviews	1	1	2
Number of formal classroom observations	12	8	20
Number of Circles	2	2	4
Days spent conducting informal and formal observations	9 days	7 days	16 days
Estimated hours spent in each school	40 hours	32 hours	72 hours

the Circles, I did not take notes; I was fully present as a participant and recorded my observations and reflections privately after leaving the Circle. However, because the purpose of one of the faculty Circles was to determine how SWRPs were working for teachers and what additional support they needed, I requested and received their permission to observe and take written notes during the Circle.

During the initial stage of analysis, I kept what I learned from each school separate. However, to address the overarching research questions, I later merged the views to gain a total picture. Chart A1.2 shows the number of people who participated at each school as well as the number of Circles in which I participated.

Using both quantitative and qualitative methods, I learned from people who played different roles in the schools. I organized their insights around the themes in the literature, the theoretical framework, and the research questions. Then I made every effort to fairly and accurately represent their opinions and beliefs about the schools' relational ecologies and how they experienced change.

Limitations of the Study

My study had several limitations, including time, access, limited perspectives, and the study design.

Time. The physical distance between me and the OUSD posed financial challenges, which limited the amount of time I could spend in the schools. I spent seven to nine days in each school conducting interviews, focus groups, surveys, and observations, so what I present here is, as I said, a mere snapshot in time. I was not able to observe events that might have affected the study findings, nor was I able to observe teachers in their classrooms more than once.

Access. I did not have access to all meetings, mediations, conferences, classrooms, or other events that might have affected the research findings. I observed as much as possible during each school day as I was permitted and as was appropriate. To respect students' privacy, I did not observe or ask to observe conferences or conversations between students and RJ facilitators unless these events occurred in a public setting.

Limited Perspectives. Because I selected the study participants based on my study's purpose, the study was informed by a small number of people at each school, and all focus group participants were advocates of school-wide restorative practices. I did not hear all of the voices and perspectives in the schools. Because the survey was voluntary, it reflected the perspectives only of those who chose to respond. My own bias toward restorative justice limited my role as participant-researcher in some instances, especially when I participated in Circles. I had to manage the tension between being engaged and detached, while negotiating access to enough spaces to paint a thick and accurate description of the school's relational ecology.

Study Design. This was a multisite case study of perceptions. I did not compare my findings to other research and evaluations on SWRPs in the OUSD, nor did I have access to data on students that might have contradicted my findings. I also did not have access to data on fighting and suspensions that may have strengthened or disconfirmed my finding on decreased conflict. Additionally, I had no pre-SWRP implementation baseline to compare changes in the relational ecology. I had to rely on participants' perceptions, recollections, and reflections.

Limited Exploration of Racial Biases. Because the OUSD was most concerned with exploring what was behind the disproportionate disciplining of African American males, I focused questions about racial bias and perceptions only on African American students. I did not explore racial bias toward any other group. I also did not identify the race/ethnicity of those who responded to my questions. It is not safe to assume those respondents were White, since both the students and staff were very diverse. The decision to focus on African American students was not intended to exclude others, but was intended to attempt to hone in on a previously identified problem.

Circumscribed Findings. My purpose in this study was not to prove anything about RJE or to make claims about it. The study was too circumscribed and the schools too new in their RJE practice to support such conclusions. My focus was simply to learn about the journey to implement RJE in these two schools through the perceptions people had along the way. I am assuming they are not alone in their struggles to create restorative schools.

On Becoming a Restorative Researcher

This book is based on my own research of RJE. In scientific research, "objectivity" means that, somehow, the human beings conducting research are able to extricate their own stuff (ideologies, assumptions, opinions, attitudes, values, and beliefs) from what, who, or how they are researching. Social science researchers are trained to believe they can be neutral: that phenomena—people, behaviors, and situations—can be observed entirely from the outside and that the observer's viewpoint does not enter into the findings. Yet, many of us believe that it is metaphysically impossible to keep ourselves out of our research. How can we be objective or neutral when we, as living beings, are profoundly connected with each other and who I am affects what I see?

Critical researchers do not claim to be objective, at least not in the traditional sense. We believe that research should be done *with* people, not on them. Critical researchers like myself embrace what the researcher brings to the research. We bring a position, self-reflection, moral purpose, a view of research as praxis, and a commitment to advocate for the marginalized and oppressed populations being studied in order to advance social justice and equity. We believe that research should be done to change lives, particularly to transform power dynamics and end oppression. Those who participate in our critical research studies should be empowered to become changemakers in their own communities. Certainly, the research should not cause harm or damage. Critical research is, like traditional scientific pursuits, conducted systematically by gathering and analyzing data, but the intention is to have a positive impact on the lives of those participating in the study.

This is my research lens. I positioned myself as a "participant-researcher"—one who is included in the restorative processes of the schools. I would not sit outside the Circle taking notes. What I did not know was that I, too, would change as a result of doing this study: I evolved from critical researcher to *restorative researcher*. This means that, as a researcher, I place relationships at the very heart of my study, my methods, my interactions, and my writing. I am acutely aware that I am the vehicle for the many voices in this study and that I must honor them by representing their words accurately, in context, and with integrity.

I came to this realization after talking about my field experiences in the schools with Dr. Sonia Jain, the OUSD's RJ evaluator and consultant. She helped me to see that, *because* I embraced restorative justice, I could elicit information from the people in the schools. I did not walk into the schools as a typical "objective" researcher (although I do constantly carry a clipboard and digital recorder!). I walked in knowing what a Circle is and how to be in one. I knew what to look for in terms of how people related to each other (smiles matter). I knew what language to listen for. I understood what questions I needed to ask and why I needed to ask them. I brought myself into the research. I did not hide the fact that I advocate for change or that I am a staunch supporter of RJE. I developed relationships with the people in my study—relationships that I maintain to this day.

Because I embrace restorative justice values, it did not take long for people in the schools to trust me. They believed me when I told them I was there not to find things wrong, but to learn and to share what I learned, so that their experiences—good and not so good—could help other schools self-transform into restorative schools. Even though some of the teachers had had bad experiences with researchers in the past, they soon realized that I took a genuine interest in who they were as human beings and that I listened carefully to what they had to say. I respected their space, asked for their permission, and honored their boundaries. Sometimes I wept openly when I was touched by something they said in Circle. RJ is something one *experiences* and *feels*. I think to be a good researcher of restorative justice, we need to experience it, feel it, and believe in it. For these reasons, when I have observed problems in implementing restorative practices with fidelity, I have named them not to criticize but to stand with these RJE change-makers to help move implementation forward—to carry the paradigm shift deeper. What they are undertaking is both enormous and the hope of the future, and they have my enduring gratitude and admiration.

I share this about myself and my approach because I want my readers to understand who wrote this book. I chose to conduct this research study and write this book—and Living Justice Press chose to publish it—because we believe that this study about implementing RJE contributes to the national and, indeed, global movement to create restorative schools.

Notes

Foreword

1. Giroux, "Racial Injustice and Disposable Youth in the Age of Zero Tolerance."

Introduction: Creating a Restorative School in Stages

1. The Active Implementation (AI) Hub, created by the University of North Carolina at Chapel Hill, is a helpful resource for learning implementation science.
2. Riestenberg, "Restorative Implementation," 2.
3. Ibid.

Chapter 1: From Zero Tolerance to Restorative Schools

1. See, for example, Sanchez Fowler et al., "Association between Behavior Problems, Teacher-Student Relationship Quality, and Academic Performance"; Day-Vines and Terriquez, "Strengths-Based Approach to Promoting Prosocial Behavior"; and Michail, "Understanding School Responses to Students' Challenging Behaviour."
2. See, for example, Dohrn, "Look Out Kid/It's Something You Did"; Cassella, "Zero Tolerance Policy in Schools"; Ladson-Billings, "America Still Eats Her Young"; and Skiba and Peterson, "School Discipline at a Crossroads."
3. See, for example, the website of the Minnesota Department of Education: "Restorative Practices": http://education.state.mn.us/ MDE/dse/safe/clim/prac/ and "Data and Assessment": http:// education.state.mn.us/MDE/dse/safe/clim/Data/. See also Kidde, "Outcomes Associated with Restorative Approaches in Schools."

4. See, for example: IIRP Graduate School, *Improving School Climate*. See also: Coldren et al., *School-Based Restorative Justice Data Template*.

Chapter 2: Zero Tolerance—A Disastrous Policy

1. Simon, *Governing Through Crime*, 214.
2. Ibid, 216.
3. Ladson-Billings, *Crossing Over to Canaan*, 80.
4. No Child Left Behind (NCLB), Sec. 2344, (a), 1, B, (iii).
5. See, for example, Zembroski, "Sociological Theories of Crime and Delinquency."
6. Hulac et al., *Behavioral Interventions in Schools*.
7. Hopkins, *Restorative Classroom*, 92.
8. See, for example, Michael, *Raising Race Questions*.
9. Howard, *We Can't Teach What We Don't Know*, 127.
10. See, for example, Zimmerman et al. "Teacher and Parent Perceptions of Behavior Problems." See also Wald and Casella, "Battle Each Day."
11. Skiba, "When Is Disproportionality Discrimination," 180.
12. See, for example, Gregory and Weinstein, "Discipline Gap and African Americans." See also Day-Vines and Terriquez, "Strengths-Based Approach to Promoting Prosocial Behavior."
13. Sue, *Microaggressions and Marginality*, 229–33.
14. Skiba, "When Is Disproportionality Discrimination," 182.
15. See, for example, Zimmerman et al. "Teacher and Parent Perceptions of Behavior Problems"; Wald and Casella, "Battle Each Day"; Gregory and Weinstein, "Discipline Gap and African Americans"; and Day-Vines and Terriquez, "Strengths-Based Approach to Promoting Prosocial Behavior."
16. Blad, "New Federal School Discipline Guidance Addresses Discrimination, Suspensions."

Chapter 3: Understanding Restorative Justice in Education (RJE)

1. Zehr, *Little Book of Restorative Justice*, 37.
2. Morrison, *Restoring Safe School Communities*, 73–75.
3. See Sullivan and Tifft, *Handbook of Restorative Justice*.
4. Morrison, *Restoring Safe School Communities*, 75.
5. Zehr, *Little Book of Restorative Justice*, 35.

6. Morrison, *Restoring Safe School Communities*, 76.
7. Evans and Vaandering, *Little Book of Restorative Justice in Education*, 8.
8. In some situations, these questions may reflect a bias toward Western values. Also, in modifying these questions, facilitators may unwittingly interject their own cultural or racial biases. Another consideration is that these questions do not take stakeholders to the deeper levels where the brokenness that often leads to harm-causing can be brought to light and healed.
9. This chart cannot capture the nuanced ways in which practitioners use these processes in different contexts. These are just basic descriptions. Some schools have purposely moved away from mediation or now use peer mediation only for minor conflict resolution. For fuller descriptions of each process, please see three of *The Little Book Series: of Circle Processes* (Pranis), *of Restorative Discipline* (Stutzman Amstutz and Mullet) and *of Family Group Conferences* (Macrae and Zehr). In any RJ process, participants share, acknowledge, honor, and incorporate each others' cultural values; Western values are not the automatic default or presumed "norm."
10. Restorative Justice Colorado, *Colorado Standards of Practice*.
11. Hopkins, *Restorative Classroom*, 22.
12. Riestenberg, Minnesota Department of Education, "School Restorative Practices." Brochure.
13. See, for example, Freire, *Pedagogy of the Oppressed*; Hopkins, *Just Schools*; Boyes-Watson, *Peacemaking Circles and Urban Youth*; Boyes-Watson and Pranis, *Circle Forward*; Evans and Vaandering, *Little Book of Restorative Justice in Education*; and Tosolt, "Gender and Race Differences in Middle School Students' Perceptions."
14. Morrison, "Schools and Restorative Justice," 332.
15. Hopkins, *Restorative Classroom*, 15.
16. Morrison, *Restoring Safe School Communities*, 155.
17. Evans and Vaandering, *Little Book of Restorative Justice in Education*, 105.

Section 2: Setting the Stage

1. From the website of the Oakland Unified School District: http://www.ousd.org/cms/lib07/CA01001176/Centricity/Domain/1/OUSD%20District%20Docs/OUSD%20Fast%20Facts%202014-15.pdf.

2. See: Jain et al., *Restorative Justice in Oakland Schools*.
3. Rusby et al., "Observations of the Middle School Environment."

▨ Chapter 6: What Do the Schools' Relational Ecologies Look Like?

1. See, for example, Fullan, "Future of Educational Change"; Fullan, *Change Theory*; and Hall and Hord, *Implementing Change*.

▨ Chapter 7: Changes in the Schools' Structures

1. Nor and Roslan, "Turning Around At-Risk Schools."
2. See, for example, Fullan, "Change Theory" and Hall and Hord, *Implementing Change*.
3. See: Morrison, "From Social Control to Social Engagement."

▨ Chapter 10: Putting It All Together: Relational Ecology and Change

1. Bryk et al., *Organizing Schools for Improvement*, 137.
2. See, for example, Storz and Nestor, "Insights into Meeting Standards from Listening to the Voices of Urban Students."
3. See, for example, Tosolt, "Gender and Race Differences"; also Sanchez Fowler et al., "Association between Externalizing Behavior Problems."
4. See, for example, Fullan, "Change Theory"; Hall and Hord, *Implementing Change;* Nor and Roslan, "Turning Around At-Risk Schools"; and Hemmings, "Four Rs for Urban High School Reform."
5. Raible and Irizarry, "Redirecting the Teacher's Gaze."
6. See, for example, Weissbourd, "'Quiet' Troubles of Low-Income Children."
7. Kay Pranis in a conversation with Denise Breton, St. Paul, MN, August 2016. See Boyes-Watson and Pranis, *Circle Forward*.
8. See: Evans and Vaandering, *Little Book of Restorative Justice in Education*.
9. See, for example, Riestenberg, *Circle in the Square*; Tosolt, "Gender and Race Differences"; and Day-Vines and Terriquez, "Strengths-Based Approach to Promoting Prosocial Behavior."
10. Freire, *Pedagogy of the Oppressed*, 79.
11. Morrison and Vaandering, "Restorative Justice."

Chapter 11: Mapping the Shift to a Restorative School

1. Restorative Solutions website offers a list of implementation guides for restorative practices that various schools and districts have developed. These can be used as a basis for customizing an RJE strategic plan. See: Compton and Childs, "Implementation Guides for Restorative Practices in Schools."

2. See, for example: Bryk and Schneider, "Trust in Schools"; Bryk et al., *Organizing Schools for Improvement*; and Hemmings, "Four Rs for Urban High School Reform."

3. See, for example: Gregory and Weinstein, "Discipline Gap and African Americans"; and Day-Vines and Terriquez, "Strengths-Based Approach to Promoting Prosocial Behavior."

4. Higgins et al., *Impact of School Environments*.

5. Pranis, Stuart, and Wedge, *Peacemaking Circles*, 34–35.

6. See: Hopkins, *Just Schools* and *Restorative Classroom*; Riestenberg, *Circle in the Square*; and, Evans and Vaandering, *Little Book of Restorative Justice in Education*.

7. Compton, "Enhancing PBIS and SEL with Restorative Practices," para 1.

8. Riestenberg and Price-Ellinstad, "Restorative Implementation," 8.

9. Ohlenberg, "Why Schools Need to Be Trauma Informed," 12.

10. OUSD, 2015. http://www.ousd.org/Page/13002.

11. Brown, *Daring Greatly*.

12. Llewellyn et al., "Imagining Success for a Restorative Approach to Justice," 282–83.

13. McClain, *America Needs More Black Men Leading Its Classrooms*.

14. Skiba and Peterson, "School Discipline at a Crossroads," 342.

Appendix 1: Methodology

1. See Ladson-Billings and Tate, "Toward a Critical Race Theory of Education."

Bibliography

This bibliography offers sources that may be of interest and practical support to those engaging the paradigm shift to RJE in schools. A full bibliography of the entire body of work that contributed to this narrative is available in Martha A. Brown's dissertation, *Talking in Circles* (see below).

Ahmed, Eliza, and Valerie Braithwaite. "Forgiveness, Reconciliation, and Shame: Three Key Variables in Reducing School Bullying." *Journal of Social Issues* 62, no. 2 (2006): 347–70. doi:10.1111/j.1540-4560.2006.00454.x.

AI Hub: The National Implementation Research Network's Active Implementation Hub: http://implementation.fpg.unc.edu/.

Alexander, Michelle. *The New Jim Crow*. New York: The New Press, 2012.

Ayers, William, Bernadine Dohrn, and Rick Ayers, eds. *Zero Tolerance: Resisting the Drive for Punishment in Our Schools*. New York: The New Press, 2001.

Bandura, Albert. *Social Learning Theory*. New York: General Learning Press, 1971.

Beckman, Kara, and Nancy Riestenberg. *Trainer's Guide for Working with Schools to Implement Restorative Practices*. Minnesota Department of Education. Retrieved 2.14.17 from http://education.state.mn.us/MDE/dse/safe/clim/prac/index.htm.

Blad, Evie. "New Federal School Discipline Guidance Addresses Discrimination, Suspensions." *Education Week*, 8 January 2014. Retrieved from http://blogs.edweek.org/edweek/rulesforenwwagement/2014/01/new_federal_school_discipline_guidance_addresses_discrimination_suspensions.html?cmp=ENL-EU-NEWS2.

Boyes-Watson, Carolyn. "Community Is Not a Place but a Relationship: Lessons for Organizational Development." *Public Organization Review* 5, no. 4 (2005): 359–74.

————. *Peacemaking Circles and Urban Youth: Bringing Justice Home.* St. Paul, MN: Living Justice Press, 2008.

Boyes-Watson, Carolyn, and Kay Pranis. *Heart of Hope:* A Guide for Using Peacemaking Circles to Develop Emotional Literacy, Promote Healing & Build Healthy Relationships. St. Paul, MN: Living Justice Press and Cambridge, MA: Institute for Restorative Initiatives, 2010.

————. *Circle Forward: Building a Restorative School Community.* St. Paul, MN: Living Justice Press and Cambridge, MA: Institute for Restorative Initiatives, 2015.

Brown, Brené. *Daring Greatly: How the Courage to Be Vulnerable Transforms the Way We Live, Love, Parent, and Lead.* New York: Gotham Books, 2012.

Brown, Martha. A. "Talking in Circles: A Mixed Methods Study of School-Wide Restorative Practices in Two Urban Middle Schools." PhD diss., Florida Atlantic University, 2015. Order No. 10154934. Available from ProQuest Dissertations and Theses Global. 1817925195. Also retrievable from: https://fau.digital.flvc.org /islandora/object/fau%3A32067/datastream/OBJ/view/Talking_ in_Circles__A_Mixed_Methods_Study_of_School-wide_ Restorative_Practices_in_Two_Urban_Middle_Schools.pdf.

Bryk, Anthony S., and Barbara Schneider. "Trust in Schools: A Core Resource for School Reform." *Educational Leadership* 60, no. 6 (March 2003): 40–44.

Bryk, Anthony S., Penny Bender Sebring, Elaine Allensworth, Stuart Luppescu, and John Q. Easton. *Organizing Schools for Improvement: Lessons from Chicago.* Chicago, IL: University of Chicago Press, 2010.

Cassella, Ronnie. "Zero Tolerance Policy in Schools: Rationale, Consequences, and Alternatives." *Teachers College Record* 105, no. 5 (2003): 872–92.

Centers for Disease Control and Prevention. *The Adverse Childhood Experiences (ACE) Study.* 2014. Retrieved from http://www.cdc .gov/violenceprevention/acestudy/index.html.

Childs, Karen E., Donald Kincaid, and Heather P. George. "A Model for Statewide Evaluation of a Universal Positive Behavior Support Initiative." *Journal of Positive Behavior Interventions* 12, no. 4 (2010): 198–201. doi:10.1077/1098300709340699.

Claassen, Ron, and Roxanne Claassen. *Discipline That Restores.* South Carolina: BookSurge Publishing, 2008.

Coldren, James R., Chelsea Haring, Andrew Luecke, Christina Sintic (all of the Governors State University) and Sara Balgoyen (The Illinois Balanced and Restorative Justice Project). *School-Based Restorative Justice Data Template: Final Report to the Illinois Criminal Justice Information Authority.* ICJIA Grant #407301. 15 November 2011. http://www.ibarj.org/docs/SchoolRJFinal Report.pdf.

Collaborative for Academic and Social and Emotional Learning (CASEL). (n.d.). *Success in Schools. Skills for Life.* Retrieved from http://www.casel.org/.

Compton, Randy. "Enhancing PBIS and SEL with Restorative Practices." Web log comment, 5 November 2014. Retrieved from http://restorativesolutions.us/restorative-justice-blogposts /pbis-and-restorative-practices.

Compton, Randy, and Catherine Childs. "Implementation Guides for Restorative Practices in Schools." Restorative Solutions (website). Retrieved 2.25.17 from http://restorativesolutions.us /implementation-guides-for-restorative-practices-in-schools.

Crimmins, Daniel, Anne F. Farrell, Philip W. Smith, and Alison Bailey. *Positive Strategies for Students with Behavior Problems.* Baltimore, MD: Paul H. Brookes Publishing, 2007.

Day-Vines, Norma L., and Veronica Terriquez. "A Strengths-Based Approach to Promoting Prosocial Behavior among African American and Latino Students." *Professional School Counseling* 12, no. 2 (2008): 170–75.

DeFur, Sharon H., and Lori Korinek. "Listening to Student Voices." *Clearing House: A Journal of Educational Strategies, Issues and Ideas* 83, no. 1 (2010): 15–19.

Dohrn, Bernadine. "Look Out Kid/It's Something You Did." In Ayers, Dohrn, and Ayers, *Zero Tolerance,* 89–113.

Duckworth, Angela L., Tamar Szabó Gendler, and James J. Gross. "Self-Control in School-Age Children." *Educational Psychologist* 49, no. 3 (2014): 199–217. doi:10.1080/00461520.2014.926225.

Dutro, Elizabeth, and Andrea C. Bien. "Listening to the Speaking Wound: A Trauma Studies Perspective on Student Positioning in Schools." *American Educational Research Journal* 51, no. 1 (2014): 7–35. doi:10.3102/0002831213503181.

Durlak, Joseph A., Roger P. Weissberg, Allison B. Dymnicki, Rebecca D. Taylor, and Kriston B. Schellinger. "The Impact of Enhancing Students' Social and Emotional Learning: A Meta-Analysis of

School-Based Universal Interventions." *Child Development* 82, no. 1 (2011): 405–432. doi:10.1111/j.1467-8624.2010.01564.x .

Elias, Maurice. J., Joseph E. Zins, Patricia A. Graczyk, and Roger P. Weissberg. "Implementation, Sustainability, and Scaling Up of Social-Emotional and Academic Innovations in Public Schools." *School Psychology Review* 32, no. 3 (2003): 303–19.

Evans, Katherine R., and Jessica. N. Lester. "Restorative Justice in Education: What We Know So Far." *Middle School Journal* 44, no. 5 (2013): 57–63.

Evans, Katherine R., and Dorothy Vaandering. *The Little Book of Restorative Justice in Education.* New York: Good Books, 2016.

Fallon, M. L., B. V. O'Keefe, and G. Sugai. "Consideration of Culture and Context in School-Wide Positive Behavior Support: A Review of Current Literature." *Journal of Positive Behavior Interventions* 14, no. 4 (2012): 209–19.

Freire, Paulo. *Pedagogy of the Oppressed.* New York: Continuum International Publishing Group,, 1970; rev. ed., 2008.

Fullan, Michael. "Change Theory: A Force for School Improvement." *Seminar Series Paper,* no. 157 (November 2006). Victoria, BC: Center for Strategic Education. Retrieved from http://www.michaelfullan.com/media/13396072630.pdf.

———. "The Future of Educational Change: System Thinkers in Action." *Journal of Educational Change* 7, no. 3 (2006): 113–22. doi:10.1007/s10833-006-9003-9.

———. "Curriculum Implementation and Sustainability." In *The Sage Handbook of Curriculum and Instruction,* edited by F. M. Connelly, 113–22. Thousand Oaks, CA: Sage Publications, 2008.

Gay, Geneva. *Culturally Responsive Teaching: Theory, Research, and Practice.* New York: Teachers College Press, Columbia University, 2000.

Giroux, Henry A. "Racial Injustice and Disposable Youth in the Age of Zero Tolerance." *Qualitative Studies in Education* 16, no. 4 (2003): 553–65.

Goleman, Daniel. *Emotional Intelligence: Why It Can Matter More Than IQ.* New York: Bantam Books, 1995.

Gregory, Ann., and Rhona S. Weinstein. "The Discipline Gap and African Americans: Defiance or Cooperation in the High School Classroom." *Journal of School Psychology* 46, no. 4 (2008): 455–75.

Hall, Gene E., and Shirley M. Hord. *Implementing Change: Patterns, Principles, and Potholes.* 3rd ed. Upper Saddle River, NJ: Pearson Education, 2011.

Hemmings, Annette. "Four Rs for Urban High School Reform:

Re-eEnvisioning, Reculturation, Restructuring, and Remorali-
zation." *Improving Schools*, 15, no. 3 (2012): 198–210. doi:10.1177
/1365480212458861.

Higgins, Steve, Elaine Hall, Kate Wall, Pamela Woolner, and Caro-
line McCaughey. *The Impact of School Environments: A Literature
Review*. Report. Newcastle upon Tyne, UK: Research Centre for
Learning and Teaching, School of Education, Communication and
Language Sciences, Newcastle University, 2005.

Hirschfield, Paul J. "Preparing for Prison? The Criminalization of
School Discipline in the USA." *Theoretical Criminology* 12, no. 1
(2008): 79–101. doi:10.1177/1362480607085795.

Hopkins, Belinda. *Just Schools: A Whole School Approach to Restorative
Justice*. London: Jessica Kingsley Publishers, 2004.

———. *The Restorative Classroom: Using Restorative Approaches to
Foster Effective Learning*. London: Optimus Education, 2011.

Hoppey, David, and James McLeskey. "A Case Study of Principal
Leadership in an Effective Inclusive School." *Journal of Special
Education* 46, no. 4 (2013): 245–56. doi:10.1177/0022466910390507.

Howard, Gary R. *We Can't Teach What We Don't Know*. New York:
Teachers College Press, Columbia University, 2006.

Hulac, David, Joy Terrell, Odell Vining, and Joshua Bernstein.
Behavioral Interventions in Schools: A Response-to-Intervention
Guidebook. New York: Routledge, 2010.

IIRP Graduate School. *Improving School Climate: Findings from Schools
Implementing Restorative Practices*. Bethlehem, PA: International
Institute for Restorative Practices, 2009.

Jain, Sonia, Henrissa Bassey, Martha A. Brown, and Preety Kalra.
Restorative Justice in Oakland Schools: Implementation and Impacts.
Report. 2014. Retrieved from http://www.ousd.k12.ca.us/cms
/lib07/CA01001176/Centricity/Domain/134/OUSD-RJ%20
Report%20revised%20Final.pdf.

Johnstone, Gerry, and Daniel W. Van Ness, eds. *Handbook of Restorative Justice*. Cullompton, UK: Willan Publishing, 2007.

———. "The Meaning of Restorative Justice." In Johnstone and Van
Ness, *Handbook of Restorative Justice*, 5–23.

Kempf-Leonard, Kimberly. "Minority Youths and Juvenile Justice:
Disproportionate Minority Contact after Nearly 20 Years of Reform
Efforts." *Youth Violence and Juvenile Justice* 5, no. 1 (2007): 71–87.

Kidde, Jon. "Outcomes Associated with Restorative Approaches in
Schools." Selected_RJ_in_Schools_Outcomes_J_Kidde.docx.

Ladson-Billings, Gloria. *The Dreamkeepers: Successful Teachers of*

African American Children. San Francisco, CA: Jossey-Bass Publishers, 1994.

———. "Just What Is Critical Race Theory and What's It Doing in a Nice Field Like Education?" *Qualitative Studies in Education* 11, no. 1 (1998): 7–24.

———. "America Still Eats Her Young." In Ayers, Dohrn, and Ayers, *Zero Tolerance*, 77–85.

———. *Crossing Over to Canaan: The Journey of New Teachers in Diverse Classrooms.* San Francisco, CA: Jossey-Bass, 2001.

———. "Race Still Matters: Critical Race Theory in Education." In *Handbook of Critical Education*, edited by Michael W. Apple, Wayne Au, and Luis Armando Gandin. New York: Routledge, 2009, 110–22.

Ladson-Billings, Gloria, and William F. Tate, IV. "Toward a Critical Race Theory of Education." *Teachers College Record* 97, no. 1 (Fall 1995): 47–68.

Lederach, John Paul, and Angela Lederach. *When Blood and Bones Cry Out: Journeys Through the Soundscape of Healing and Reconciliation.* New York: Oxford University Press, 2010.

Levine, Daniel U., and Lawrence W. Lezotte. "Effective Schools Research." In *Handbook of Research on Multicultural Education*, edited by James A. Banks and Cherry A. McGee Banks, 525–45. New York: Macmillan, 1995.

Llewellyn, Jennifer J., Bruce P. Archibald, Donald Clairmont, and Diane Crocker. "Imagining Success for a Restorative Approach to Justice: Implications for Measurement and Evaluation." *Dalhousie Law Journal* 36, no. 2 (2013): 281.

Macrae, Allan, and Howard Zehr. *The Little Book of Family Group Conferences: New Zealand Style.* New York: Good Books, 2004.

May, Henry, Jason Huff, and Ellen Goldring. "A Longitudinal Study of Principals' Activities and Student Performance." *School Effectiveness and School Improvement* 23, no. 4 (2012): 417–39. doi:10.10 80/09243453.2012.678866.

McClain, Dani. *America Needs More Black Men Leading Its Classrooms.* Retrieved 2.14.17 from http://www.slate.com/articles/life /tomorrows_test/2016/06/only_2_percent_of_teachers_are_ black_and_male_here_s_how_we_might_change.html.

Michael, Ali. *Raising Race Questions: Whiteness and Inquiry in Education.* New York: Teachers College Press, 2015.

Michail, Samia. "Understanding School Responses to Students' Challenging Behaviour: A Review of Literature." *Improving Schools* 14, no. 2 (2011): 156–71.

Minnesota Department of Education. "Data and Assessment." http://education.state.mn.us/MDE/dse/safe/clim/Data/.

———. "Restorative Practices." http://education.state.mn.us/MDE/dse/safe/clim/prac/.

Mirsky, Laura. "SaferSanerSchools: Transforming School Cultures with Restorative Practices." *Reclaiming Children and Youth* 16, no. 2 (2007): 5–12.

Morrison, Brenda E. "School Bullying and Restorative Justice: Toward a Theoretical Understanding of the Role of Respect, Pride, and Shame." *Journal of Social Issues* 62, no. 2 (2006): 371–92.

———. *Restoring Safe School Communities: A Whole School Response to Bullying, Violence and Alienation.* Sydney, Australia: The Federation Press, 2007.

———. "Schools and Restorative Justice." In Johnstone and Van Ness, *Handbook of Restorative Justice*, 325–50.

———. "From Social Control to Social Engagement: Finding the Time and Place to Talk." In *Contemporary Issues in Criminal Justice Policy,* edited by Natasha A. Frost, Joshua D. Freilich, and Todd R. Clear. Policy Proposals from the American Society of Criminology Conference, San Francisco, CA, November 2009. Belmont, CA: Wadsworth, 2010.

Morrison, Brenda E., Peta Blood, and Margaret Thorsborne. "Practicing Restorative Justice in School Communities: The Challenge of Culture Change." *Public Organization Review* 5, no. 4 (2005): 335–57.

Morrison, Brenda E., and Dorothy Vaandering. "Restorative Justice: Pedagogy, Praxis, and Discipline." *Journal of School Violence* 11, no. 2 (2012): 138–55.

Musaifer, Sara, Nancy Riestenberg, and Carol Thomas. *Restorative Measures in Schools Survey.* Report. 2011. Minnesota Department of Education. Retrieved from http://education.state.mn.us/MDE/StuSuc/SafeSch/RestorMeas/.

Nor, Sharifah Md, and Samsilah Roslan. "Turning Around At-Risk Schools: What Effective Principals Do." *International Journal on School Disaffection* 6, no. 2 (2009): 21–29.

Oakland Unified School District. *OUSD. Trauma Informed Practices.* http://www.ousd.org/Page/13002.

———. *Resolution of the Board of Education of the Oakland Unified*

School District No. 0910-0120. 2010. Retrieved from http://www .ousd.k12.ca.us/cms/lib07/CA01001176/Centricity/Domain/156 /Resolution_0910-0120_Districts_Restorative_Justice_ Initiative_.pdf.

———. *OUSD Fast Facts 2013-2014*. 2014. Retrieved from http:// www.ousd.org/cms/lib07/CA01001176/Centricity/Domain/4 /OUSDFastFacts2013-14.pdf.

———. *Restorative Justice*. 2014. Retrieved from http://www.ousd .k12.ca.us/restorativejustice.

———. *Home*. 2015. Retrieved from http://www.ousd.org/site /default.aspx?PageID=1.

Oehlberg, Barbara. "Why Schools Need to Be Trauma Informed." *Trauma and Loss: Research and Interventions* 8, no. 2 (2008): 12–16.

Pranis, Kay. *The Little Book of Circle Processes*. New York: Good Books, 2005.

———. "Restorative Values." In Johnstone and Van Ness, *Handbook of Restorative Justice*, 59–74.

Pranis, Kay, Barry Stuart, and Mark Wedge. *Peacemaking Circles: From Conflict to Community*. Saint Paul, MN: Living Justice Press, 2003.

Raible, John, and Jason G. Irizarry. "Redirecting the Teacher's Gaze: Teacher Education, Youth Surveillance and the School-to-Prison Pipeline." *Teaching and Teacher Education* 26, no. 5 (2010): 1196–203.

Reimer, Kristin. "An Exploration of the Implementation of Restorative Justice in an Ontario Public School." *Canadian Journal of Educational Administration and Policy* 119 (2011). Retrieved from http:// www.umanitoba.ca/publications/cjeap/pdf_files/reimer.pdf.

Reinke, Wendy M., Keith C. Herman, and Melissa Stormont. "Classroom-Level Positive Behavior Supports in Schools Implementing SW-PBIS: Identifying Areas for Enhancement." *Journal of Positive Behavior Interventions* 15, no. 1 (2013): 39–50. doi: 10.1177/1098300712459079.

Restorative Justice Colorado. *Colorado Standards of Practice*. Retrieved 2.16.17 from http://www.rjcolorado.org/restorative-justice /colorado-standards-of-practice.

Restorative Practices in Schools Resources: http://education.state .mn.us/MDE/dse/safe/clim/prac/index.htm.

Restorative Practices in School Toolkit: www.restorativeschoolstool kit.org.

Reyes, Augustina H. *Discipline, Achievement, Race*. Lanham, MD: Rowman and Littlefield Education, 2006.

Riestenberg, Nancy. *Seeding Restorative Measures in Minnesota: Chal-*

lenging Opportunities. 2003. Retrieved from http://www.educ
.cam.ac.uk/research/projects/restorativeapproaches/ seminarfour
/N%20Reistenberg.pdf.

———. *Circle in the Square: Building Community and Repairing Harm
in School*. St. Paul, MN: Living Justice Press, 2012.

———. Minnesota Department of Education, "School Restorative
Practices." Brochure.

———. "The Restorative Implementation: Paradigms and Practices."
*Restorative Practices in Action Journal: For School and Justice Practi-
tioners*. 2015. New York State Permanent Judicial Commission on
Justice for Children, Albany NY. pjcjc@nycourts.gov.

Riestenberg, Nancy, and Debra Price-Ellingstad. "The Restorative
Implementation: Paradigms and Practices." Paper presented
at Restorative Practices in Action: A Conference for School and
Justice Practitioners. May 2015. John Jay College, New York.
Retrieved from http://johnjay.jjay.cuny.edu/restorativepractices
/resources.asp.

Rusby, Julie C., Ryann Crowley, Jeffrey Sprague, and Anthony Biglan.
"Observations of the Middle School Environment: The Context
for Student Behavior Beyond the Classroom." *Psychology in the
Schools* 48, no. 1 (2011): 400–415. doi:10.1002/pits.20562.

Sanchez Fowler, Laura T., Tachelle I. Banks, Karla Anhalt, Heidi Hin-
richs Der, and Tara Kalis. "The Association Between Externalizing
Behavior Problems, Teacher-Student Relationship Quality, and
Academic Performance in Young Urban Learners." *Behavioral Dis-
orders* 33, no. 3 (2008): 167–83.

Scanlon, Lesley. "'Why Didn't They Ask Me?': Student Perspectives
on a School Improvement Initiative." *Improving Schools* 15, no. 3
(2012): 185–97. doi:10.1177/1365480212461824.

Simon, Jonathan. *Governing through Crime: How the War on Crime
Transformed American Democracy and Created a Culture of Fear*.
London, UK: Oxford University Press, 2007.

Skiba, Russell J. "When Is Disproportionality Discrimination? The
Overrepresentation of Black Students in School Suspension." In
Ayers, Dohrn, and Ayers, *Zero Tolerance*, 176–187.

Skiba, Russell J., Mariella I. Arredondo, and M. Karega Rausch.
"New and Developing Research on Disparities in Discipline." *Dis-
cipline Disparities: A Research-to-Practice Collaborative*. Report. The
Equity Project at Indiana University, Center for Evaluation and
Education Policy, March 2014.

Skiba, Russell J., Robert H. Horner, Choong-Geun Chung, M. Karega

Rausch, Seth L. May, and Tary Tobin. "Race Is Not Neutral: A National Investigation of African American and Latino Disproportionality in School Discipline." *School Psychology Review* 40, no. 1 (2011): 85–107.

Skiba, Russell J., and Reece L. Peterson. "School Discipline at a Crossroads: From Zero Tolerance to Early Response." *Exceptional Children* 66, no. 3 (2000): 335–47.

Solomon, Benjamin G., Suzanne A. Klein, John M. Hintze, James M. Cressy, and Sarah L. Peller. "A Meta-analysis of School-Wide Positive Behavioral Support: An Exploratory Study Using Single-Case Synthesis." *Psychology in the Schools* 49, no. 2 (2012): 105–21.

Storz, Mark. G., and Karen R. Nestor. "Insights into Meeting Standards from Listening to the Voices of Urban Students." *Middle School Journal* 34, no. 4 (2003): 11–19.

Stutzman Amstutz, Lorraine, and Judy H. Mullett. *The Little Book of Restorative Discipline for Schools: Teaching Responsibility; Creating Caring Climates.* New York: Good Books, 2005.

Sue, Derald Wing. *Microaggressions and Marginality: Manifestation, Dynamics, and Impact.* Hoboken, NJ: Wiley, 2010.

Sullivan, Dennis, and Larry Tifft, eds. *Handbook of Restorative Justice: A Global Perspective.* Abingdon, UK: Routledge, 2006.

Sumner, Michael D., Carol J. Silverman, and Mary Louise Frampton. *School-Based Restorative Justice as an Alternative to Zero-Tolerance Policies: Lessons from West Oakland.* Report. Berkeley, CA: Thelton E. Henderson Center for Social Justice, 2010. Retrieved from http://www.law.berkeley.edu/files/11-2010_School-based_Restorative_Justice_As_an_Alternative_to_Zero-Tolerance_Policies.pdf.

Tosolt, Brandelyn. "Gender and Race Differences in Middle School Students' Perceptions of Caring Teacher Behaviors." *Multicultural Perspectives* 12, no. 3 (2010): 145–51.

Uhlenberg, Jeffrey, and Kathleen M. Brown. "Racial Gap in Teachers' Perceptions of the Achievement Gap." *Education and Urban Society* 34, no. 4 (2002): 493–530. doi:10.1177/0012450203404006.

United States Department of Education. *U.S. Department of Education Announces Voluntary Resolution of Oakland Unified School District Civil Rights Investigation.* OCR Case Number 09125001, version 2, September 17, 2012. Retrieved from http://www2.ed.gov/about/offices/list/ocr/docs/investigations/09125001-b.pdf.

———. *U.S. Departments of Education and Justice Release School Discipline Guidance Package to Enhance School Climate and Improve School Discipline Policies/Practices.* 2014. Retrieved from http://www .ed.gov/news/press-releases/us-departments-education-and -justice-release-school-discipline-guidance-package-.

Vaandering, Dorothy. "The Significance of Critical Theory for Restorative Justice in Education." *Review of Education, Pedagogy, and Cultural Studies* 32, no. 2 (2010): 145–76. doi:10.1080/10714411003799165.

———. "Student, Teacher, and Administrator Perspectives on Harm: Implications for Implementing Safe and Caring School Initiatives." *Review of Education, Pedagogy and Cultural Studies* 35, no. 4 (2013): 298–318. doi:10.1080/10714413.2013.825514.

Wadhwa, Anita. *Race, Discipline, and Critical Restorative Justice in Two Urban High Schools.* PhD diss., 2013. ProQuest LLC. (UMI 3579002).

Wald, Johanna, and Ronnie Casella. "A Battle Each Day: Teachers Talk about Discipline, Suspensions, and Zero Tolerance Policy." In Reyes, *Discipline, Achievement, Race,* 89–104.

Weissbourd, Richard. "The 'Quiet' Troubles of Low-Income Children." *Harvard Education Letter* 24, no. 8 (2008): 6–7.

Zamudio, Margaret. M., Caskey Russell, Francisco A. Rios, and Jacuelyn L. Bridgeman. *Critical Race Theory Matters: Education and Ideology.* New York: Routledge, 2011.

Zehr, Howard. *Changing Lenses: A New Focus for Crime and Justice.* Harrisonburg, VA: Herald Press, 1990; 3rd ed. 2005.

———. *The Little Book of Restorative Justice.* New York: Good Books, 2002.

Zembroski, David. "Sociological Theories of Crime and Delinquency." *Journal of Human Behavior in the Social Environment* 21, no. 3 (2011): 240–54. doi:0.1080/10911359.2011.564553.

Zimmerman, Rick, Elizabeth L. Khoury, William A. Vega, Andres G. Gil, and George J. Warheit. "Teacher and Parent Perceptions of Behavior Problems among a Sample of African American, Hispanic, and Non-Hispanic White Students." *American Journal of Community Psychology* 23, no. 2 (1995): 181–97.

Zins, Joseph E., and Maurice J. Elias. "Social and Emotional Learning: Promoting the Development of All Students." *Journal of Educational and Psychological Consultation* 17, nos. 2 and 3 (2006): 233–55.

Martha A. Brown, PhD

Dr. Martha A. Brown is a renowned author, consultant, presenter, researcher, teacher, and advocate of restorative justice. She earned her doctorate in Curriculum & Instruction from Florida Atlantic University after first exploring restorative schools in the United Kingdom and then ultimately conducting her dissertation research in partnership with the Oakland Unified School District in California.

Dr. Brown is the Lead Instructor for Simon Fraser University's Continuing Studies Restorative Justice Certificate Program, where she facilitates learning for adult students in Canada, United States, Australia, Africa, and other countries worldwide. She has published several peer reviewed articles, book chapters, and book reviews regarding restorative justice, correctional education, and evaluating art education programs. She has also presented nationally at conferences sponsored by the National Association of Community and Restorative Justice (NACRJ) and the International Conference on Conflict Resolution in Education (CRE).

In 2016, Dr. Brown founded RJAE Consulting, Intl. to provide planning, evaluation, and other consulting services to schools, school districts, correctional facilities, and organizations focusing on restorative justice or art education.

EMAIL: martha@rjaeconsulting.com
WEBSITE: www.rjaeconsulting.com

Index

academic achievement: and Circles, 200–205; gap in, 129–30; and meaningful learning, 218, 255; and racial biases impact on, 40–41; and relational pedagogies, 201, 255; SEL skills promote, 58–60; and social and emotional needs, 59–60. *See also* student-teacher, teacher-school bond.

academic discourse, 119

accountability: collective and individual, 29; of community, 29, 217; and guilt, 258; for making things right, 176; mutual, 60, 217, 220, 227; personal, 187; vs. punishment, 29, 160; in repairing harm, 175, 178, 219; and RJE, 52, 219; in a restorative school, 176; sharing, 154, 218, 227

activism: and art, 129–30; and Oakland, 128

administrators, *see* school administration

adolescent(s): African American, 40; behavior punished, 19, 34, 38; and development, 38; and "super-predator" narrative, 32

adult(s): care for students, 22, 123, 125–26, 195; change before students change, 6, 43, 162, 185, 194, 248; and cultural competency, 133–34; and deepening RJ practice, 230, 234; as disciplinarians, 219–20; as foundation of school change, 6, 185, 190; participation

in Circles, 63, 111; racial biases of, 134–142, 228, 256; relationship-building among, 151; and relationships with students, 60, 71, 122–23; and response(s) to youth, 59; and restorative process, 219; and role in school-wide change, 6, 43, 162, 185, 248; and staff Circles, 247; training of, 149, 216–17; and trust, 107–108, 111–12, 212; and voice in school, 154

advisory period: as Circle time, 81, 95, 113, 118, 173–75, 202

African American/Black male youth, 221–30; as disproportionately disciplined, 132, 135–36, 148, 183, 221, 277, 279, 283; as harmed by zero tolerance policies, 41–42; and high school failure and exclusion rates, 277; interventions that did not "work" with, 221–30; in leadership RJE roles, 256; as not "the problem," 226–28, 256; RJE's effectiveness with, 221–30, 256; stereotypes about, 37; and "super-predator" narrative, 32; as suspended for defiance, 243; as targets of racial biases, 132, 135–43, 221–23

African American/Black staff, 132, 267

African American/Black students: attitudes toward, 137–43; behavior issues with, 41; as belonging to school community, 222; as

keeper(s), 51; students as, 251; teacher practice as, 164

language: restorative, 48, 53, 56, 250, 279; of restorative school, 56, 61, 152, 286

laws: changing, 19; and enforcement policies, 21; and impact on schools, 33–34; and role of in RJE paradigm shift, 19; and White supremacy, 223; of zero tolerance, xxviii, 20

law enforcement, 21, 41–42, 271. *See also* school resource officers (SROs).

leadership, 153–63; and accountability, 154; by African American/Black students, 256; and balancing conflicting priorities, 156–57; caring, 126; changes in, 99, 155–56, 179; democratic, 214–15; diversity (racial) of, 267–68; educating in RJE, xxvii, 57, 264–67; effective, 105; and empowering others, 155, 158, 214; in implementing RJE, 179; with local community, 238–39; of parents, 92; in policies and procedures, 149; of principal, 108; and priority on RJE, 157–58; and race critical awareness, 265; and recruiting RJE minded, 244, 266–67; and reflective action, 172; and relational capacity, 154; as RJE advocate, 157; as shared, 154, 214; of students, 78, 188, 196, 220; styles and strategies of, 117, 153–55, 182; support from, 5, 153, 157, 216; of teacher, 117, 155; of teams, 159, 243; and training, 170; and trust, 108; turnover of, 168, 228, 245; visionary, 155, 214

learning: and belonging, 255, 258; changes us, 218; through Circles, 26, 54, 56, 200, 217–18, 220, 269; as collaborative, cooperative, 25, 31, 197–98, 205, 215, 255; as

communities, xxii, xxvi, 12, 48, 64, 184, 217–218, 237–38; about conflict resolution, 26, 53, 71; in context, 169–73, 179, 254; environment for, xxii–xxiv, 4, 18, 22, 25–26, 41, 49, 88, 215, 225, 255, 278; and feedback, 219, 260; as meaningful, 255; in middle school, 70–71; about mutual accountability, 29; and reintegration, 258; and relational pedagogies, 56, 197; and relationships, 255, 262, 264, 268–69; RJE and, 24–27, 29, 31, 43, 49, 56, 63–64, 70, 255, 262, 265, 267, 278; and safety, 88–89; and school culture, 2; SEL and, 25, 57–63; as student-centered, 198, 269; students engaged with, 84; and SWRPs, 6; theory of, 185; and tier 1 RPs, 56–57, 256; and traditional education model, 18, 265; and trauma, 193, 225; and zero tolerance, xxvii, 22, 41, 56. *See also* Albert Bandura, social and emotional learning (SEL).

Lederach, Angela, 117

Lederach, John Paul, 26, 106, 117

listening: as active, 119; assess school for, 242; and being heard, 115–21; in Circle, 113, 118, 189, 193–94, 213, 217, 233, 237, 239; culture of, 1, 115–17, 119, 144, 247, 263; and democratic governance, 214; and personal changes, 196, 234; and skepticism, 159; and students, 185, 195; and SWRPs, 183; and teachers, staff, 112, 247; and trust, 115; survey on, 116

The Little Book of Restorative Justice in Education (Evans and Vaandering), xxi, xxii, xxv, 47, 222

local education leaders: building relationships with, 238–39; collaborating with, xxi; and teacher education programs, xxi, 267

room, 178, 197–205; as creating positive, caring school culture, 52; as expanding SEL competencies, 60–62; and feedback flow, 219; and repairing relationships fosters change, 218–21; and SEL, 57–62; skepticism about, 159–62; on three-tiered pyramid model, 53–57; used with PBIS and SEL, 57–60. *See also* Circles, implementation, school-wide restorative practices (SWRPs).
restorative principles, 24, 50, 52, 63, 246
restorative/RJE processes: adapt to communities and cultures, 52; affirm student value, 25–26; and Circles, 26, 49–50, 53–54, 201, 220–21; develop community, 24; develop students' capacities, 56; principles shared among, 50, 52; questions used in, 49; as rejecting behavior while supporting person, 53; to repair harm, 52–57; and SEL, 57–62, 68; and "sharp-end" uses, 52–53, 56–57; as teaching conflict resolution, 26, 53; on three tiers of pyramid, 53–57, 63, 147, 250; three types of, 49–51; at tier 1 universal, school-wide, 56; as trauma-informed, 193; as using conflicts to build or repair relationships, 24, 53; as value-based, 45–47. *See also* Circle(s), restorative language, restorative questions, SWRPs.
restorative questions, 49, 53, 186, 251
restorative school(s), 18; begins with adults, 162, 185, 248–49; benefits students, 121–23, 144; builds skills for a globalized economy, 29; and celebrating milestones, 258–59; and change based on relationships, 105–106; and changes in classroom, 179, 197–205; changes required in,

147–62; Circle use in, 54–56, 63, 118–19, 174–75, 201–202, 247–48; costs of, 26–27; as creating learning environment, 25–26; and creating time for RPs, 27; as democratic and humanizing, 214; and documenting progress, 259–60; and evaluation and research, 260–62; and federal RJ guidelines, 42; and fidelity of implementation, 5–7, 162–79, 230, 254; and funding RJE, 75, 263; and hiring RJE-minded leaders and staff, 127–28, 243–44; and instructional strategies, 268–69; and integrating RPs with daily school life, 54; and preparing for implementing RJE, 242; from punitive to restorative, 17; and racial biases, 131–44; and "in recovery" from zero tolerance, 31; relational ecology of, 106–45; and RJ room, 82, 97; and safety, 79; and scheduling, 244–45; sharing power in, 62–63; and social justice, 128–35; staff prefer working in, 124–25; and stages of implementing RJE, 5–8; students as change agents in, 62, 121–22; and telling the school's story, 259–60; training and support necessary in, 215–16, 250–54; trauma-informed practices integrated in, 253; turnover challenges for, 245; and voluntary participation in RJE, 248–49. *See also* authority, implementation, Oakland Unified School District, relational ecology.
restorative values, 18, 45–49, 56, 196; in strategic planning, 241
"restore the referral," 176, 178, 219. *See also* referrals.
Riestenberg, Nancy, 55, 185, 205, 209, 248, 252; on counting smiles, 262; on implementation science, 5, 6,

Living Justice Press (LJP)
Other LJP Books for Schools

Living Justice Press has evolved with the restorative justice (RJ) movement. The roots of restorative justice lie with Indigenous philosophies and practices worldwide. During the 1970s, a movement began to explore how to respond to harms in more positive ways. Punishment gave way to problem-solving, and dialogues about values took the lead.

Young people caught in the system became a special concern. So RJ practitioners, parents, and educators began taking restorative justice practices into schools. Not only students' academic studies but also their social and emotional development benefited, as school climates and cultures changed. Here are some LJP books that support restorative ways of doing school.

Circle Forward: Building a Restorative School Community by Carolyn Boyes-Watson and Kay Pranis. By far LJP's bestseller to schools, *Circle Forward* provides model Circles or Circle plans that bring Circles into every aspect of school life.

Circle in the Square: Building Community and Repairing Harm in School by Nancy Riestenberg. Another high seller to schools, *Circle in the Square* helps a school's adults understand what doing school restoratively means and looks like day to day.

Heart of Hope by Carolyn Boyes-Watson and Kay Pranis. Like *Circle Forward*, *Heart of Hope* offers Circle plans designed to develop social and emotional awareness and skills.

Peacemaking Circles: From Conflict to Community by Kay Pranis, Barry Stuart, and Mark Wedge. Often referred to as "the bible of Circles," *Peacemaking Circles* explores the inner and outer practice of Circles for those of us not raised in Circle-based cultures.

Please visit LJP's website for more information about books, free downloads of Circle graphics, Circle practitioners and trainers, and the training schedules of LJP authors. Thank you for your support and for the restorative and Circle work you do.

www.livingjusticepress.org